CW01497339

TO SEE OURSELVES

Also by Alistair Moffat

TO SEE OURSELVES

A Personal History of Scotland since 1950

ALISTAIR MOFFAT

BIRLINN

First published in 2025 by
Birlinn Limited
West Newington House
10 Newington Road
Edinburgh
EH9 1QS

www.birlinn.co.uk

ISBN: 978 1 78027 947 3

British Library Cataloguing-in-Publication Data
A catalogue record for this book is available from the British Library

Typeset by Initial Typesetting Services, Edinburgh

Papers used by Birlinn Ltd are from well-managed forests
and other responsible sources

Printed and bound by Clays Ltd, Elcograf S.p.A.

For my mum, Ellen Irvine
The memory of her smile never fades

Contents

Foreword

Winter Lights

Out in the early dark with my little dog in a deep December, rain, snow or moonlight, ice, mud or good footing, the world seems at once vast and formless yet also to stretch no further than the edge of the blackthorn hedge on the other side of the track. When we head up to Windygates, along the ridge above our farm, the vistas lengthen and the valley opens below. Even though all I can make out against the midnight-blue sky are woods and the humps of hills on the horizon, there's no need to see it. This land lives in my mind's eye. Its invisible winter rhythms begin the day, begin another cycle, advance the week, the month, the year, laying down the sediment of everyday experience, the stuff, the habits, the base material of history.

On this cloudless morning, the sun is rising over the faraway North Sea. The eastern horizon glows yellow and pale blue, and on the single-track road that snakes along the foot of the valley I watch a car's headlights flicker behind the wood of sitka spruce and swing into the neighbouring farmstead. I can make out someone in a high-vis jacket moving around, then rows of strip lights begin to flare and fire up in sequence, as hay is pulled out of bales to feed the stabled horses. When Maidie and I turn south down the long track, I look west to the high country, to the wind-scoured uplands of the Scottish Borders. Up on the flanks of Huntly Hill a pinpoint kitchen light clicks on in another farmhouse. I murmur 'good morning'. Other lives are beginning their day, waking, washing, switching on a kettle. The darkness edges away, the moon sets, another day dawns and another page of Scotland's story turns.

I walk back, and after boiling my own kettle, sit down at my desk and turn on the Anglepoise lamp. Until I begin writing in the pool of light, or at least make some scribbled notes, I have little idea of what I think: only scraps, adjectives, images, sometimes flashes of colour and atmosphere, occur to me. Until I start to write sentences, always in longhand, with plenty of scoring out, I don't know what's in or on my mind. To communicate, even with myself, I need words on paper, the beginnings of a story.

After a series of what feel like episodes – some recent, some remote, some recurring, some fleeting, some like gossamer islands in the distant past – I find myself in the winter of my own life. There will be no second spring. That's why understanding the last seventy-odd years is so important to me now, this urge to comprehend something of how with dizzying speed the world has changed utterly since I was born in 1950, a war baby, one of the last of the boomers. I want to connect the great sweep of unprecedented societal change with my own half-forgotten experience of it, the microcosmic and the macrocosmic, and relate my experience of growing up in a small town to the worlds beyond it. We rarely stop to notice history happening, the wheel of time turning every day, changing, bringing darkness and light like wind-blown clouds scudding up the flanks of the western hills.

What follows is the sum of a process, a mosaic assembled from fragments of a life and the experiences that revolved around it, like standing in the centre of a fairground carousel as the wooden horses spin, bobbing up and down in time with the jaunty oompah music. This is a personal chronicle of the most radical and rapid changes in Scotland's history, the dizzying and sometimes disorienting changes that have affected every one of us deeply.

The book begins with basics, with shelter: houses, flats, towns and cities, and how the look and nature of the built environment has been profoundly altered. Shopping might seem at first glance a trivial topic, but everyday habits have reshaped our society. Since 1950, education, the greatest gift any community can bestow on young people, has expanded and then contracted; doors have been opened and then firmly closed again. Television began to flicker in the corners of sitting rooms in the late 1950s, and its programmes simultaneously opened our eyes and minds to new worlds and ideas, and introduced new norms, erasing or diminishing parts of our cultural identity. Horizons shrank as an empire disappeared almost overnight off the maps on every schoolroom wall, and the heavens became the sky as the Church of Scotland shrivelled, its influence all but gone. No society devoured daily, evening and weekend newspapers as avidly as the Scots, but readerships once counted in seven figures now barely achieve five. The story of change is long and labyrinthine – and sometimes unnoticed – but as examples are added to the mosaic, a clearer picture emerges, the carousel slows down and we begin to see ourselves.

I

Up in a Day

Against a backdrop of shining white walls with climbing roses and broadleaf trees behind, there are four photographs taken in the densely packed lanes and pathways of the New Jerusalem. Everyone is smiling, their faces radiant in the sunshine, their eyes set on the dawn of a golden future, a better, fairer world, the outset of new lives, the darkness of the past banished behind them.

Photographs sometimes invent memories. Frozen, posed moments, they prompt us to remember before, after and behind; what happened before the shutter clicked and after the camera was put back in its case, sometimes long after. Wherever the people pictured sit or stand, we feel we can inhabit the background, fill out the wider scene, clearly recall the whole house, every corner of the garden, the park, the riverside path, the occasion, whatever it was that caused expensive film to be exposed and the moment captured. In these glossy, precious rectangles, amongst my most prized possessions, it is hope that was captured, the radiant promise of a better future, one that could now include everyone – or everyone who had survived. And yet I have no memory at all of those early days and all that promise, only intuition, only a sense of atmosphere, one that has never left me.

The earliest photograph was taken on a day of high summer, sometime in July 1950. Beside the shiny, corrugated metal wall of an Anderson bomb shelter repurposed as a garden shed, my grannie, Bina Moffat, sits, almost remembering to smile, peering at the camera through the new National Health specs balanced on the end of her nose, her head tilted slightly backwards. To her right stands my big sister, Barbara, four years old at the time, cuddling into Bina, her mouth half open as through she had just spoken. Her hair has been caught up by a broad ribbon tied at the back, and she stands beside a climbing rose, its blooms at their fullest burst. I am cradled in the crook of my grannie's arm, asleep in the warmth, my left hand reaching out of the baby blanket, my tiny fingers curled inwards. But someone else is there. As we look at these fading, black-and-white memories, inhabiting and investing in them, we often forget the person who took the picture, whose idea it probably was, who sat my grannie down beside the rose, who spoke to Barbara. My mother, Ellen Irvine, almost certainly framed the scene, insisting on smiles from those who were not asleep. It was a good day, one that needed to be captured and remembered.

About a year later, in the summer of 1951, she took her Box Brownie outside once more. Seated on the step of our house, our address in one of the streets of the New Jerusalem, is my dad, like his mother, wearing National Health specs. This time I am awake, much bigger and smiling as he holds me upright. But under a mop of blond hair, I have blinked at the moment the shutter clicked. Barbara, holding my other hand to steady me, is also smiling, a wonderful smile that has never faded. In a third picture, I am in my pram, secured to the sides with reins over my shoulders and a broad, white belt, and my eyes are still closed, blinking at a brilliant sun beating down on a chubby, round, chuckling face browned in the good weather. Barbara has folded her hands on the side of the pram and her forearms are clearly tanned.

The fourth and final photograph was taken in the summer of 1952. This time I am walking, clutching the handle of the pram. There are tall broadleaf trees behind the houses of the New Jerusalem, rows of what those who never experienced the liberating joy of living in them might have dismissed as prefabs. At least 50 of these little houses were built at Inchmyre, on the eastern edge of Kelso, a small market town on the banks of the River Tweed in the Scottish Borders, probably in 1945, the year when a better future began.

In 1944, when it was clear that Germany would be defeated and that the Second World War would soon come to an end, Winston Churchill's National Government voted through the Housing (Temporary Accommodation) Act. It promised the rapid production and erection of 300,000 new homes for returning servicemen and the families they would then have. In a twentieth-century version of beating swords into ploughshares, the same factories that had built artillery, tanks and aircraft would adapt their methods to prefabricate houses. One design (christened AIROH after the Architectural Industries Research Organisation on Housing) was designed to use the stockpile of scrap aluminium that had been salvaged from the wrecks of bomber and fighter planes.

In 1944, the Tate Gallery in London mounted an exhibition to show what these little bungalows would look like, what amenities they might have and how they could be constructed very quickly. On a bombsite in Oxford Street, an AIROH was erected in four hours. So that those outside London might also be informed, Pathé News made a feature to show off the new prefabs. The houses were endorsed by a pretty, dark-haired, young woman whose cut-glass accent suggested she might never have cause to actually live in one: 'I think it is very good indeed, for a small house, for the men who are coming home and the women who have been working hard in the factories and want to get back to family life. I think it is an ideal house.'

Sitting in the darkness of the cinema, my mum must have smiled at the daftness of inviting someone who sounded like

Joyce Grenfell to hymn the praises of prefabs (although the dark-haired woman never called them that), but she would have agreed. Those families who moved to Inchmyre in 1946 loved these detached houses, 'ones you could walk around, with your own front door and back door'. The former Labour Party Leader Neil Kinnock lived in an AIROH in Tredegar in South Wales: 'It had a fitted fridge, a kitchen table that folded into the wall, and a bathroom. Family and friends came visiting to view the wonders. It seemed like living in a spaceship.'

The Ministry of Works took charge of production and paid for its costs while local authorities supplied the sites and installed common services like water and electricity. There were more than 25 different designs of prefabs but each had to have a minimum floor space of 635 square feet and sections (usually each house had been made in the factory in four sections) could be no more than seven and a half feet wide so that the loads of the lorries that delivered them did not project across the white lines of Britain's road network, such as it was.

The service unit was cleverly designed and exactly the same in all versions of the prefab. It concentrated all the water and waste pipes and the electrical cables in the same place at the back of the house, making construction much easier – and much faster than the traditional method of laying one brick on another. A fitted kitchen with built-in shelving and units that included a cooker and a fridge was backed onto a bathroom with a separate toilet. A coal fire in the sitting room had a boiler behind it that supplied constant hot water and central heating for all the rooms, at least during the day and in the evenings when the fire was burning. Bedrooms had built-in shelving and wardrobes.

When the lorries arrived at sites, a team of builders aimed to erect at least three prefabs in a week, something completely unheard-of in Britain. With wartime efficiency, collapsible gantries or five-ton cranes were waiting to lift each section off the lorries and set them on temporary rails so that they could be moved to the precise place where the prefab was to be put together. It must have been a magical transformation, streets of houses appearing on empty sites within days, often with the future occupants watching. In one of my photographs, taken at the front doorstep, it is possible to make out the three or four courses of brickwork the house was bolted onto. That was the only preparation needed for building and the sole vestige of traditional methods. All the prefabs looked very similar, painted magnolia white inside and out, and with green gloss for the door facings, skirting boards and other wooden trimmings. Some even came with curtains already hung. The speed of production and construction was achieved on a wartime footing, and the Ministry of Works insisted that 'the [housing] emergency is to be treated as a military evolution handled by the government with private industry harnessed in its service. As much thought will go into the prefabricated housing programme as went into the invasion of Africa.'

What also endeared these little houses to their new occupants was more than the fridge. It was their location. Many people who moved in, like my parents, were raised in tenements, often with no internal water supply, where four or five routinely slept in the same room and had no choice but to use communal toilets. The prefabs were built on greenfield sites at the edges of towns and cities, sometimes even on municipal parks, and they gave the sense of living in the clean, clear air of the countryside and a new start. And unlike the crowded urban tenements, each house had a small garden where vegetables, and climbing roses, could be grown. It was for many the New Jerusalem.

The prefabs were much loved, but their design was by no means perfect. Condensation was the principal difficulty, caused by the use of asbestos and aluminium. My mum remembered the bitter winter of 1947 when snow fell in January and lasted until the end of March. Temperatures plummeted and stayed low.

When my mum went to pick up Barbara from her cot on one of those winter mornings, ice had formed on her blankets. The aluminium window frames conducted the cold and caused the condensation on the window panes to freeze in solid sheets that she could not shift without risking breaking the glass.

Almost all of these new clusters of prefabs shared something, an inheritance from the closeness of tenement life: a real sense of community. Occupied by returning servicemen and their wives who began, at last, after five years of war, to create a family life, they blossomed as potatoes and flowers were planted and washing fluttered in the breeze. My photos show how close to each other the prefabs were and how close at hand neighbourly support was. Almost all had young children or babies like me, and the Nisbets next door were very friendly, as were the Ainslies whose garden backed on to ours. In those days, mums were at home and child care was informal: 'Can you keep an eye on them while I nip down the street for some messages?' In good weather, neighbours sat outside in the warm evening air, smoking, talking to each other, drinking tea. Over milk and two sugars, problems were aired and shared, and stories told as a better and different future began to unfold.

Designed to have a life of only ten years, the prefabs lasted much longer. Those at Inchmyre were only demolished in the 1960s, and some lasted even longer. There are still pockets of prefabs surviving in the suburbs of Scotland's cities, all of them spruce, spick and span. And full of memories.

Two years after my parents and my sister moved to the little garden suburb at Inchmyre, another series of photographs was taken. They shone a brilliant, unflinching light on darkness, on lives without hope, on despair and almost unimaginable poverty. In January 1948, in the midst of another bitter winter, Bert Hardy came to Glasgow on an assignment for *Picture Post*. With a huge circulation that sometimes reached 1.5 million copies each week, the paper carried photographic features that covered news, sport and more general aspects of life in post-war Britain. Before the advent of television documentaries, *Picture Post* showed as well as told, using images, captions and articles to tell stories. Bert Hardy's photographs were by themselves balefully eloquent, scarcely needing the accompanying words by A. L. Lloyd.

Published on 31 January 1948 and headlined 'The Forgotten Gorbals', the feature became enormously influential, opening the nation's eyes to extraordinary deprivation as it documented life in some of Europe's worst slums. One of the most haunting images is of Mary, a 16-year-old bakery worker. With a life waiting to be lived, it seemed that her dreams could not escape the nightmare of her surroundings. She sits at a table with her chin and cheek resting on her hand, staring at nothing in particular, her eyes dead, her face without expression as futility and frustration stretch out into an inevitable future. Behind Mary, her little brother sleeps in a curtained bed recess, his stockinged feet hanging over the side. Beside her stands another brother, and across a filthy table covered with crockery and a half-eaten loaf of bread is another sister, a toddler. Their mother sits by the table, having just fed a baby wrapped in a blanket. Six people are crammed into a tiny corner of what appears to be a very small room. The woman looks as blank as her oldest daughter. Details leap out of Hardy's photograph. Shoes have no laces, wallpaper peels, bed clothes are makeshift and rumpled.

In the article that accompanies the photographs, there is shock, even outrage:

They live five and six in a single room that is part of some great slattern of a tenement, with seven or eight people in the room next door, and maybe eight or ten in the rooms above and below.

The windows are often patched with cardboard. The stairs are narrow, dark at all times and befouled not only with mud and rain. Commonly, there is one lavatory for thirty people, and that with the door off . . .

Living as they commonly do, huddled together with adults often in the same bed, youngsters find few mysteries among the facts of life.

By and large, the youngsters have plenty of pride and few illusions. Said one girl, 'I hate it in the Gorbals. If I meet any-one new, I have to give a false address.'

Another said, 'We're eight in one room. We go to bed in relays. My elder brothers walk around the court while we girls undress. Then they come back and kip down on the floor beside us. The cat sleeps with us. If a rat runs over the blankets, he springs out and has it.'

At midnight, if you stand on any of the four bridges that run across the Clyde into the Gorbals, you see the windows still lit – for when the gas goes down, the rats come out in strength.

So the lights burn dimly all night and they shine on the huddled sleepers, on the delicate faces of the girls, on the rav-aged faces of the women who once were girls and on the men's faces that look like the broken slabs of every commandment in the Decalogue.

Let no one think the residents of the Gorbals like the way they live or are apathetic to any agitation for change. They have an unusually deep awareness of their plight and a hot anger for listless authority.

In another of Hardy's photographs a teenage Madonna sits on a chair in the middle of a small room. On her lap is a baby, a little brother or sister. The girl's face is streaked with dirt, her hair unkempt, but she looks directly at the camera with a steady, heartbreaking defiance. Aware of her plight even at that age, in her eyes there is a cold anger. More than any of the more documentary pictures, this one seems like a deliberate statement. All the other family members are absent, perhaps behind Hardy and his tripod, and the effect is to make the image, her isolation, even more powerful.

Many families lived in what were known as single-ends, essentially one room, rarely larger than fourteen feet square, often even smaller. Born in the Gorbals in 1938, Frances Walker emigrated with her family to Australia in 1963. Her rage at her early upbringing burned for the rest of her life. Here is an extract from an interview she gave in 1999:

> Can I say now that it was hell living in Mathieson Street? My father was in the RAF serving in India but he rarely sent us any money. We were seven in one room. We had one cold water tap when the pipes were not burst and shared one toilet with all of the close. At night when all the beds were down the only things that could move were the rats and, believe me, they ran all over us. The rat-catcher came one night and in our single-end, he caught fourteen. I almost lost my leg in a rat bite. It took months to heal. We never had enough to eat – to be honest, we were starving. I have a few photographs of us slum kids in the back courts – we looked like tinkers.

Bert Hardy's photographs are not silent freeze-frames, and the testimonies of Frances Walker and others are not full stops but prompts to a wider understanding of what daily – and nightly – life was like. Fourteen rats caught in a small single-end room must have been only a fraction of the population that scratched and snuffled behind skirting boards and in ceiling cavities. The noises of the night must have terrified little ones holding their bedclothes up to their chins. And when Frances Walker's cat caught a rat, it will have squealed inches from faces as the cat bit it and shook it, its blood spattering on the blankets. Did the cat

eat its kill? Food needed for starving children will have been frequently fouled by the swarms of night-time predators and their
close and constant presence behind walls, floorboards and in
ceilings must have made for a life of constant fear and vigilance.

The stench of poverty, of decaying tenements and their overflowing communal toilets, was another unwelcome constant.
John Wotherspoon remembered:

> We stayed on a five floor landin', so that there could be anythin'
> up to thirty-five, forty people usin' that toilet, so you were aye
> queued up for it, so if you were caught short – and in these
> days the lack of food and everythin', it affected your bowels,
> you know, diarrhoea and such like – you had a terrible job,
> you know, if you were caught short, somebody in the toilet
> and you were waiting to get in.

And when you did, it could be very unpleasant. Here is Robert
Douglas's recollection:

> Jeez! The place was minging. One of the neighbours must have
> been in shortly before me. I opened the small, steel, mesh-
> covered window above the toilet. A breeze straight from the
> Arctic blew in. As I peed, I leaned forward, one hand on the
> wall, to bring my face near to the window, better freezing than
> being gassed.

Inside single-ends may not have been much better. In the late
1960s, I worked with a plumbing company renovating old council flats in the Borders. They had been evacuated, but in some of
them the strong smell of what one plumber called 'pishy pyjamas' had not departed. Young children will have wet the beds
they shared with siblings and parents in single-ends and two-
room flats, and without any running water and only the use of

a communal washhouse in the back court, it was very difficult to keep anything clean. The photographs of Hardy and others sometimes show families who had all but abandoned any effort at washing themselves, their clothes and sheets or keeping their tiny rooms tidy.

These images of lived experience are startling, but statistics show that they were by no means confined to the Gorbals or to Glasgow, and the deprivation they reveal was not a recent phenomenon. In 1917, the Royal Commission on Housing in Scotland spoke of 'unspeakably filthy privy-middens in many of the mining areas, badly constructed, incurably damp labourers' cottages on farms, whole townships unfit for human occupation in the crofting counties and islands . . . groups of lightless and unventilated houses in the older burghs, clotted masses of slums in the great cities.'

In 1936, another survey reckoned that 50 per cent of Scotland's housing was 'inadequate'. During the Second World War there was no house building, no repairs or renovation of existing stock and also a good deal of bomb damage. Already extreme, problems in Scotland had become acute by 1945. More than 120,000 houses needed immediate replacement, 200,000 were overcrowded, 64,000 had suffered various degrees of damage during the war, and with the return of servicemen who started families, like my mother and father, a further 134,000 households needed accommodation. In total, half a million new houses were required, and the scale of the problem was almost doubled when 405,000 more, considered 'unfit for habitation', were taken into account. These usually had no private toilets or water supply.

In 1950, a survey concluded that across Scotland, 1.4 million people out of a population of just over 5 million were 'denied a reasonable home life'. Overcrowding was at its worst in Glasgow and the industrial towns of the lower Clyde Valley. The census of 1951 revealed that of all those in Scotland who lived in

To See Ourselves

single-ends, 49 per cent were in Glasgow, while in Edinburgh, Dundee and Aberdeen only 16 per cent of their total population were crammed into one room. For the first time, the census also asked respondents about piped water, baths and toilets, and once again Glasgow found itself pre-eminent – and by some distance. Housing was an enormous problem, a national emergency. While Bert Hardy's photographs and A. L. Lloyd's words shocked the rest of Britain – only 5.5 per cent of Londoners were living in one or two rooms compared with 50.5 per cent in Glasgow – the feature can have come as no surprise to Glaswegians who did not live in the Gorbals or the other inner-city slums. In his *Scottish Journey*, published in 1935, the poet and novelist Edwin Muir related what he saw:

> . . . it was several weeks after I came to Glasgow, when I found a post in an office, that I first came into contact with the slums as I walked to and from my work. After that I passed through one of the worst of them twice daily. For it is almost impossible (or was at that time) for anyone working in [central] Glasgow to avoid passing through a slum on his way to and from work, unless he lives in the West End. The people I met did so, for they lived on the South Side, and all the main thoroughfares leading from the town to the South Side were slums or semi-slums.

After the Labour Party landslide in the general election of 1945, political action on housing was rapid and undertaken on a vast scale. In addition to the erection of 32,000 prefabs in Scotland, more than 100,000 new houses had been built by 1950, and the pace of completions was quickening. It had to. With the return of servicemen and the passing of the Family Allowances Act of 1945, the baby boom began. The number of live births in Scotland jumped from 86,924 in that year to 104,413 in 1946 and then to 113,147 in 1947.

In Glasgow, where housing problems remained critical, politics began to interfere. Compiled in 1945/46 by Sir Patrick Abercrombie and Robert H. Matthew, and supported by the Westminster Government, the Clyde Valley Regional Plan proposed radical solutions. New towns would be built to rehouse inner-city populations and thin out the oppressive, unhealthy overcrowding. In the Gorbals, there were 40,000 crammed into a small area, a density of 281 people to the acre. To the south-west, East Kilbride was designated as a new town in 1947. Its streets would be lined with low-rise housing and separated from the city by a green belt where building was forbidden. In Fife, Glenrothes was begun in 1948. Between 250,000 and 300,000 Glaswegians would eventually be rehoused in these and other new towns.

Robert Bruce, Glasgow's Master of Works and the City Engineer, disagreed. He believed that the 316,000 new houses needed could be built within the city boundaries. Many of these would have to be in the form of high-rise flats in order to accommodate all those who needed urgently to move out of the slums. Those areas would be cleared and new housing built in place of the crumbling, unsanitary tenements. While Bruce and the convener of the city's housing committee, David Gibson, eventually came to believe that the tower blocks were the best and fastest solution to acute hardship, they were also engaged in a power struggle. The corporation was determined to avoid the loss of a quarter of Glasgow's population of just over 1 million – and the consequent weakening of political clout – and after 1951, the Labour-controlled administration was forced to deal with Winston Churchill's re-elected Conservative Government. Friction caused delay and confusion.

In the event, there was no resolution, and both approaches moved forward. New towns were not only established at East Kilbride and Glenrothes; another was designated at Cumbernauld in 1955 and later two more at Livingston (1962) and Irvine (1966).

In addition, a series of what were known as overspill agreements were made with 57 towns across Scotland. Families who could not be housed in Glasgow or the satellite new towns would move to places as far apart as Stranraer and Wick. Houses would be built for them by the Scottish Special Housing Association, which had been formed in 1937 to create a programme of social housing across the country. At the same time, Glasgow Corporation began the construction of four huge schemes on the periphery of the city at Pollok, Castlemilk, Drumchapel and Easterhouse.

By the late 1940s, building was well underway at Pollok, to the south-west of the city centre. It had a huge target population of 40,000, approximately the same as the teeming rookeries of the Gorbals, and larger than many Scottish towns. Most homes were not in tower blocks but in three- or four-storey flat-roofed modern tenements. Work was complete by 1951, and the bulk of the new residents came from the Gorbals or Govan. Many had been on council-house waiting lists for years, and one woman later recalled:

> We were on the waiting list for over fourteen years. When you were offered a house, you jumped at it.
>
> It was pretty grim and cold when we first arrived in 1947. The gardens were all bare, no street lights and the roads were dirt tracks. But it was great to get away from the smoke of the Gorbals though it took us a while to get used to it out here.

Most important to all who moved were not so much the surroundings but the plumbing:

> We moved from a room and kitchen to this four-apartment. It was great to have hot running water and an inside toilet for the first time.

The one thing that stood out was the bathroom. It made a change from having to get washed in an old bathtub.

These early, positive impressions did not persist. By 1962, Glasgow Corporation resolved to speed up the process of house building, and the solution was reckoned to lie in a renewed focus on high-rise flats. Industrial building methods were much faster than the laying of traditional bricks and mortar, but the short-term fix this approach promised gave rise to severe longer-term problems. Like the new residents of Pollok, many were delighted to have toilets they did not have to share, hot running water and good waste disposal. But the tower-block estates and low-rise buildings around them had very few amenities for the community, sometimes no shops or local schools. Residents complained that they had to catch a bus into the city centre to get a haircut, and Glasgow Corporation banned the building of public houses on their property until 1969.

As the towers began to age, serious design faults and the results of shoddy, rushed workmanship surfaced. These very tall buildings, often more than 20 storeys, were unsuited to the wind and heavy rain of the West of Scotland's Atlantic climate. Residents complained that the noise of the howling wind sometimes made it impossible to listen to the radio or the television, or even have a conversation. Rain did not run off the flat roofs of the towers but instead pooled and created reservoirs that seeped down through poorly sealed joints to create damp on walls. External cladding had been fixed by metal pins that rusted badly, and some heavy, half-ton panels were blown off to shatter on the paving hundreds of feet below. Windows with steel frames corroded and leaked, and thin partition walls meant neighbours could clearly hear each other (when it was not windy), while uninsulated outside walls leaked heat. And as buildings aged, lifts often broke down.

By the 1980s, only decades after the first of them had been built, the towers began to fall. Demolition carried on into the 1990s, and the 300 blocks built in Glasgow were thinned out. Perhaps the most notorious were the Red Road Flats. Eight multi-storey towers (the 31-floor point blocks were the tallest buildings in Glasgow at the time) were constructed in the north-east of the city, the first of them completed in 1966. After a bizarre proposition to demolish five of the blocks in 'a dramatic explosive display' to celebrate the opening of the 2014 Commonwealth Games was dismissed after an outcry, the Red Road Flats were finally brought down in 2015. Film of this moment shows an eerie, symbolic effect. Explosions near the base of each tower make them seem to sink slowly rather than topple. They disappear from view behind a screen of trees before huge dust clouds billow upwards. It is like watching the simultaneous sinking of several *Titanic*s – and the death of a dream of renewal.

Despite the politics and the rivalries, David Bruce, David Gibson and the town planners across Scotland's local authorities acted on what seem to me to have been the best of motives. In order to get families out of the rat-infested slums of the Gorbals and elsewhere, they moved quickly and decisively. In 1961, Gibson said:

In the next three years the skyline of Glasgow will become a more attractive one to me because of the likely vision of multi-storey houses rising by the thousand . . . The prospect will be thrilling, I am certain, to the many thousands who are still yearning for a home. It may appear on occasion that I would offend against all good planning principles, against open space and Green Belt principles – if I offend against these it is only in seeking to avoid the continuing and unpardonable offence that bad housing commits against human dignity. A decent home is the cradle of the infant, the seminar of the young and the refuge of the aged.

House completions were like victories, the daily creation of different versions of the New Jerusalem that my family benefited from. Catastrophic mistakes were clearly made and vast amounts of taxpayers' money wasted. But the memories were by no means all bad. Rose MacLean and her family had been offered a flat in Castlemilk but the duties of child care prevented her from viewing it. Her husband and daughters went to look at it and reported back.

In fact, I didn't see the house until the night we moved in. When they came back and said the house was on the ground floor I thought I was getting a back and front door you know – but it was a corner house with a big garden in Ardmaleish Road. They talked about the white sink in the kitchen and the BATHROOM – we only had a toilet on the stair. They were all thrilled . . . To this day I've been happy and I haven't regretted moving to Castlemilk.

Between 1945 and 1984 the look of Scotland's towns and cities changed dramatically. In less than forty years more than a million new houses and flats were built, 76 per cent of them by the public sector, by local authorities and housing associations. Not only were Scottish townscapes transformed, they looked very different to those of the rest of Britain. Most of the new building was concentrated in the Central Belt. And the proportions are startling. More than 80 per cent of the people of Coatbridge, Wishaw, Motherwell, Clydebank and Irvine lived in council houses and flats in the 1980s. In Airdrie, Alloa, Greenock, Falkirk, Hamilton, Kilmarnock, Johnstone, Glenrothes and East Kilbride, it is 70 per cent, and in Glasgow, Dundee, Paisley, Kirkcaldy and Dunfermline 60 per cent.

The density and scale of council-house building has generally made for a monotonous uniformity, a loss of any distinctive local identity, neighbourhoods that could have been anywhere. This huge construction programme was a sustained, massive, even heroic, response to the post-war housing emergency, but its nature – and the way it looked – created problems as well as solving them.

Between 1952 and 1968, when I left home to go to university, I lived on a council estate built, as most were, on the periphery of a town. But it was relatively small, perhaps only 250 low-rise houses in terraces of four and five with front and back gardens. The open countryside was close and so was the town centre and its shops. Transport was not an issue, and most people walked to work or to the shops. In our scheme tenants competed each year for a trophy for the best, most colourful front garden, and almost all grew vegetables in their back plots. I can remember only two problem families, their issues signalled and symbolised by tall weeds and litter instead of primulas, asters or roses at their front door. But my dad and several others had a word, gently suggesting that if they did not wish to grow flowers, then at least they had to tidy up. 'Just letting the place down,' I remember him saying. And if there were any drink-fuelled nighttime incidents, fighting or shouting and swearing, the group of vigilantes used less gentle methods.

A smaller scale and amenities close at hand, as well as community continuity, allowed a strong sense of identity and investment in our council estate to grow. Even if no residents owned their houses, they took pride in them.

In the big towns and cities of the Central Belt, it could be very different. Local shops, pubs, schools and, eventually, leisure facilities like swimming pools did appear, but often too late. The schemes were simply too large for any social control to be exerted, too anonymous to allow a positive sense of identity to grow and be reinforced. As a reporter at Scottish Television, I went with a film crew to do a story in the Easterhouse estate on the periphery of Glasgow in 1981. The address I'd been given didn't exist. All the street names had been removed from the buildings on the corners, and I had not thought to bring a map with me. All I could see were long avenues of identical low-rise flats or rows of terraced houses and very few people to ask for directions. Those I did manage to stop just shook their heads and moved on. It felt – and looked – like comedian Billy Connolly's famous description of 'a desert wi' windaes'.

Like Easterhouse, many schemes were built on greenfield sites on the edge of towns and cities, and this only deepens the sense of colourless anonymity, of living nowhere in particular. The apparently endless duplication of distinctively Scottish pebbledashed weatherproofing and the prevalence of grey made for a monolithic, forbidding look, especially in the winter or bad weather. Even though the vast majority of council housing stock, with the exception of the tower blocks, was initially sound and serviceable, the townscape of Scotland suffered, and was occasionally submerged. A car journey from Wishaw through Motherwell to Bellshill and across the M8 to Coatbridge and Airdrie can be monotonous, even depressing, and it leaves the driver uncertain where one town begins and another ends. Falkirk, Larbert, Stenhousemuir and Bonnybridge all look much the same, and quite different from housing in England and Wales. By 1981, 54.6 per cent of all Scotland's homes were council houses or flats; in the south that figure drops by half to 26 per cent.

Change came in 1979 with the election of a Conservative Government led by Margaret Thatcher. A year later the Tenants' Rights, Etc. (Scotland) Act became law. It gave council tenants the option to buy their houses on very favourable terms, and many in Scotland exercised it. It allowed those who had been tenants for three years to buy a house at a 33 per cent discount on the market price (which itself was low because it was without precedent) and a flat at a 44 per cent discount. Tenants of over 20 years' standing were given a whopping 50 per cent discount.

During the 1980s home ownership shot up from 55 per cent to 67 per cent. By the time the scheme was wound up in 2013, 455,000 Scots had bought their council houses. The grey streets brightened as the pebbledash was painted, porches and extensions built and new front doors fitted. But such was the depletion of the council-housing stock, there now exists a chronic shortage, one that will not easily or quickly be made up. Between 1970 and 1980, Westminster Governments financed 34 per cent of the cost of new Scottish council housing, but the Conservatives were determined, on both economic and ideological grounds, to reduce the level of these grants. By 1986, the housing subsidy had collapsed to only 7 per cent, and building programmes consequently shrivelled.

*

In the southern suburbs of Edinburgh, there exists a gigantic time capsule, a social and architectural palimpsest of the history of post-war housing in Scotland. In Craigour Avenue, in Moredun, twelve AIROH prefabs have survived, at least one of them passed on like a family heirloom. The little houses were part of a large estate of 565 prefabs erected on the greenfield site. Alan Bass, whose uncle was the first tenant in 1948, is the current owner-occupier of number 35. Betty Campbell moved to number 76 from the tenements of the inner city and she has golden memories:

> I loved it there as it was still countryside at that time. There was a farm behind us where the cows came right up to the fence at the back of our house. The farmer had a pony named Trigger who all us kids loved. When he saw us around, he would come to us for treats.

The prefabs survive in small clusters along the avenue, interspersed with solid, semi-detached council houses built in the

1950s. All have generous front and back gardens, and the planners allowed room for green, open spaces where children could play and the community could breathe. Behind Craigour Avenue rise four tower blocks, each one fourteen storeys high, with wide, sweeping views to the south and the Pentland Hills. To the west of Moredun runs Gilmerton Road and a deposit of ribbon development that predated the flats. It is lined by bungalows built by private companies, one of several developments in the Edinburgh suburbs. When restrictions were lifted in 1954, the likes of Miller Homes and Mactaggart & Mickel began to contribute significantly to townscapes. Initially, their bungalows were not much bigger than council houses. It was the finish that attracted a premium, with central heating, an integral garage and fitted kitchen often standard.

Other deposits of history can be found in Craigour Avenue. All the surviving prefabs had been purchased in the wake of the 1980 Tenants' Rights Act. The walls of three were still off-white (or was it magnolia?), while others had been painted in cheery colours. One was a startling midnight blue. Several of the council houses had also been bought by their tenants. Various non-standard features like new front doors and extensions marked them out.

The chairman of Edinburgh Corporation's housing committee from 1962 to 1965, Councillor Pat Rogan, declared: 'It is a magnificent thing to watch, as I did many times, whole streets of slum tenements being demolished, just vanishing into dust and rubble' and their occupants moved to modern, immeasurably better housing. Craigour Avenue is more than a palimpsest. It is a monument to hope and decades of determination to rid Scotland of the foul stain of slum living. There were of course serious difficulties and many poor policy decisions, but in the prefabs, the council houses and even the high flats, many Scots at last found dignity and a much better life in decent modern homes. When I

first walked down Craigour Avenue, it was a sunny spring morning, and I suspect for many of the earliest residents, the sun shone
more brightly than it had ever done.

2

Green Grass

Early memories are like pools of sunshine in the dark mists of the past, frozen at first and then suddenly animated by a splash of sound, a shout, a murmur or a snatch of conversation. For me it was a loud bellow, the deep, chesty lowing of cows in the early morning, their udders swinging, bulging with milk, plodding along Inch Road behind our house, sometime in the early 1950s.

Our streets of council houses were completed in 1952, built on the low-lying land to the north of Kelso. Inch Road, Inchmead Drive, where I lived from the age of 2 until I was 18, Inchmead Crescent and Inch Gardens were laid out on an old meadow, an 'inch' in Scots, land once flooded by the River Tweed. There were still fields around the houses, and on the other side of Inch Road, three tree-lined grass parks provided grazing for Sandy Purves's cows.

Early every morning, I heard them. Sandy walked along the road with his two collie dogs and opened a wide double gate in the wall that bordered the park. Just as much creatures of habit as Sandy, the black-and-white Ayrshire cows were waiting behind it, lowing, snorting plumes of snotty breath in the cold morning air, anxious to be milked. Once the old man had pulled back the pale-blue gates, the cows jostled onto the empty road, the dogs and Sandy's shepherd's crook not needed. They knew where they were going. If there was any traffic, it stopped, and Sandy would wave and tap the backside of the hindmost cow with his crook, just to make himself look useful. The collies circled behind, and I walked along the pavement beside this little herd. There might have been a dozen, maybe a few more. I don't remember ever saying anything to Sandy or him even acknowledging me. Wee boys did things like that in those far-off days, just looked on, hands in pockets, scuffing along on the edges of life.

Back projection might be at work here, but my image of Sandy is that he resembled Wilfred Bramble's Albert Steptoe, the rag-and-bone man in the BBC comedy series of the 1960s and 70s. Wearing round, rimmed National Health specs, the ones that hooked around the ears with bendy curved legs made from wire, he was small and stooped, probably an old man when I was young. Like every other man in the 1950s and 1960s, he wore a bunnet, a cloth cap pulled tight to the scalp, its brim outshot, pointing the way, and also an old three-piece suit, and to add sound effects, tackety boots that hit the tarmac of Inch Road with a rhythmic clack. Maybe there was the silver chain of a pocket watch across the waistcoat, glinting in the morning sun. Sometimes Sandy answered the cows' bellows with a throaty grunt and a half-hearted wave of his shepherd's crook. I suppose it was encouragement for both parties.

Once the procession reached Bowmont Street, the collies got ahead of the cows. The SMT bus garage was just up on the left, and early buses left the town by that road. If a driver saw the dogs, he'd brake and stop to let the herd cross and bunch up to get down narrow Winchester Row to the dairy, where Sandy's daughter, Agnes, was waiting. In wooden stalls with hay stuffed in the mangers at the far end, they attached teat cups to the cows' udders and production began. The smell is what I remember best: creamy, warm milk and cow shit.

On the internet, I looked up the average daily milk yield of a dairy cow and was amazed to see it's about 40 pints (litres still don't mean much to me apart from being more than a pint). If Sandy and Agnes milked a dozen cows each morning, then that's almost 500 bottles of milk. And it was milk in those days. No one had heard of selling skimmed milk to human beings. But Purves's dairy had two kinds: milk with rich, yellow cream at the top, about two inches, and milk with even more cream.

When I was a bit older, Agnes (I don't ever remember seeing her smile) gave me a job as a delivery boy. Each morning before school I pushed a heavy metal barrow carrying four milk crates (48 pint bottles in total, I think) up Roxburgh Street. After I'd dinked down one or two bottles on a doorstep, and picked up the empties, I pushed the ever-lighter barrow on up the street until it was empty and then shoogled and clinked back down to the dairy to put the empties next to the steam of the washer. On the bottles was printed *A. B. Purves, Tweedview Dairy* (if you poked your head out of the gates and looked to the left, you could see a bit of the river) in red letters; some of them had been filled, washed and refilled for so many years that the words had almost completely faded.

What strikes me now about those sunshine splashes of memory is distance. Sandy's cows grazed in fields about 200 yards from the dairy where their milk was put into bottles and then delivered to the streets around it. There were no food miles involved, not even one. And of course the freshness and the taste of the milk and the yellow cream is nowhere to be found now. The Tweedview Dairy is no more, and the fields on the other side of Inch Road now contain a medical practice, a swimming pool, a primary school and houses, all good and necessary additions as history washes over communities, change and loss not measured in centuries but in the span of a single lifetime. In my mind's bright eye, I see the daily journey of the cows to the dairy as they plod on into the past, their colour fading, their bellows echoing, vanishing like autumn leaves into the darkness and memories of an older Scotland that has all but disappeared.

In late September 1968, my own world changed utterly. I left all the familiar comforts and frustrations of home in Inchmead Drive to go to university in St Andrews. Despite indifferent Highers results I had been given an unconditional acceptance to study English, History – and rugby, as it turned out. A few weeks before term started at the beginning of October, I received a post-card from the impressively named Dick Rawlinson, the captain of the university's First XV. Would I like to come up to Fife early to take part in a pre-term rugby training week? He'd heard that, as a precocious schoolboy, I'd played for Kelso.

Only three or four years before, Dr Richard Beeching's cuts had wrecked the coherence of Britain's transport infrastructure, and so after a day-long, complicated bus, train and bus journey, I arrived in St Andrews at last, in the late afternoon. Having had no lunch, nothing since porridge with the top of Sandy Purves's milk for breakfast, I looked for something to eat. The baker's shop I found in Market Street was closed, and from its window display of salamis and a sign that advertised 200 different types of cheese, I didn't hold out much hope of getting a sausage roll in Geddes Fine Foods. Further along the street I came across Wm Low. There was nothing in the windows. All I could see through them were aisles of shelves and people who didn't look like shop assistants taking items off them and putting them in large plastic baskets.

'Self-service, sir,' said a man who looked like he might be the manager. 'You take what you want off the shelves and pay on your way out.'

I was baffled. I'd never been in a self-service shop before, and in truth never gone shopping for food before if you didn't count fish and chips. What I did know was that Wm Low (or Willie Low's as it was affectionately known) wasn't a grocer's shop, at least not like any I'd ever seen. Self-service shops, what eventually morphed into supermarkets, had bypassed the Borders, where a grocer's was a place you went to the counter and the man in the white apron asked you what you wanted. Then he, not you, took it off the shelves behind the counter, or sliced it up, or poured it out, weighed it and wrapped it. And spoke to your mum as he did all that.

Pettigrew's in Bridge Street made their own chutney (the stink in Oven Wynd next to the shop could be eye-watering). MacDonald's in The Square had rows and rows of different brands of whisky and the Co-op had a different department for everything. But in a Wm Low, it was apparently up to you to find stuff, and when I did find it, I had no idea what it was or how to get into it, whatever it was. Behind the glass door of a cabinet, I eventually came across a Melton Mowbray (*where?*) pork pie. It looked faintly familiar, like something that might quell the pangs. But after a couple of greasy bites, I threw it in a bin.

*

Radical changes in shopping habits brought about seismic change in culture and society, changes that were not trivial or incidental but absolutely central to how late twentieth-century and early twenty-first-century Scotland took shape. The journey from the cornershop, the greengrocer and the local butcher to the hypermarket and its vast car park on the edge of town began in the 1950s, but not before the shadows of war had finally begun to recede. Food rationing continued for nine long and frustrating years after VE Day and VJ Day, only ending when the unrestricted sale of butter was permitted in July 1954. The year I was born, 1950, eggs, meat, cheese, tea, cooking fats, sugar, sweets and butter were all rationed, sometimes severely. Families continued, as they had during the war, to depend on their gardens – and allotments if they could be had – for vegetables, berries and whatever could be grown in greenhouses or under makeshift frames, often constructed with a few bricks and an old window frame whose panes were still intact. Many people still foraged, picking berries from reluctant, prickly bushes by the roadside to make jam or looking for mushrooms in old horse pasture on misty, late summer mornings.

Rationing could be unpredictable, and grocers and butchers were supplied erratically with goods that were sold on a first-come, first-served basis. This partly explains a remarkable statistic. In 1957, housewives, or whoever cooked meals, went out shopping an average of 7.6 times a week. When Sunday closing and early closing at lunchtime on Wednesdays and Saturdays are taken into account, that means women often picked up their shopping baskets twice a day.

The other determinant, of course, was food storage. In 1955, only 8 per cent of British households owned a fridge, a percentage that was almost certainly substantially lower in Scotland and very much influenced by income and social class. The tiny amounts of rationed meat, eggs, cheese and cooking fats were too precious to risk their going off, and so they were usually cooked or consumed on the day of purchase, or the day after in wintertime. Most larders had a thick stone shelf that stayed cooler, where perishables could be safely stored. Many people also had meat safes. Ours was a small wooden frame whose door and sides were made from a fine wire mesh. This allowed the cool air on the stone shelf to circulate and kept out flies. My grannie routinely put milk, eggs, butter and meat in it. Most of the shelf space was taken up with jars of preserves, jellies and jams from wild fruit and pickles of all sorts. In the long years of rationing, there was often little choice or variety and a great deal of repetition: mince and tatties on a Monday, fish on a Friday. But nothing was wasted or thrown in a bin. A recent survey showed that in Britain almost 40 per cent of food is thrown away as it moves beyond sell-by or use-by dates. Such a statistic would have appalled my grannie.

Shopping habits began to change slowly as more and more

people were able to afford to buy fridges, either outright or on hire purchase. Reasonably full employment meant that when women went out to work, they had both a greater need for a fridge and the means to pay for one, or at least make a down payment. But it was a very gradual process. Even if they had a job, most women still shopped most days, and in Kelso, the archaeology of these frequent journeys can still be traced. On Roxburgh Street, which leads from the town square in the centre to the grand, imposing gates of Floors Castle, the stately home of the dukes of Roxburghe, there were several grocers' shops at intervals. On the corner of Winchester Row, near the dairy, was Jack Donaldson's, and only a hundred yards further north was Gow's, another, slightly grander emporium that also sold whisky, sherry and may have bottled their own port. And yet in each establishment, tills and doors tinkled often as small but frequent purchases were made each day. Housewives were busy raising families as well as trying to make ends meet, so long shopping expeditions could be difficult to manage. A grocer close at hand, within walking distance, was very useful. In addition to Sandy Purves's dairy, there were at least three others in Kelso. Milk could be heavy to carry, and if families brought their own jugs or containers, it was easy to spill, especially if little ones were sent out to get it. This was an early version of convenience shopping.

'Seven out of ten people can't tell Stork from butter!' ran the catch-line of advertisements for a brand of margarine. Oh yes, you could. As a child, I thought Stork was disgusting, its oily texture, its sour, fake taste repellent, and I refused point-blank to eat bread smeared with it. It was also rationed, but more generously than butter. And it was a lot cheaper. When all restrictions on food shopping were finally removed in 1954, people lit bonfires to ceremonially burn their ration books. But relief took time. Even though it was possible to buy as much butter as any customer liked, it was initially very expensive, and vile Stork clung on as an unwanted staple. Scottish cookery in the 1950s tended to be more about bulk and thrift than taste; as little meat as possible was used to make the likes of stovies (potatoes and onions flavoured with fat, gravy and tiny morsels of mutton), and stews and soups were made from boiled bones or the very cheapest cuts. Bread, potatoes and oatmeal padded out meals and filled hungry bellies. You need 'to kitchen your meat' my grannie said, every day, as we sat down in the kitchenette. Slices of bread seemed to accompany everything. When, much later, I worked on a building site, I watched one man at the lunch break put a sausage roll into a buttered bread roll and devour it, a carbohydrate bomb.

In the 1950s and well into the 1960s, the Co-op dominated British retailing. It had 13 million members in 1965, but slow decline had already set in. Its share of the grocery market was dropping across the United Kingdom, from 23.2 per cent in 1950 to 20.8 per cent in 1961. This trend was less marked in Scotland, where the Co-op was known as the Store. One of the great attractions was that its founding principles made not only for lower prices (since there were no private shareholders to satisfy with good profits), but also provided an annual or sometimes quarterly dividend for members. The 'divi' could amount to as much as a shilling in the pound, and so if members loyally shopped at the Store, they might receive a substantial cash payment at the year's end, or quarter. In a digital age, the process of calculating this amount sounds cumbersome, unlikely and untidy, but it worked, and the servers never crashed.

My grannie's membership or divi number was 495 (an early adopter) and my mum's was 2168. I remember both because I was often sent 'down the street for messages' to the Store. Accompanying the shopping list was the relevant divi book and the cash (the exact amount plus a penny extra for a gobstopper from Baikie's sweetie shop next door). The routine is printed indelibly on my memory. With a basket, I went into the grocery department and solemnly, wordlessly, handed the list and the divi book to a man behind a broad mahogany counter. On one side were sets of scales with different sorts of panniers and a row of metal weights arranged in order of size, like a rank of toy soldiers. The grocers all wore high-waisted white aprons, and once the list had been handed over, they began fulfilling it. Flour, sugar, tea and other dry goods were not prepackaged but scooped loose out of large containers or jars and poured carefully into pound, half-pound or quarter-pound paper bags before being dunted on the counter so that the contents settled. Then the tops were deftly folded and turned down. Bacon was surgically sliced on a whirl-ing, sliding machine and laid precisely on a sheet of greaseproof paper. This was then folded neatly and tight enough to be sealed. In an age before sticky tape, the grocer's origami sufficed.

As the grocer worked, placing each package in my mother's shopping basket, he made an entry in the divi book with the goods purchased and the price opposite. Under that page was a sheet of blue carbon paper. It had a strange smell all of its own, like something medical. Once all was complete and I had handed over the money, a clutched handful of half-crowns, or two-bob bits, sixpences and pennies (except for one), the page was carefully torn out (the spine of the little green book was perforated) and a carbon copy of the transaction was left for the Co-op member (never a 'customer'). At the end of the day, all the torn-out pages of the divi books were gathered up by the ladies of the ledger department. The following morning, each page would be entered under the member's name and number in a series of monthly ledgers. These were large and had marbled covers with the name of the Co-operative Society embossed on them. At the end of the month, and eventually the year, the purchases of each member would be calculated, and, depending on the percentage rate agreed for that year, the amount of the divi would then be paid out in cash. I know all this because my mum worked in the Store's ledger department with the other ladies who all wore what looked like smocks. Her handwriting always reminded me of those times. It was immaculate, precise, and it had to be. The divi depended on it.

Before the age of the hypermarket dawned, the Co-op in Kelso worked like a dispersed version of one. There was much more on offer than groceries. Next door in Roxburgh Street was the Ladieswear Department. It also sold children's clothes, wool and sewing materials such as coloured threads, needles, pins, silver thimbles, darning stools and small blocks of beeswax. Up a broad flight of stairs at the back was the Hardware Department and also a small but extremely attractive toy shop. I coveted, almost salivated at the rows of Dinky Toys and boxes of little lead soldiers. It must have had a chimney because Santa came down it every Christmas. On the other side of the grocery was the Fleshing Department, or butcher's shop, and beyond that, a shoe shop. It contained a wonder, a Pedoscope, something that would probably be banned now. It fascinated me. Having clumped up to it in a new pair of shoes and pushed my feet into a rectangular aperture at the bottom, I looked down an eyepiece that resembled something that might have been attached to a submarine's periscope. And you could see the bones of your feet, black inside the fainter outline of the new shoes. It was in essence an X-ray machine, and they were definitely my feet because when I wiggled my toes, I saw them wiggle. Shoes were very expensive and needed to fit properly. At the bottom of Roxburgh Street was the Menswear Department, run by a man who was the embodiment of dapper. Always with a measuring tape around his neck and in a three-piece, pin-stripe suit, he could make one for you. The Store made my kilt, and I still have it.

The whole town, small and compact in the centre, was far more comprehensive and varied in its retail offerings than any contemporary hypermarket or shopping mall. Customers only had to walk a little further. There were two more tailors in the town who made suits, and I vividly remember watching a bespectacled little man sitting cross-legged in a large window, where the light was good, sewing the seams of a jacket turned inside out. There were five bakers' shops: one that specialised in confectionery (custard slices, fairy cakes, Victoria sponges and fly cemeteries); all of them baking their own bread, buns, biscuits, cakes; and, most important of all, five slightly different versions of the little, very savoury delights now known as Scotch pies. Frank Frost was a tobacconist who sold British, American, French and Turkish cigarettes as well as Havana cigars and many brands of pipe tobacco. There was a fishmonger, a florist, two greengrocers, several grocers (some of them catering for the tastes of the better-off), a music shop, a seed merchant, a pet shop, several newsagents, two furniture shops, branches of four banks and much else. Almost all of these businesses prospered in a small town of around 4,000 inhabitants with a substantial hinterland of farms, small villages and estates. Those who worked on the land could not make 7.6 visits to the grocers each week, and they were served by a fleet of mobile shops and delivery vans. Big houses in the town and close by had groceries brought to them by a small posse of boys pedalling bicycles with large iron frames attached to the front to hold rectangular wicker baskets. It was a varied, high-quality retail economy that worked, but one that was doomed to wither.

'Pile it high and sell it cheap!' was Jack Cohen's business mantra when he founded Tesco in London's East End in 1919. He combined the initials of his tea merchant, Thomas Edward Stockwell, with the first two letters of his own surname to create the famous brand. Moving on from market stalls, Cohen opened his first shop in 1931, and in 1956 the first self-service grocery was set up in St Albans. The same year, the first recognisable Tesco supermarket opened in a disused cinema in Maldon, Essex. Business boomed, and Cohen's internal motto of YCDBSOYA (You Can't

Do Business Sitting On Your Arse) appeared to inspire rapid expansion, much of it by acquiring other chains of grocery shops.

Based in Dundee, Wm Low also began to expand, and the self-service shop I failed to negotiate in St Andrews opened in the mid 1960s. It was too small to be considered a supermarket, and there was nowhere to park except on the street outside, but it operated on the same principle. Almost everything was pre-packaged, some of it frozen or chilled. Wm Low had 70-odd shops of varying sizes across Scotland and the North of England, but there were none in the Borders, and self-service remained a mystery to me until I bought the greasy Melton Mowbray pork pie.

In 1994, after a takeover battle with Sainsbury's, Tesco bought Wm Low. They restructured and expanded, often opening brand-new, much larger supermarkets on the edge of towns with car parks.

In 1960, there were about 5 million private cars registered in Britain, used by 31 per cent of all households. By 1970, the number of cars on the road had doubled. It should be remembered that, in the 1950s, Britain was the second largest car manufacturer in the world. The major companies were BMC (formerly Austin and Morris), Ford, Vauxhall and the Rootes Group, and by 1963, their combined annual output had climbed to 1,867,641 new cars. A huge, new, computerised plant was opened by the Rootes Group at Linwood near Glasgow, and in 1963 the first Hillman Imps rolled off the assembly line. Along with BMC's Mini, Ford's Anglia and then Cortina, and Vauxhall's Victor, the production of affordable new models quickly created a second-hand market, making cars accessible to working people for the first time. This in turn radically reshaped shopping patterns across Scotland. More and more households had acquired fridges and freezers for cold storage, and instead of the daily, local shop, cars allowed families to do a single, weekly 'big shop', and to buy more when they did. Supermarkets with car parks expanded rapidly, and their proliferation brought about profound change in shopping habits as one domino fell after another.

People needed to leave their houses much less often. The 7.6 weekly visits to shops very quickly became a thing of the past, and Scotland began to abandon local retailers in favour of what they saw as convenience. The Co-op in Kelso eventually closed all its departments except grocery and moved that to a new building on the opposite side of Roxburgh Street, one that looks and feels like every other supermarket. The divi book has become a swipe card that records sales, and amounts can be redeemed not in cash but against future purchases. There is even a small car park behind the new Co-op, and nobody seems to call it the Store any more.

Much was lost in this accelerating process. Variety and, perhaps, quality were sacrificed on the altar of time-saving convenience. Shopping was once a vital part of the social glue that held communities together, and now these bonds are much slacker and less nourishing in every sense. Sandy Purves's milk travelled less than one food mile and it was delicious. Now, the seasons appear to have disappeared as fruit and vegetables from around the world miraculously fill supermarket shelves all year round. Some may look like tomatoes and apples, bright and shiny, but often they taste of nothing. And God knows where the milk comes from.

Partly as a consequence of the COVID-19 pandemic and its restrictions, those high street shops that survived the tidal wave of supermarket expansion have recently suffered very badly as change accelerated once more. In the last five years, across Britain, more than 6,000 have closed, and one in seven lie empty. Many have become charity shops. Because of the justified fear of the threat of COVID infection, a switch to online shopping (and the vast fleet of delivery vans that follow in its wake) rocketed, and it now accounts for a staggering 34 per cent of all retail sales, a large proportion of which are groceries. As we move into a world of faceless, keyboard transactions, the heart is being torn out of communities. Most social activities are planned in advance, and fewer spontaneous, chance interactions and encounters take place. Fewer people go out to shop, to walk along high streets. The information, news and gossip that passes between people is now rarely face to face, and it loses much of its flavour, nuance and reliability as a result. France has doggedly retained twice as many high street retailers as Britain, and the Mayor of Paris recently announced measures to ensure that every resident should be within a fifteen-minute walk from shops. A similar proposal is gaining support here. This new urban planning concept is designed to ensure that everyone is within a fifteen-minute walk or cycle ride to banks, shops, schools and other amenities.

Old habits die hard. Like most people I do a weekly supermarket shop, but I also buy things in my local high street. Never having lost the habit of reading printed newspapers, I go into town most days. While I queue at the only butcher still in business, I can read the headlines and, still a loyal Co-op member, I buy things there most days – often as much as I can carry, wine bottles being heavy. And I stop in the street to talk, to hear news, exchange views, ask questions, to feel like I belong.

3

Breaking Out

Early childhood memories are rarely pin-sharp, detailed or indelible. Mostly, they are atmospheres that drift in and out of focus, sunny games of Japs and British amongst the whin bushes in the steep meadows above our council estate, or rainy Sunday afternoons staring out of the window at the grey houses opposite. But the night of 20 August 1955 was different, unforgettable. Because that was when my grannie explained the rest of my life to me.

It was a Sunday night, and it had begun to rain, big drops pattering on the windowpanes. Our house had three bedrooms, one for my mum and dad, one for my sisters, Barbara and Marjie, one for my gran and none for me. But Bina had a big double bed with a horsehair mattress on squeaky springs, and there was room for me to sleep with her, clinging onto the side nearest the window, my head on the long bolster pillow we shared. As it grew dark and the rain fell, my gran tried to console me. 'Dinnae greet, ma wee lamb.'

The following morning was to be my first day at the Inch Road Infants School, and I didn't want to go. 'But you have to go,' she said. It didn't matter if you didn't like it. They learned you things at the school. That was it and all about it. You had to be learned to read, write and count. And do what you were told. It rained harder and harder, overflowing the guttering above Bina's window. The long summer of my life with my grannie was ending.

Raised on a farm, Bina never understood the need for curtains. As I stared at the grey skies, she told me something else that I didn't want to hear: that after you finished the school, you had to go to your work. Every Monday morning, and do what you were told. And if you didn't like your work, well, that was normal. Most folk didn't. But you had to do it. And that lasted, every Monday morning, until you got the Old Age Pension, if you were spared. And that was it. Life.

The following morning, I joined a line of thirty or more 5-year-olds, at the end of a long, grey queue that would eventually lead to the Post Office and the Old Age Pension, if you were spared. I hated the Inch Road Infants School and soon learned how easy it was to play truant. When I did turn up, almost always when it was raining, I made up prodigious lies about being sick, and when asked at home about what we learned in Primary 1, I created more fantasy. As a result, I soon fell behind. In those days, classes were streamed into A, B, C and D. Slow or disruptive children like me were generally to be found in C and D classes where we made raffia mats or cork coasters and occasionally rioted. Miss MacDonald's sense of justice could be summary. For laughing and pointing at a girl who had peed her pants, the urine pooling under her desk, I was made to stand in the rubbish bin. For swearing I was locked in the chalk cupboard. When Miss MacDonald heard me tipping out all the green cardboard boxes onto the floor and smashing the chalk, I was dragged along to the headmaster's room to get the belt, three on each hand. In the 1950s, pupils as young as 7 and 8 were often punished with the tawse, a thick leather strap with the business end split so that it stung.

Schools did not communicate well with parents in those days. Education was none of their business and teachers knew best, as well as being a cut above. My dad once told me that I should salute any teachers I passed in the street. And if the headmaster happened to come into our classroom, we all stood up. But when my mum found out what had been going on, there was none of my dad's daft deference. She insisted on seeing the headmaster. Having been scrubbed, warned to behave and keep quiet, I was to accompany her. Perhaps because of the need to concentrate on what she sternly called 'behaviour', I have no memory of what she said to Mr Scrimgeour. Much later, she told me that the gist of it was that my sister, Barbara, was very clever, first in the A class (she would eventually be dux of the school), and that meant I could not be as stupid as the school thought I was. It was the teachers' job to educate me, to get it out of me and that wasn't going to happen in the wilds of the D class. My mum must have been persuasive because, like a miracle, it all happened. I was moved to the A class.

It was a life-defining moment, a determined act of love I shall never forget. My mum fought for me and we both won.

*

In 1951, Ted Brocklebank left his infant school and went to the Burgh School in St Andrews. It was an unusual mixture of primary school classes and secondary, with children up to 15 years old. His first recollection of his time there was one shared by many hundreds of thousands of Scottish schoolchildren:

'Chinky' Chalmers was the headmaster . . . and he wielded a mean Lochgelly 'heavy'. Discipline and belting seemed to be more important than learning at this new school. All the teachers belted, some with less reason than others. If the crime had been particularly heinous, it was: 'Wait outside the door till Mr Chalmers collects you.' What seems unfair even at this great remove was that pupils were belted for simply not knowing the answers to questions posed. I'm sure I deserved all the beltings administered. I was lippy and seemed to be in fights all the time. I ran with a group that vowed never to let our belters see us in tears. Later, as we ran cold tap water on our blistered wrists we strutted our youthful macho. Hardly felt it! But there was something sickening about watching shy, obedient classmates reduced to tears, not because they had been cheeky or disruptive, but because they had failed a long division sum or misspelt a word. Miss G was the worst belter. She had rimless glasses, thin lips and wore no makeup. No Nazi interrogator ever inspired more terror. She only became animated when yanking out her belt from her desk, shrieking: 'Come out to the front, boy.' Mr A, the woodwork teacher, was normally a bluff old cove. But even he could lose it when, for example, a victim withdrew his hand at the last minute or refused to accept the belt. I can remember Mr A chasing one culprit around the woodwork benches with an 18-inch-long Lochgelly 'heavy'. Even at ten we knew the real loser was Mr A.

Not far from St Andrews, Lochgelly was where the belt ('tawse') used by Chinky Chalmers was made. The saddler Robert Philp began to produce them in bulk sometime around 1884, when both his son and his daughter qualified as teachers. Usually about two feet long and a little over an inch wide, the leather was split at one end into what frightened children called the 'tawse taes'. As I discovered, these ensured that each stroke would sting. The heavy, and therefore even more painful, version preferred by Chinky Chalmers was made from thicker leather. There was also a 'super-heavy' available that was half an inch thick. So that children's hands were not cut and unseemly blood spilt, Philp smoothed the edges of the tawse taes. Despite Chalmers' preference, the Lochgelly tawse was lighter and easier to use and also stiffer so that it did not wrap around the victim's hand.

'Tawse' is a Scots word that derives from 'taw', to whip, and sometimes the punishment of children in front of the class resembled the ritual cruelties of the Colosseum even more closely. When a child was thought to deserve 'six of the best', the class would occasionally chant 'Taw them! Taw them!' As a student teacher in 1972, observing lessons from the back of the class, I saw this more than once. It was disturbing, a young mob chanting for blood, or at least red welts. In 1982, a two-tailed Lochgelly heavy retailed for £5.90. That same year, a female teacher offered advice on how to use one correctly:

> You make sure that their cuff is pulled up to the edge of the wrist so that you don't injure their wrist when you belt them. Then you put the belt over your shoulder, you line yourself up in front of the kid, you make sure your leg is out of the way because you look pretty stupid if you hit your leg. You don't use an enormous movement from the shoulder, you just let the length of the belt follow through and you hit them. It was barbaric but it did work, and we don't have it now and we're having enormous problems in the classroom.

Other accounts of technique noted that before they were hit, the children were instructed to fold one hand under the other. That was thought to make it more awkward for the victim to pull back their hands at the last moment, the reaction that provoked the woodwork teacher in St Andrews to run in a rage around the benches of his classroom. Others insisted that the child lay their hand on their desks so that the pain would be even greater as their knuckles rapped against the wood when the tawse struck their palms. Other items were used, often in a moment of anger. Wooden blackboard dusters were hurled at children, rulers used to rap knuckles, bottoms spanked, legs slapped and pencils jabbed into ribs.

The spectacle of children suffering the pain and humiliation of corporal punishment was not rare in post-war Scotland: it was commonplace. In a survey of 40,000 school leavers in 1980, only 5 per cent of boys had never had the tawse. And an analysis of another sample showed that 60 per cent of girls had been punished in the same way. Corporal punishment was heavily used in Edinburgh's schools, where punishment logs were kept, and the tawse was swung more than 30,000 times in one year. In a 1977 study, more than 30 per cent of 12–15-year-old boys suffered the tawse once every ten days and 20 per cent were belted three or more times during the same period. Which suggests that the female teacher who advised on technique was wrong. It didn't work.

As Ted Brocklebank remembered, this epidemic of violence against children, some as young as 5 or 6, could be arbitrary. In 1968, a code of practice was issued to schools that insisted the tawse was not to be used as a punishment for academic failure but only to enforce discipline. Yet, at the Burgh School and beyond, many teachers largely ignored the guidance.

The writer and historian Carol Craig makes the important point that the corporal punishment of children in Scotland did not happen in a vacuum. Policemen, neighbours, even shopkeepers, thought nothing of giving a child 'a clout round the ear' or 'a kick up the backside'. Professor Richard Finlay has observed that Scots have a particularly wide vocabulary for the inflicting of violence: words like leathering, battering, skelping, tanning, loundering, hammering, bleaching, whipping, roasting, thrashing, dishing out a hiding, getting a doing and many more terms were often used.

Corporal punishment in schools was banned by most European countries before the Second World War, sometimes long before, but in Scotland it was practised for a considerable time, and was much more common than it was in England. Carol Craig believes that there were three main reasons for this persistence. Severe overcrowding in poor housing creates stress that can easily spill over into violence against children, normalising it. Until recently,

Scotland was a more religious society and, as such, more readily embraced the notion of sparing the rod and spoiling the child. And finally, in large towns and cities violence sometimes spilled onto the streets and was therefore more visible as a part of life.

In 1980, Mrs Margaret Maguire of Clydebank was prosecuted because she refused to allow teachers to belt her son. In the hope of some sympathy, she turned to her church and sought an interview with the Catholic Archbishop of Glasgow, Thomas Winning. But when they met, he told Mrs Maguire that corporal punishment had 'done him no harm'. That appears to have been the prevailing view, and few challenged it. But when they did, dark aspects of what amounted in some cases to sadism emerged.

The journalist Kate Kinloch wrote: 'The other week I was visiting a friend whose husband is a teacher. He came home from school while I was still there, and flung his briefcase on the floor. "The teacher next door sent in teenage girls again today to borrow my strap so that he could use it on them." His face showed all the disgust he felt.' Kate asked how old the girls were, to which he replied: 'Oh, about fourteen. And the teacher is young, in his early thirties. It's kinky, I tell you, kinky. There's no other word for it.'

Despite this, and other cases of excess and abuse, widespread support in Scotland for the belting of children persisted. The distinguished historian Professor Sir Tom Devine believes that many parents still support the use of the tawse. When, in 2018, the Scottish Government began to formulate legislation to outlaw physical punishment of under-16s, making it a criminal offence for parents to smack their children, there was powerful opposition. Nevertheless, the bill became law in 2020.

More than 40 years before, the attitudes of the authorities were very different. In order to protect their children from violence, two more mothers took on the educational and legal establishments in Scotland. In September 1976, 15-year-old Jeffrey Cosans was caught taking a shortcut through a cemetery. He refused to accept being punished with the tawse and was suspended from Beath High School in Cowdenbeath, Fife. His mother Jane argued that the school was breaching his human rights and also those of his parents because they refused to respect their opposition to corporal punishment. Jeffrey was preparing for his O-grade examinations, but his suspension went on so long that he never sat them. After leaving school with no qualifications, he was unemployed for six years. In fact, Jeffrey's suspension had been entered into the records of his local employment exchange, and that probably discouraged employers from interviewing him. His lack of qualifications also meant he could not gain entry to a college of further education.

Earlier in 1976, Mrs Grace Campbell asked Strathclyde Regional Council to guarantee that Gordon, her 7-year-old son, would never be belted by his teachers at Bishopbriggs Primary School. The council refused and the situation remained unresolved.

The two mothers made common cause, but they had great difficulty in funding the costs of their case. The Campbells were forced to borrow money, and one evening they returned home to find graffiti sprayed all over their front door. Bricks were thrown through their windows more than once. When Jeffrey Cosans was suspended, the *Glasgow Evening Times'* editorial was unequivocal: 'The case might seem like a storm in a tea cup. But there's an important principle. The headmaster did the right thing – and set a good example.'

Not everyone agreed. Mrs J. Small wrote to the editor:

Since the beginning of the new school term my seven year-old daughter has had the belt twice. Once it was for talking in the line before going into school, the next time for holding a door open to let children in from the playground, which it seems contravened some school law. When I questioned the punishment I was told it was necessary for discipline. I am sure that generations to come will look back in amazement to think that in 1976 this type of punishment was still being used in our schools.

In 1982, Grace Campbell and Jane Cosans took their case to the European Court of Human Rights and, against all the odds, won. The effect was confused but rapid. From the beginning of 1983, no child in Strathclyde or Lothian Region was ever belted again, and other local authorities quickly followed suit. In between the mothers' case being heard and a judgment being made, the Secretary of State for Scotland, George Younger, gave a commitment that the use of the tawse in schools would cease. The Education Act (No. 2) of 1986 finally banned corporal punishment in schools and became law in 1986.

Grace Campbell paid a high price for her dogged fight for the rights of children. In the same year as they won their case in Strasbourg, she had a stroke; she died in 1989, only 47 years old. Her son Gordon is now a doctor, and his brother, Andrew, is a human rights lawyer. In 2022, he said: 'The greatest legacy is the one my mum gave my children, who are happy and relaxed to go to school; who are incredulous at the idea of violence in a classroom; and who are deeply inspired by what their granny did for them and others.'

In 1962, I moved from the Abbey Primary School all the way across Kelso to the big school, the High School. My own mum's efforts had worked. I had, mostly, behaved myself, even learned a little, and I found myself in the A class. But when I sat down in Mr Cowe's classroom to learn how to do algebra, I was baffled. I couldn't grasp the point. None of the symbolism made any sort of sense. Letters didn't add up. ax+bx+c= 0. Really? I was able to do mental arithmetic well enough, but its principles of addition, subtraction, multiplication and division seemed not to apply to this maze of equations.

That was bad enough, but it wasn't the main problem. Sandy Cowe was known as Sandy Bull because he could be very aggressive with those, like me, who made mistakes. Using derision as well as the tawse, he created an atmosphere of constant fear in his classroom, and I came to dread Monday morning maths periods. The arbitrary nature of Mr Cowe's rages meant that every child, especially one like me who had difficulties, was always on their guard. It was more important than anything, certainly learning, to avoid being belted, derided or having a board cleaner hurled across the classroom at you. If I didn't understand something, and that was often, I never dared ask a question.

Every week, it seemed, Mr Cowe set us short tests that he marked there and then so that the results could be read out to the class. Towards the end of the first term, I remember that I had somehow picked up enough of how equations worked to get some of the answers right, or nearly right. But it made no difference. Because I had failed to put a full stop at the end of each set of workings, Mr Cowe announced to the class that I had scored 2 per cent. And three strokes of the tawse on each hand.

When children are scared, or even apprehensive, they learn very little. In later life, I became interested in quantum physics, managed to read Stephen Hawking's *A Brief History of Time* almost to the end and understood that mathematics is the language of the universe, even if I didn't understand precisely what black holes are. But it took a long time for that frightened little boy to escape the shadow of violence that darkened Scottish schools for far too long. Many are nostalgic for the best days of our lives. They were too often not. The dictionary derivation of nostalgia notes that the first element is from the Greek *nóstos,* meaning homecoming, and the second from *álgos,* which means pain.

Before any of us in Primary 7 went on to Kelso High School, there was a high hurdle to clear. What we knew as the Control was more generally called the Qually across the rest of Scotland, the Qualifying Examination, the equivalent of England's 11 Plus. Its purpose in Kelso was to determine streaming, where children would be allocated according to ability, the A, B, C or D class. Everyone would go to Kelso High School; it was the sole secondary school in the town, and the expectation was that those in the C and D classes would leave at the age of 15 to go into apprenticeships or do manual labour of some sort. The As, and perhaps some of the Bs, might stay on longer at school, take O-grade and Higher exams and then go on to further education of some sort. In most larger towns and the cities, the division was more stark, more defining. For example, in St Andrews, those who did well at the Qually would expect to go to Madras College, while the rest would go to the Burgh School into the care of Chinky Chalmers and the female teacher with the rimless spectacles. The equivalent in England was a secondary modern school.

As well as pupils being streamed, so were schools in Scotland, and Edinburgh supplies a good illustration today. The A class comprises Fettes College, Merchiston Castle School and Loretto in nearby Musselburgh. These are all fee-paying and have many boarders. Since they are private schools not funded directly by the state, except for the advantage of having charitable status, they opt for the English curriculum with pupils sitting A-levels rather than Highers. This makes it easier to gain entrance to Oxford and Cambridge universities.

The B class is peculiar to Scotland, and some are known as Merchant Company Schools; all of them were founded by philanthropists, and almost all of them take their names. George Watson's is one of the largest, and it is joined by George Heriot's, Daniel Stewart's (now Stewart's Melville College) and Mary Erskine's all-girls' school. Other private schools in the B class are Edinburgh Academy and St George's School for girls. The tartan skirts, purple blazers and other uniforms brighten a winter afternoon when pupils board Edinburgh's buses at the end of another school day.

Between B and C were the Royal High School and Trinity Academy, schools that used to charge a nominal fee but are now in the public sector. In the C class are the likes of Boroughmuir High School, James Gillespie's High School, Leith Academy and seventeen other schools. The D class is no more but used to be made up of junior secondary schools like David Kilpatrick's in Leith and others. These classifications are, of course, no reflection on academic standards; they relate only to cost.

The Education (Scotland) Act, 1918 had introduced the principle of universal free schooling and created 38 education authorities across the country. They seemed to adopt different versions of the Qually. At Ardrossan Academy Primary School, pupils took an IQ test and then the usual school exam results were taken into account. In Fife, there were two IQ tests taken months apart and also an English essay. Roxburgh County Council opted for an IQ test, an arithmetic paper and an English paper. Known as the Moray House Test after Edinburgh's teacher training college, the IQ paper was baffling as it asked me to make deductions about different sorts of shapes: squares, circles, triangles and the like. It looked like a different, more solid version of algebra. But I managed to do better in the English and arithmetic papers.

Educationists insisted that no one ever failed the Qually, some simply did less well than others. Once all the papers were in, an 'adjusted average' was worked out, and those above it went into the A and perhaps B classes (these were often very large at 30 or more pupils, following the post-war baby boom) and those below it went into the C and D classes. Of course, the pious semantics that allowed the spurious claim that no one ever failed the Qually made not a jot of difference.

*

There were other rites of passage at the end of primary school. Not in Kelso, but across the rest of Scotland teachers organised the Qually Dance. Boys were expected to invite girls to be their partners, a process printed indelibly on many memories. Here is one: '[I invited] Alison Boyd. She's a pharmacist now, apparently, but I haven't seen her since taking her for fish and chips after our Primary 7 Qually Dance. She hasn't returned any of my calls.'

Even though these examinations ceased in the late 1960s, some Edinburgh primary schools still hold Qually Dances at the end of the year. Annoyingly, to me at least, some have adopted the Americanism, the end of year 'prom'.

Looking back at that time, despite my problems with algebra, I can see that I was lucky. Those children consigned to the B, C and D classes saw very important life choices taken out of their hands and made for them by the vagaries of a set of exams, some of which, like the IQ tests, are now discredited. At the age of 12, it was decided that young boys would be manual workers, either in the building trade or similar, and for young girls, it was shop work or jobs in the textile mills of the Borders. Much too young to question these judgements and with little or no input from parents (unless they were blessed with a warrior mum like mine), those in the lower streams were forced to accept their fate. Exams are competitive and comparative, and those below the 'adjusted average' lost. And they were about to lose out on even more opportunities.

In 1963, Lord Robbins published his report on the future of Britain's universities. The old core of the system had been Oxford, Cambridge and the four ancient Scottish universities. In effect, they had been a finishing school for the elite, for public school-boys and a few girls, or the Scottish Merchant Company schools, and they were places where political, financial and social leaders took their degrees. England's great Victorian civic universities, often founded by local philanthropy, in the likes of Manchester, Birmingham and Leeds were more or less the preserve of the middle classes, people who would take up roles in the professions and industry. It was an academic landscape that had to change – and quickly. The tidal wave of the baby boomers was about to surge through higher education, and Lord Robbins and his committee put forward proposals for expansion that would cope with significantly higher demand.

The recommendation – and the quickest fix – was to convert all colleges of advanced technology and other respected higher education institutions into universities. Pieces of paper and legislation would do it. In the 1960s, charters were granted to Keele, Sussex, the University of East Anglia, York, Lancaster, Essex, Kent, Warwick, Salford, Ulster and, in Scotland, Strathclyde and Heriot Watt. Dundee broke away from St Andrews in 1967. Stirling University was the sole new foundation in Britain at that time, and Lord Robbins became its first chancellor.

Of more immediate significance to me and my family was the Anderson report of 1960. It proposed that British residents on first degree courses should be entitled to public support for their living costs as well as the payment of tuition fees. And these grants – not loans – should be available 'to all who were qualified for them by ability and attainment'. And not the ability to pay for schooling.

Linked to Robbins' expansion of universities, this was a turning point for many thousands of young Scots. Bursaries for schoolchildren with ability but no money had long been available, but these were, of course, competitive since the amount of funding was finite. Even philanthropist Andrew Carnegie's spectacular endowment of $10 million in 1901 to the universities of Scotland was insufficient to provide what became known as maintenance grants. But by 1910 the Carnegie Trust was paying the tuition fees of half of all the students at the four ancient universities, and while some working-class children did break through, they were very much the exception. The Anderson Report changed all that.

In 1963, Nanny Hall won the dux medal at Kelso High School. What made that achievement more remarkable was that he and his family lived at the bottom of our street, in a council house. No doubt now known as Mr Ian Hall, he was a hero, and he took advantage of the new legislation, the first person I knew who went to university. The next person to do this in our street was my big sister. Barbara won the dux medal in 1964 and caused a row.

Even though she was highly qualified, even though she was eligible for both a maintenance grant and the tuition fees were paid by the local education authority, and even though she had been offered a place at Edinburgh University, my dad didn't want her to go.

The illegitimate son of a single mother (my grannie, Bina), Dad had powerful but unarticulated difficulties with social status. One of these edged around the notion of 'not getting above yourself'. And going to university was definitely getting above yourself. My dad was a very clever man who had served his apprenticeship as an electrician and was reckoned to be an excellent tradesman. But he was a tradesman. The sons, and increasingly the daughters, of solicitors, doctors, teachers – they were the sort to go to university. But not his daughter. And there was something else, an unwritten contract. When children left school at 15 (and even though Barbara was often first in her class, Dad objected to her staying on at school), and before they got married and started their own families, they lived at home where they were expected to contribute a sizable proportion of their weekly pay packet for 'bed and board'. If Barbara went to Edinburgh, that would not happen.

As she did for me, my mum made the difference. After a titanic struggle, Dad relented, and my big sister became the second person in our street to matriculate at a university. It was the beginning of a brief window in history, one that remained open for less than 20 years, a time when there was no bar to educational advancement for those young people with ability. Any nation's greatest resource is its people, and at last the potential of the people of Scotland was being realised. But not for long.

When my turn came in 1968, it was much easier. Barbara had graduated, immediately got a good job as a teacher and vindicated all that my mum had argued for. Only a handful of years before, the futures of working-class children raised on a council estate were usually predetermined. Now, new horizons opened.

When I left Wm Low's in St Andrews with my pork pie, there were 197,000 students in British universities. By 1980, the number had climbed to 524,000. The year before, Margaret Thatcher's Conservative Government was elected, and a different view of higher education began to prevail. The state needed to shrink, the Conservatives believed, and it would no longer pay the whole cost of a university education. As time went on, more and more of the financial burden fell on the students and their families. The principles of the Anderson and Robbins Reports were largely abandoned, a situation that the Labour Government of 1997 to 2010 did little to remedy. The window through which my sister and I, and many other working-class children, had glimpsed a brighter future had closed.

I graduated from St Andrews in 1972, and to my great joy and pride, I returned 40 years later to be installed as the university's fifty-first Lord Rector. It is a grand title, and the costume, the gowns and the hat, as well as the ceremonials, with maces and processions, are all splendid. My dad would have been horrified. All that was well above the likes of me. But it was not a real job, and there were few responsibilities. The Rector chairs the university court, sitting on a piece of furniture that looks more like a throne, in a room lined with portraits of titled luminaries who, unlike me, seemed comfortable. It turned out that the court's business was not run by the person chairing it but by the Senior Governor, someone who, so far as I could work out, was elected by no one. This probably happened because in the past so few Rectors actually visited St Andrews. I had decided to engage closely with the students and came up every fortnight, but that made no difference and I was excluded from the decision-making process.

What I loved, and what made it all worthwhile, was working with the students. The Rector is elected by the undergraduates, and in October 2011 we fought an exhilarating, week-long campaign. Brilliantly orchestrated by young people who had a mastery of social media, my job was to meet as many students as possible, make stump speeches at halls of residence and generally get our message across. At the count it turned out that we had won by a country mile, soundly defeating a former Secretary of State for Scotland, an international footballer and a TV reporter amongst others. It was an unforgettable experience.

Unable to make any headway with the academic establishment, I spent my time helping students as much as I could, raising money for a Rector's Fund and holding fortnightly surgeries to sort out problems. Over three years I met many hundreds of students and was continually struck by how very different St Andrews had become. When I graduated in 1972 there were plenty of middle-class students, many of them English, but there were also lots of young people with similar backgrounds to mine receiving their degrees and celebrating with their families. Forty years later, the student population having more than doubled, there were very many fewer. The gentrification of the town, immediately evident in the expensive shops and restaurants in Market Street and on South Street, the accents I heard, the stories I was told, and the high cost of accommodation all combined to present a very different picture. I liked almost all the students I had dealings with, but the vast majority of them came from comfortable, even very wealthy, backgrounds. I know these are only anecdotal impressions, but they were gathered consistently over a long period. And the statistics support them.

From meetings of the university court and the vast documentation around them, I saw that the other striking difference was
the commodification of higher education. A degree is now a
product, a very expensive purchase, and academic standards were
immeasurably higher than 40 years before. The latter can only
be an improvement. The teaching of English was shockingly bad
when I was a student. In my rectorial address of 2012, I made
myself even more unpopular with the academics when I encouraged students to work less and meet more people. Spending time
with those from different backgrounds and different countries
was one of the most enduringly valuable elements in my education at St Andrews. I learned more than one important life lesson
there. But now, because degrees are so expensive, every ounce of
academic value has to be wrung out of them. And that ought not
to be the only point of going to university.

In 2007, there were hopeful signs that Scottish universities might
see a return to the situation before the withdrawal of government
support. The new SNP Government voted to abolish the payment of
tuition fees by Scottish students. Two years earlier, Nicola Sturgeon,
who would later become First Minister, had said that the average
accumulated student debt of £11,000 would 'impede access to education' and would have discouraged her from going to university.
But in reality that debt did not disappear: it doubled. The Scottish
Government paid only for tuition fees and did not give the sort of
maintenance grants I received. By 2015, the least-well-off students
owed about £22,000 when they graduated. Nowadays, it is more
likely to be around £15,000 (in England, £45,000); however, the
total student debt in Scotland in 2023 was a staggering £7.6 billion.
The new measures had the unintended effect of making a university
education cheaper for more wealthy families who could afford to
support their children. The percentage of less-well-off students at
Scottish universities remains unchanged. And the doors that opened
for so many in the 1960s and 1970s remain firmly closed.

4

Show Business

At the end of one of the long summers of the late 1950s, the world suddenly shrank. Evenings were no longer spent playing chasey around the rugby ground or standing below the glow of the lamppost at the top of Inchmead Drive chanting 'Truth, dare, double dare, promise or repeat'. My mum no longer had to come to the front garden gate to call us indoors at bedtime. We already were indoors, early. My sisters and I sat on cushions on the floor, leaning against the sofa where my parents were waiting in anticipation. Bina was looking out of the window. The rest of us were looking at a set of small wooden shelves in the corner of the sitting room. On it sat a television, and that night the world both shrank and expanded.

It wasn't the first time I'd watched. Each summer, two brothers roughly my age came to Kelso for part of the school summer holidays. Barrie and Pete were from the West of Scotland, one of the large towns near Glasgow, and they seemed like city sophisticates to me and our gang. The boys stayed with their grannie, Nana Hawkins, and after a game of football (rugby was a mystery to them), they announced they were going to watch something called *Boots and Saddles* on TV. We had seen men fixing a large aerial onto the chimney of the Hawkins' house. But when Nana saw us all, a bunch of local scruffs, marching up her garden path behind Barrie and Pete, she called an instant halt. We could watch *Boots and Saddles*, but only through the sitting-room window.

At first there was nothing to see. Then Mr Hawkins opened two little doors to reveal a screen not much bigger than the window panes we were looking through. After switching it on, he stood waiting for the set to warm up, like our old radio. Then fuzzy diagonal black and white bars appeared. With more twiddling of knobs, what I later discovered was the horizontal hold, a small grey picture finally appeared. It was a posh-looking and posh-sounding woman sitting next to a table with a vase of flowers on it. Mr Hawkins came over and opened the sitting-room window about six inches so that the scruffs could hear her say something like, 'Now, children, are you sitting comfortably? It's time for another exciting story from the Wild West.'

We were mesmerised. Standing next to a well-trained horse, a trooper sounded a bugle call (somehow, I found out that the call was 'Boots and Saddles', the order to muster and mount up), and moments later, behind an officer, 30 cavalrymen trotted out of the fort. The subtitle of the show was 'The Story of the Fifth Cavalry'.

We had all seen westerns at the Saturday matinees at the Roxy and the Playhouse, but this was very different. There weren't scores of other kids yelling and carrying on, no farting competitions in the front row, no squabbles over ice lollies, no teenagers snogging and grappling in the back row. In your own house, you could watch loads of stuff for free and without having to go anywhere. It was somehow yours, ours.

It wasn't free, of course, but what allowed Nana Hawkins, and a few months later, the Moffats, to have a TV was the rapidly expanding rental market. Sets, often called receivers in those early days, were very expensive to buy, but companies like Radio Rentals and DER began to offer much more affordable deals, both hire purchase and rentals. My mum and dad may have paid seven shillings and sixpence a week, a sizable chunk of their combined weekly wages, but it turned out that the telly would save them money elsewhere.

More than 2.1 million households in Britain had a TV licence in 1953, many of them acquiring sets so that they, and many neighbours and visitors crowding into sitting rooms, could watch the Queen's Coronation on 2 June. By 1960, the number had jumped to 9.3 million, even though the rollout of BBC transmitters and services was gradual (as was the launch of the regional ITV companies after 1955).

Watching TV was not straightforward. Instead of clicking the remote and sitting down as we do now, the set often needed tuning. Knobs for vertical and horizontal holds were twiddled, the contrast adjusted and sometimes an indoor aerial had to be placed in exactly the right spot, often a different spot from the night before. Sometimes my mum stood in the middle of the sitting room, holding up the aerial like the Statue of Liberty holding her torch. I remember my dad, bad-tempered, balancing it on the top of the half-open sitting-room door. If the signal strength was poor or the weather bad, the screen could become snowy. And there was a test card to help with tuning. But we put up with all of that because TV was magnetic, pulling us into other worlds – and it changed society radically.

The BBC was at first the sole provider, and in Scotland it was not particularly keen to be that. The gloriously named Controller, Scotland, the Reverend Melville Dinwiddie, wrote this extraordinary piece in the *Radio Times* of March 1952:

Sound broadcasting as such is upsetting enough when reading and school lessons and other home tasks have to be done, but here is a more intensely absorbing demand on our leisure hours, and families in mid-Scotland will have to make a decision both about getting a receiver and about using it. At the start, viewing will take up much time because of its novelty, but discrimination is essential so that not every evening was spent in a darkened room, the chores of the house and other occupations neglected. We can get too much even of a good thing.

No one was listening, as the curtains were drawn and the sets warmed up. The paternalistic, patronising Controller, Scotland was swimming against the tide. So rapid and remarkable was the introduction of TV sets into millions of homes (75 per cent in Scotland had them by 1965) that many can clearly recall the first programmes they saw.

My parents were so dazzled that at first they let me and my sisters, Barbara and Marjie, watch virtually anything and stay up until it was finished. The Reverend Dinwoodie was right. It was completely absorbing. We vividly remember hiding, terrified, behind the sofa when *Quatermass and the Pit* was on. In London, workmen find what they at first think is an unexploded bomb in a crater. And, in reality, there were many of these, even ten or more years after the end of the war. But it isn't a bomb. It's an alien spaceship. Martians. This scene may be entirely apocryphal, but I can remember it very clearly. When the scientists bore a hole in the spacecraft, they look into it. And they see another eye looking at them! I nearly fainted with fright.

At the other end of the spectrum, as far from the terrors of the Pit as it is possible to be, was the *Watch with Mother* series. Even though it was clearly for younger children, we watched *Andy Pandy* and the *Flower Pot Men*. We watched *everything* for the first few months. Despite being able to clearly see the strings that made Andy dance around and despite the fact that the songs and music with Teddy and Looby Loo were dire, I liked it. The woman who narrated the show (and who sounded posher than the Queen) seemed to talk simultaneously to Andy and the children watching. When the puppets climbed back into the wicker basket at the end, she always sang the same thing: 'Time to go home, time to go home. Andy is waving goodbye, goodbye.' It didn't matter that we were all already at home. I waved back as my grannie tutted at the daftness, shook her head and looked out of the window.

An extraordinary convention had grown up, perhaps at the intervention of the Reverend Dinwiddie, that TV would shut down for an hour each day between the end of children's programmes at 6 p.m. until 7 p.m. when general output would begin. Known as the Toddlers' Truce, it was intended to allow parents to get their little ones off to bed without distraction. But problems arose when the first ITV companies began broadcasting in late 1955. If they were forced to close down transmission in what came to be known as peak time, they would lose advertising revenue, and in those early years ABC, ATV, Granada and Associated Rediffusion (all of them broadcasting in England – the Scottish ITV companies began slightly later) struggled to be viable. After pressure from the Independent Television Authority, the governing body, the Toddlers' Truce was abandoned from 16 February 1957, which gave the BBC a scheduling problem, one that they solved brilliantly. Two days after the shutdown ceased, the first edition of *Tonight* with Cliff Michelmore was broadcast. It was wonderful, and I watched every night: even when it was sunny outside, even when Barrie and Pete were on holiday. At more than 50 years' distance and having spent most of a working life in TV, I can see now that Michelmore was a terrific presenter. He set the tone for the show. Genial, relaxed and often sitting not behind but on the edge of his desk, his style was very different from the stiff, cut-glass formality of the BBC's presenters and announcers up until then. Michelmore looked as though he was enjoying himself, and the topics and other material in the show were worth knowing about, not over my head and sometimes even fun. He also seemed unflappable. When the black Bakelite phone on his desk rang to tell him there was a problem with the next item, he would smile, sometimes raise an eyebrow and then improvise, seemingly amused with the backstage problems. The Guyanese musician Cy Grant would perform live on the programme, singing the news in the calypso style. If production problems persisted, Michelmore would call on the singer to do more and sooner. The programme also ran live interviews which could be extended as needed. None of these difficulties were ever covered up, and no secret was made of the fact that this was a live show made in a TV studio. Cameras and cameramen were often visible as presenters moved around, and these moments often added to my enjoyment. You never knew what was coming next.

On an evening when all was going smoothly, Michelmore would introduce a series of filmed reports from around Britain and elsewhere. There was a team of excellent, sometimes quirky, reporters. Alan Whicker, Kenneth Allsop, Brian Redhead and Julian Pettifer all went on to stellar solo careers in broadcasting. My own favourite was Fyfe Robertson. Sporting a goatee beard and always wearing a tweed trilby hat, his pinched, dyspeptic features seemed to speak of persistent heartburn. Making no attempt to hide or modify his Scottish accent, which we all liked, he always seemed to begin each report with 'Hello, there. I'm Fyfe Robertson'. We know, we know, we saw you last week. Cliff Michelmore called him 'our roving reporter'.

What *Tonight* did for me, and I suspect many others, was to expand our horizons. Before the coming of TV, the only non-Scots, even non-Borderers, I knew anything about were cowboys, Indians and Nazis. *Whicker's World* was at first a series of reports that later became a series by itself, but Alan showed me places and people I knew nothing of and made them interesting. Although I didn't realise it at the time, the effect of all this new information, so well presented and so easily accessible, was simple: it made me curious, it made me want to know more about *out there* – the world beyond Inchmead Drive and Kelso. It was a great gift.

The Television Act of 1954 was intended to end the monopoly of the BBC. More than that, it was designed to make provision for a regional network with the first franchises awarded to companies that would serve London, the Midlands and North West England. The whole of Scotland, with STV, Grampian and Border TV would not be covered until 1962.

At first, only London received programmes from Associated Rediffusion, and the service began with an unlikely opening ceremony at the Guildhall. Instead of *Pomp and Circumstance*, which might have been more appropriate, ITV's first programme started with Elgar's *Cockaigne Overture* played by the Halle Orchestra. After some speeches and the national anthem, the schedule began with a variety show, some professional boxing from Shoreditch Town Hall and three snippets of drama that included Dame Edith Evans as Lady Bracknell.

The BBC's spoiler to the competition was scheduled not on TV but on radio. On 22 September 1955, the same day as ITV's launch, 20 million tuned in at 6.45 p.m. to hear *The Archers*. Described as 'one of the most controversial events in Ambridge's history', listeners were shocked when Grace Archer rushed into a burning stable to rescue Midnight, her horse. It all went terribly wrong, and on the way to the hospital she expired in Phil Archer's arms. This sudden piece of melodrama in what had been regarded by most listeners as a bucolic haven caused a sensation. There were letters to *The Times* and thousands of complaints, and few people outside London paid much attention to the birth of ITV.

Very soon, four companies were broadcasting, and all were finding it difficult to make their new businesses work. Not all TV sets could receive ITV, and the early adverts were poor, even amateurish, affairs. They tended to be shouty and feature salesmen who were less than persuasive, and some of them were far too long. Amongst the most successful were animations with catchy jingles such as 'Murray Mints, Murray Mints, the too-good-to-hurry mints', Rice Krispies' 'Snap, Crackle and Pop' and Rowntree's 'Don't forget the fruit gums, Mum'. Surveys found that viewers began to look forward to the ad breaks and often chanted the slogans.

Border TV did not begin broadcasting until 1961, but for two years before that we could receive a signal from Tyne Tees Television in Newcastle. The local news was mostly baffling, but the programmes were wonderful. *The Adventures of Robin Hood* began with an arrow hitting a tree with a very satisfying thwack. Outlaw Robin was played by former matinee idol Richard Greene, and for 143 episodes he was feared by the bad and loved by the gooooooood, was Robin Hood.

The BBC had a policy of not giving prizes in any of its quiz shows, but ITV had no such qualms, and *Take Your Pick!* with Michael Miles and *Double Your Money* with Hughie 'I mean that most sincerely, folks' Green were enormously popular. Because something was at stake for the contestants, these shows and others had what light entertainment producers call 'playalong'. The schedule was leavened with American imports such as *I Love Lucy* with husband-and-wife comedy duo Lucille Ball and Desi Arnaz, and *Dragnet*, a comparatively hard-edged detective series. Hard-edged compared to the BBC's *Dixon of Dock Green*, which began with the avuncular bobby Jack Warner under the lamp of a police station saying 'Evenin' all'. ITV's most popular show was *Sunday Night at the London Palladium*. It began with starbursts and the bright lights of the West End and shots of a huge audience going into the theatre, a real showbiz night out by proxy. The show was first hosted by comedian Tommy Trinder, then by Bruce Forsyth, and after him, Norman Vaughan. All had terrific stagecraft and presence, honed by years of ad-libbing in variety theatre, as well as a rich stock of catchphrases. Reflecting the argot of the early

1960s, Norman Vaughan used to do a routine with a questioning thumbs up ('swingin?') or thumbs down ('dodgy?'). Shows often began with a traditional dance act, a row of high-kicking Tiller Girls with plumes of feathers on their heads, their arms linked, and ended with the show's guests waving as they stood on a revolving stage. (The Rolling Stones refused to go on it as it was too uncool.) It now seems like entertainment from another planet, but it was immensely popular sixty years ago.

So was ITV, once all the kinks had been ironed out and the service made available across Britain. A later chair of the Independent Television Authority, Lady Bridget Plowden, summed up attitudes when she sniffed that its programmes were 'distressingly popular'. But in fact all ITV had done was to reflect popular taste, possibly not what the middle classes might have enjoyed, which was usually scheduled on the BBC. With the shining exception of Cliff Michelmore and his team, BBC presenters tended to be formal, stiff, most speaking in clipped RP tones, the language of a private education. On *What's My Line?*, a long-running entertainment show that guessed people's occupations, the regular panellists included Lady Isabel Barnet, Jerry Desmonde, David Nixon and Gilbert Harding, all RP speakers. Bespectacled, somewhat grumpy, Harding was criticised for being pompous and overbearing, but he was nevertheless one of the biggest TV stars of the 1950s.

By some quirk of geography, it had been possible for us to receive Tyne Tees TV, but STV, broadcasting from Glasgow, could be watched in Hawick, a large mill town in the west of the Scottish Borders. My mum was born and raised there, and we often visited her sisters and their families. In Auntie Mary's house, the TV stayed on, full volume, the whole time we were in the sitting room, sipping cups of tea. Which might have appeared odd or rude, but it was a blessing for me, not being much interested in conversations about who in Hawick had done what.

One day I watched *The One O'Clock Gang*. Presented by Larry Marshall and billed as 'a lunch-time menu of mirth and song', it was broadcast live from the Theatre Royal in Glasgow. I didn't understand a lot of it, but what struck me forcibly was that it was definitely Scottish, done unapologetically in Scottish accents. And what I remember very clearly was that Larry Marshall went down into the audience and talked to them. Ordinary people could be on TV! From the stage the cast also read out viewers' letters, usually marking anniversaries and birthdays. The show was distressingly popular, and thousands of editions were broadcast from September 1957 onwards. It was aired on Border TV, which had been recently launched to serve Cumbria, Dumfries and Galloway and the Scottish Borders. What I liked, instinctively, about *The One O'Clock Gang* was that it was a programme about us, not one that featured posh people, not like the BBC.

In the spring of 1960, the board of Granada Television met to discuss a new programme proposal. Not many liked it, and Denis Foreman, later to become chairman of the company, remembered the discussion: 'The sales director was dead against it. It would debase Granada's name in television putting out stuff like this and it's not going to attract viewers . . . The non-execs were against . . . There was just a majority of one . . . *Coronation Street* was given, I think, three or four slots to see what happened – and it was magic.'

Tony Warren was an actor and writer who earned £30 a week at Granada adapting scripts from books. Tired of working on Captain W. E. John's Biggles series, he decided he wanted instead to write something original, something 'from the heart, acted by genuine Northerners'. Working through the night, he wrote the first episode of what he called 'Florizel Street' (after *Sleeping Beauty*'s Prince Florizel), creating legendary characters like Ena Sharples, Minnie Caldwell, Ken Barlow and Elsie Tanner and conjuring a completely credible, very different cultural atmosphere.

Florizel became Coronation, Salford became Weatherfield, and the series was an instant success because it chimed with the lived experience of the majority of viewers. Instead of Gilbert Harding and Lady Isabel Barnet's received pronunciation, viewers heard for the first time actors playing working-class people say 'nowt' and not 'nothing', 'eh, chuck' and not 'good evening' and exclaim 'by 'eck' instead of 'gosh'. In March 1961, *Coronation Street* topped the TV ratings with 75 per cent of all viewers glued to its storylines, 15 million people watching every week. It grew into a defining ITV phenomenon, running constantly from 1961 to this day, with more than 10,000 episodes broadcast. So far.

It was a revelation to at least one occupant of 42 Inchmead Drive. Much of what I knew about England was gleaned from the comfortable, sunlit, middle-class worlds of the Famous Five and Richmal Crompton's Just William stories. But here was a completely different fictional community, one that seemed all too authentic, and *Coronation Street* quickly became popular far beyond Salford and the North West of England.

These consistently huge viewing figures had all sorts of impacts, some of them difficult to measure accurately but nevertheless indisputable. The adverts around the show and across the ITV schedule certainly stimulated the retail sector, boosting sales of everything from soap powder to drinking chocolate and white goods. When the more astute Cabinet members of the Conservative Government pushed for the ending of the BBC's monopoly, the creation of ITV and the launch of what were at first known as sponsored programmes, they hoped for just such an economic stimulus to help pull Britain out of the dismal shortages of the early 1950s and get it to the point where Prime Minister Harold MacMillan could claim before the 1959 general election that Britons had 'never had it so good'. Heightened demand forced manufacturers to respond and shops to stock what customers had seen advertised on ITV the night before. This in turn played to the co-ordinated purchasing power of the expanding grocery chains such as Tesco and Wm Low in Scotland. The very first advert on ITV was for Gibbs SR 'tingling fresh' toothpaste, a grainy, one-minute-long feature set in a wintry landscape with a posh voiceover talking about ingredients. Such was the power of novelty that often a brief recital of product brand names of the later 1950s can conjure up a lost world. Brylcreem and Silvikrin, Lifebuoy and Wright's Coal Tar, Sun-Pat and Marmite. For those old enough, it scarcely needs to be mentioned that the first two were smeared on hair, the second on skin and the third on bread or crackers. Those early adverts on ITV became firmly lodged in my consciousness at a very young age.

Statistics from other popular pastimes reflect the effects of the mass viewing of TV and how it kept millions at home. Between 1955 and 1965, attendances at football matches in Scotland declined by 30 per cent and the huge, seething, swaying crowds of a hundred thousand and more standing on open terraces quickly faded into history. For the first half of the twentieth century, Glaswegians had gone to the cinema in huge numbers, on average once a week. The rest of Scotland sat in the stalls or the balcony 36 times a year compared with 28 annual visits in England. When STV began broadcasting in 1957, the effect was immediate. In the 1930s, Glasgow had more than 130 cinemas, some of them vast. For example, Green's Playhouse could seat 4,254. Many were playful architectural extravaganzas, palaces of dreams. The art deco style was widely popular, and the Vogue Cinema in Knightswood would not have looked out of place in Andalusia, while the Toledo in Muirend looked like a Spanish cathedral. Packed into the city centre were 23 filmhouses all showing continuous daily programmes. But as people began to stay at home to watch TV or were relocated to the peripheral housing schemes where there were no cinemas, attendances began to decline sharply. Now, in the whole of Glasgow, there are only 29 cinemas.

Scotland's busy, and very male-dominated, pub culture also began to decline. In 1900, there was one public house for every 424 Scots, but by 1955 that ratio had widened to one for every 806, and since then it has climbed even higher. The gloom for landlords was not shared by the public because of one other telling comparison. In the same period, convictions for drunkenness collapsed, so to speak, tenfold to 2.6 per 1,000 in the late 1950s. Although the weekly cost of renting our TV set was high, it saved the family money because my parents went out to the cinema and my dad (only my dad) went to the pub much less frequently.

Competition was also on the minds of the Conservative MPs who voted ITV into existence in 1954. As the beneficiaries of the only predicated tax in Britain, the licence fee, the BBC had to justify its existence, and that required value and priorities to move on from the cobwebbed views of the Reverend Dinwoodie and those executives who believed that they should commission and schedule programmes the public *ought to* watch, stuff that was 'improving', what was good for them. In the early 1960s, ratings began to matter. Surveys of viewers had begun almost immediately, and only three months after its launch, a Gallup poll showed that 57 per cent thought ITV was better than the BBC and only 16 per cent held the opposite view. At the time, that view could be attributed to novelty, but it did not shift very much as time went on.

Attitudes were – and had to be – different on what became known, darkly, as 'the other side'. When ATV launched in early 1956 and experienced immediate difficulties, Richard Meyer told the ITA's Director-General that 'the lot of the pioneer programme contractor is not a very happy one financially and we do feel that we must use every possible endeavour to obtain maximum audiences in the initial stages of the development of the medium so that we can be certain of getting sales of advertising space'.

By which he meant giving the public what they want. Popular

light entertainment was not expensive to produce, and ITV wasted no time in scheduling more of the likes of Michael Miles, Hughie Green and so on. *The $64,000 Question* was adapted from the American format of almost the same title. But on a budget. Instead of $64,000, ATV's top prize was 64,000 sixpences, or about £1,600. It was nevertheless a hit, and advertisers were happy to pay more than a few sixpences to buy slots around the show.

The BBC responded slowly, almost accidentally. Two of the most memorable and remarkable TV personalities from the late 1950s were Fanny Cradock (born Phyllis Nan Sortain Pechey) and her fourth husband, Johnnie. In February 1955, the *Radio Times* described them as 'the bon viveur husband and wife cookery team [who] present an unusual style of cooking to a studio audience in the Television Theatre'. The programme has not survived, but something very like it was staged and filmed in London's Royal Albert Hall in 1956.

Wearing a dinner jacket and bow tie, Johnnie comes on stage from the left to a fanfare, and to the right Fanny appears in an off-the-shoulder, chiffon ball gown and white fur stole, caked in make-up, dripping with glittering jewellery, the earrings at least four inches long. As she peels off long evening gloves, Fanny begins to . . . cook French onion soup. Celebrity guests are invited on stage to taste it. 'Marvellous! Wonderful!' Despite the swish of the ball gown, no one was in any doubt about who wore the trousers. Domineering, occasionally irascible, eccentric and magnetic, Fanny was a star, a television natural, and audiences loved her. Her life had been a hard scrabble due to her father's gambling habits, and she had been a door-to-door saleswoman for years. Perhaps as a result of those financial struggles, her recipes were also budget-conscious. In the wake of rationing, shortages and the grey Monday-to-Friday slog of working life, this extraordinary woman provided a form of escape, a window on a life of glitter and glamour, plenty of excellent food and drink

– and laughs. Fanny memorably described herself and Johnnie approaching their new-fangled microwave oven 'with the trepidation of two people returning to a reactor station after a leak'. And it is rumoured that at the end of one programme, Johnnie turned to the camera and said, 'May all your doughnuts turn out like Fanny's.'

Competition between the BBC and ITV also drove up technical standards. In the 1950s, many TV programmes, including drama, were broadcast live. Based on the stories by Frank Richards, several series of *Billy Bunter of Greyfriars School* ran on the BBC from 1952 to 1961. The show was set in a boys' public school complete with all its conventions, obscure names and quirks. Overweight and wearing large glasses, Bunter was known as the Fat Owl of the Remove, a nickname that made no sense to me but was apparently the name of the class he was in. Regularly caned on the buttocks, he used to shout 'Yarooh! Yarooh!', which is hooray backwards. The title role was played by Gerald Campion, who was 29 when the show began and 38 when it ended. The episodes were performed live and twice in the same evening, once at 5.20 p.m. for children, and then, after the Toddlers' Truce, the actors had to do it all again at 8 p.m. Scenes were naturally very static and theatrical with actors moving far more than the cameras, and the chances of things going wrong were very high. And they often did.

In the year after Bunter was first told to 'bend over, you wretched boy', the BBC made a series of short films known as Interludes. These were mostly static shots of tranquil scenes such as horses ploughing, a waterfall, a kitten playing with a ball of wool, or the most famous of all, the potter's wheel. Lasting between five and eight minutes and accompanied by calming, peaceful music, they could be quickly broadcast if a live performance had difficulties, or if production had to move to a different studio. In live plays, they were also played during the intervals. The last Interludes were broadcast in the 1960s as more and more programmes were recorded on tape or film, and gradually live TV was reduced. Now it is more or less confined to news, current affairs, ceremonies like state funerals or coronations, and sport.

If Christmas fell on a weekday in the late 1950s or early 1960s, my dad went to work. We had a Christmas tree, and since he was an electrician, he made sure the lights always worked. On the mantelpiece hung three stockings with a half-crown, a tangerine orange and a bar of Fry's Chocolate Cream in each of them. Barbara, Marjie and I were given one present, and when Dad came home, we had a roast chicken dinner and we were all allowed a glass of shandy, heavy on the lemonade. That wasn't because my parents were mean. New Year (we never called it Hogmanay) was much more important, and on 31 December, the festivities really began. We had a celebratory dinner, the first time I ever had turkey, in the evening, and my dad had a glass of beer while my mum and my gran each had a sherry – Harvey's Bristol Cream, I think. Locked in the sideboard, a bottle could last for years. BBC Scotland ran a very good show up until 'the Bells' at midnight when we all shook hands and kissed. When the actor Duncan Macrae, having possibly had a sherry or two, recited 'A Wee Cock Sparra', it was like watching a man on a tightrope crossing Niagara Falls. Then our neighbours came round to first-foot, and the celebrations continued into the early hours of New Year's Day, often until adults 'foundered'. It was licensed excess when normal, sometimes dour, people laughed, women sometimes wanted to kiss you, and everyone generally behaved extravagantly. It was wonderful to watch. And children were included until they dropped with tiredness.

Television changed all that. Christmas used to be seen in parts of Scotland as a very English festival, a time when God rested Merry Gentlemen, who all looked like John Bull on the John Bull printing sets, and dozens of muffered people sang carols on a snowy village green lit by lamps on long sticks. The BBC began to broadcast a Christmas schedule with special festive programmes. I remember watching the film *It's A Wonderful Life* for the first time. The Queen's Christmas message went out at lunchtime, *Billy Smart's Circus* was on in the afternoon, and *Christmas Night with the Stars* featured Harry Worth, the Black and White Minstrels and Jimmy Edwards. And while all this merriment went on, my dad was at work, and so was everyone else in our street. Christmas began to look like a party Scotland wasn't invited to. But gradually the emphasis shifted. North of the border, Christmas Day became a public holiday in 1958, and by the early 1960s employers began to allow time off work. Albeit reluctantly. Not until 1974 did Boxing Day also become a bank holiday in Scotland.

In 1960, the Pilkington Committee was appointed to look at the future of broadcasting in Britain. Predictably, this gathering of the great and the good turned up its collective nose at ITV, attacking the companies for buying in too much American programming and scheduling too many crime series, all of which were 'distressingly popular'. But in a paradoxical judgement, it awarded a second channel to the BBC that would allow it, eventually, to compete more directly with ITV. BBC2 (later known as BBC Two) would commission what were seen as more culturally important programmes like the Proms at the Albert Hall. It began broadcasting in the South of England and did not launch in Scotland until 1966. The 'culturally relevant' schedule desired by the Pilkington Report allowed BBC One, as it became known, to commission more populist and popular programming so that it could compete for ratings with ITV.

In the summer of 1967, BBC2 became the first in Europe to transmit colour pictures. They came from the Wimbledon tennis championships, and two years later, the channel showed Kenneth Clark's landmark series, *Civilisation*, the story of western art and culture. Where colour was definitely needed. Those like my parents who rented their TV sets were able to switch relatively easily to the new service. By late 1969, both BBC and ITV were broadcasting in colour in Scotland, and I remember the most immediate impact was in sport. We were able to watch the football World Cup finals from Mexico via satellite in 1970 and cheer when England were beaten by West Germany in the quarter finals. Honestly? It made up for all the endless crowing about their victory in the 1966 final.

In Scotland, the three ITV companies, Grampian TV, STV and Border TV, each provided local news, some current affairs and documentary programmes for their regions while BBC Scotland covered the national news. Even though its charter characterised the BBC as a public service broadcaster, the reality was that the three ITV companies made much more local programming. BBC news rarely included items from the Borders, and even though ITV's headquarters in Carlisle was relatively distant, we saw stories from our area every week on *Border News* and *Lookaround*. Communities began to identify with their ITV contractor much more closely than with the remote BBC in Glasgow. Border TV understood that our region was not urban but rural with a network of smaller towns whose identities and rivalries were fed by a rugby union league, common ridings and other annual events. Without a trace of irony, they launched an inter-town talent competition called *Cock of the Border*. It featured singers, dancers and bands and a segment where secondary-school children took part in a quiz. As one of the hapless contestants representing Kelso, I crashed into a cultural collision. One of the questions was about the dates of English bank holidays. I had no idea, and neither did the kids from our opponents, Kirkconnel, in Dumfries and Galloway.

More terrestrial channels were added with the arrival of Channel 4 in 1982 and, in 1997, Channel 5. But the broadcasting landscape really began to change in 1983 when Rupert Murdoch's

News International took control of Super Station Europe, a pioneer of satellite TV. When broadcasting first started in Scotland, programmes went out from line-of-sight transmitters strategically placed on high ground so that they could cover as much territory as possible. Edinburgh used to receive pictures from the Craigkelly transmitter in Fife. It stands on high ground above Burntisland, on the northern shore of the Firth of Forth, and sends an unobstructed signal across the sea to the city's rooftop aerials. But sometimes reception could be poor, even when the technology improved. Satellite TV had no such difficulties. All that was needed was a dish attached to your house that was pointed at the right part of the sky.

Rupert Murdoch wanted to introduce pay TV to Britain and was much encouraged by the Conservative Governments of the 1980s in return for political support from his newspapers. By the time News International had defeated and absorbed others with similar ambitions and created Sky TV, there were difficulties. Having failed to recruit enough subscribers, it seemed that the financial model was not working. Only weeks away from seeing the business fail, Rupert Murdoch embarked on a bold strategy. He encouraged the English First Division clubs to break away from the Football League with the promise of a lucrative offer to broadcast all their live matches on Sky. ITV and the BBC showed a few games and paid only £3.2 million in 1991. The breakaway took place, the Premier League was formed, and the clubs agreed a deal worth a staggering £302 million for exclusive rights to all matches. It was a transformative moment.

Satellite TV can broadcast anywhere in the world, and now Premier League football is watched in 212 territories, in 634 million homes and with an available audience of 4.7 billion. With the injection of huge rights payments, football stadia were redeveloped, enormous transfer fees and wages paid to players, and highly lucrative merchandising deals done. Manchester United won the new Premier League six times in the 1990s, and now most of their fans are not in Manchester, let alone England. Ninety percent live in Asia: 325 million fans in total. And they are by no means unique. As a direct result of television and how it is broadcast, football has become a multi-billion, worldwide business.

It is by no means the only sport to benefit financially from the sale of TV rights. Nowadays golf tournaments and the biennial Ryder Cup, Formula 1 motor racing, rugby union, test cricket and much else are only available on pay TV.

The effects of all this have been radical. When I was growing up in Scotland sport was accessible and its heights could be scaled by anyone with enough talent and commitment. Now it feels and increasingly looks like a lucrative branch of show business where gladiators perform in vast stadia for the amusement of millions. And allegiances have become, in my view, incomprehensible. What is it that people in Singapore, Seoul or Shanghai find to identify with in their support of Manchester United? Perhaps it is enough to wear the red shirt (changed each season to keep sales of merchandise brisk) and admire the skill of the highly paid players? Perhaps it is just success, following a bandwagon?

It was all very different when I was young. Heroes walked down Inchmead Drive. On the Monday morning after he had scored the winning try at Murrayfield against France, Ian Hastie was on his way to work at Kelso railway station. As ever, seated at the sitting-room window, my gran saw him coming. We had watched the match on TV and Ian had scored from a lineout in the corner.

'Here!' my grannie shouted from the front doorstep, 'Come you here to me! What were you doing? Did you not think to run under the posts? Make the kick easier?'

The big man was forced to endure a few moments of criticism.

'Sorry,' I heard the big prop forward say. 'Sorry about that, Mistress Moffat.'

An incident from what was another age, the era of amateur sport. But it also sprang from an innate understanding of a powerful identity. Ian Hastie lived on a council estate but could ascend to the heights of glory in front of 80,000 fans in a packed stadium and many more watching on TV. He was a Kelso man, a Scot who played for his country, who also represented us, ordinary people, because he was one of us, close to us in all senses, not remote. Although on that Monday morning, I expect he wished he had been.

During the Easter school holidays of 1968, I was playing tennis at Shedden Park in Kelso when I saw Geoff Stevenson walking across the cricket ground, waving his arm, calling me over. Kelso were due to play an evening game against the Scottish Champion club, Edinburgh Wanderers, at Murrayfield and the First XV loosehead prop had called off. Geoff, the chairman of the selectors, told me that I was drafted into the side, despite being only 17 years old and still at school.

When I pulled on the black-and-white Kelso jersey with number 1 on my back, I was simultaneously proud and fearful. 'You'll be all right, son,' said Jimmy Riddell, an 18-stone second row forward. 'I'll be behind you.' We played on the international pitch in front of empty stands because all Scotland's games had been played by then, and though we lost to a team with several internationals in it, I played as hard as I knew how for my town, my community, and all that it represented. In the *Scotsman* the following morning, the match report picked me out as a promising newcomer. Life since then has been all downhill.

Forty years later, it was Kelso's turn to be Scottish champions, and at a celebratory dinner I made an unpopular speech. Working at ITV at that time, I had been involved in the negotiations over our coverage of the first Rugby World Cup, and I could see that as television money began to enter the sport, it would quickly become professional at the top level.

Our championship winning team had five current or recent Scottish international players in it, a huge number for a small club in a small town. But I told players, former players and others at the dinner something they did not want to hear. It was a source of immense pride to see our players' names with Kelso in brackets next to them in the Murrayfield programmes, but, I said, that would stop, and soon. As the game turned professional, larger clubs, almost certainly based in Edinburgh and Glasgow, and one in the Borders, only one, would replace all the historic names in those international programmes.

That detail mattered then and still matters. A Scotland team used to be a mosaic made up from players countrywide: from Stewart's Melville FP in Edinburgh, from West of Scotland in Glasgow, from Gordonians in Aberdeen, Highland RFC in Inverness and from clubs in the Borders. The team draws its support from all over the nation and brings the nation's diverse parts together to form a clear identity on days when we played Wales, France, Ireland and especially England. Like Ian Hastie, players from those clubs and many others walked down the streets of their cities and towns on the Monday morning after an international match. But perhaps not all of them had to suffer criticism from an old lady waving her stick at them.

Now that large amounts of money have flooded into rugby from the sale of TV rights to matches, and top players and coaches are very well-paid professionals, they have become detached from that collective identity. Many have only tangential connections to Scotland, having been born in South Africa or New Zealand and brought in to bolster a team with too little native talent to call on. They are all gladiators, and their matches are only accessible to those able to pay £100 or so for tickets, much more if they want the best seats.

When I worked in television in a job that involved a great deal of travel, I always looked for the Kelso result wherever I was.

And now I occasionally go down to Poynder Park to watch my old team play. Of course, I mourn the passing of the amateur era and the way in which the coming of TV money has changed the game. It is the money, and not the accident of native talent coming together once in a generation in a small town, that determines winners and losers. Money produces results, and those results are therefore more or less predictable.

Like Craigour Avenue and its prefabs, council houses and tower blocks in south Edinburgh, Poynder Park seems to me like another huge time capsule. On two sides the ground is surrounded by the council estate where we lived – I had to walk only a hundred yards with my kitbag on match days – and on the north side stands Kelso High School, the place where those who wanted a route to university in the 1960s and 70s could study. On the south side is Inch Hospital, run by the NHS, and to the west is a street of well-set houses in Poynder Place, houses one might aspire to own if you stuck in at the school. All these elements come together at Kelso Rugby Club and around its field of dreams.

Sky TV's sport and film offerings were only a prelude to even more rapid change. As the BBC and ITV tried to cope with the pressures of competition, they looked to make savings and changes. The price of the ITV franchises to broadcast in the regions had in part been regional programming, not only news but current affairs, documentaries and occasionally drama. By 1999, the companies had persuaded government to largely release them from these obligations, and an enormous amount was lost: another piece of regional identity broken off and discarded. Borderers saw themselves less and less on Border TV after its new operation was merged with Tyne Tees TV in Newcastle, and the same pattern was repeated all over Scotland and in the rest of Britain. Local diversity and the sense of a community that communicated with itself were badly damaged. And there are no signs of repair.

With the recent arrival of streaming services such as Netflix, Amazon and others, television viewing has rapidly globalised. The old schedules are now mostly ignored except for live events and news broadcasts, and what is aired on ITV, BBC, Channel 4 and the other broadcasters can in any case be found on catch-up services. In one sense, the instant availability of a new French police series or one of those multi-episode and often beautifully made American dramas has brought even more of the world into sitting rooms than *Tonight* with Cliff Michelmore did. But in another, this ever-changing array of almost bewildering new choices has excluded much of what is closer at hand.

5

The Decline of Hell

I'd never been more surprised in my life, or so confused. In the crypt of the kirk, not far from Inchmead Drive, a youth club had been set up so that during the winter months teenagers had somewhere to go and something to do instead of mooching around street corners, sharing illicit cigarettes and dreaming up mischief. In the crypt, all these youthful threats to society would be contained in one place and much closer to God under the supervision of His earthly representative, the Reverend Donald MacLeod. It was not an unmixed blessing. No music was allowed – no long-haired Beatles, and certainly not the godless Rolling Stones – but there was a dartboard, a makeshift bar selling splits, little bottles of lemonade decorously drunk through a straw, and a table-tennis table. The latter turned out to be the altar of my misfortune.

One night, for some forgotten reason, the Reverend MacLeod had to return to the manse. His departure must have been the signal for a long-laid plot to unfold, and quickly. Isobel Elliot, Evelyn Johnstone and Rae Smith suggested we play table-tennis doubles. There was a lot of colliding and giggling going on, and no one seemed to be keeping the score. Then, with no warning, Rae put down her bat, checked we were the only ones in the crypt, came back into the games room, closed the door and switched off the lights. Suddenly, three pairs of girly hands were everywhere, and after realising this was an adolescent dream made flesh, and lots of it, I was quickly doing my best with one pair. I had no idea who was doing what and no idea how long this amazing event lasted, except that it didn't last long enough.

'What's that?' whispered Rae. The heavy outside door had creaked open, and a moment later light flooded into Gomorrah, or was it Sodom, as the Reverend MacLeod came into the games room. I'd managed to pull up my jeans but not had time to do up my shirt. Isobel stood behind me holding her hands over her bra, Evelyn was tugging at the waistband of her slacks, and Rae groaned with embarrassment. Her dad was a member of the kirk session.

The Reverend's face turned an enraged red and his eyes stood out like organ stops as he took in a scene of total moral collapse. But before any of us could say anything – and what was there to say? – the minister turned on his heel without uttering a word and stamped noisily out of the crypt, slamming the metal-studded wooden door behind him like the crack of doom. As the girls adjusted their clothing, they looked open-mouthed at each other. Not a word was spoken.

Half an hour later, still dazed from the teenage orgy, I discovered what had happened, and it was something completely unexpected. Having gathered up the breaking storm of his Highland wrath, the Reverend had rung the doorbell of 42 Inchmead Drive and demanded to speak to my dad immediately. After a brief allusion – perhaps the minister lacked the vocabulary or, more likely, was unable to describe the scene of wantonness he had just beheld in God's house for all of ten seconds – he told my dad I would be expelled from the youth club and I would not be going on next summer's church outing to Spittal Beach. My dad waited until the Reverend MacLeod ran out of rant and then threw him out.

When I got home and heard what had happened, I braced myself for at least a bollocking, maybe a clout round the ear, but to my amazement, my dad did not wag his finger at me, ask a single question or say a word of reproof. 'Bloody hypocrite,' was what he said. 'Who does he think he is that he can barge into my house and go on about one of mine?'

It was the winter of 1964. And fifteen, frantic, fumbled minutes in the crypt of a kirk was a tiny symptom, a moment that marked of the end of an era.

*

Since the Reformation of 1560 and the wars of the sixteenth and seventeenth centuries that established its independence, the Church of Scotland had intervened in the life of Scotland in many more ways than at births, deaths and marriages. A central tenet of the First Book of Discipline, the new church's constitution, compiled by John Knox and a group of ministers, was the idea of the priesthood of all believers. Each of God's children, male and female, was to be responsible for their own salvation and no longer to be dependent on the mutterings of priestly Latin on their behalf. That involved reading the Bible, the sacred Word of God. Which in turn needed literacy and a 'school in every parish', a goal that took more than a century to achieve. The Kirk was therefore in control of Scotland's schools and education system until as late as 1872, and retained great influence even after that.

The parish kirk session, a council of elders who wielded great power, even over ministers, also administered the poor relief fund and did what it could to help those who found it difficult to help themselves. This facet of Christian obligation was bound up with matters of public morality, something that still greatly concerned the Reverend MacLeod in the winter of 1964. As he stormed along the street to bark at my dad, he may well have pined for the great power the Kirk used to wield. For almost three centuries, public shaming was the principal instrument of control. If a parishioner was accused and thought to be guilty of fornication, sex outside wedlock, these poor souls were required to stand on the Stool of Repentance at Sunday church services and be rebuked by the minister for their crimes. In the seventeenth century, fornicators were required to wear sackcloth and the standard tariff was three appearances on the Stool in front of a congregation, who were mostly quietly thanking the Lord that it was not they who were hanging their head. It was six appearances for a repeat offence, and an interminable twenty-six for adultery. Those such as the gentry, who could afford it, sometimes had their appearances commuted or even rendered unnecessary by the prompt payment of 'buttock mail'. The latter element is the old Scots word for rent or payment, as in blackmail, and the first is less obvious than it seems. 'Buttock' was another name for a loose woman or a prostitute.

There was certainly a degree of prurience spiced no doubt by a great deal of gossip in all this, but also an important element of social control. In an age before contraception, what Robert Burns engagingly called 'houghmagandie' had consequences, very heavy, life-changing consequences for women and their babies. Illegitimate children could be a strain on a limited amount of poor relief, and to their credit, many kirk sessions did what they could to limit the number of children in the parish who had to be raised by single mothers. Many took pains to extract admissions of paternity and force the errant father to support his offspring. Sin could be expensive, and those born as a result of it could have a difficult start in life.

With the great Disruption of the Church of Scotland in 1843, when it split into two factions, and the removal of its control of schooling 20 years later, its influence began to wane. Nevertheless, Scotland remained a nation of believers for a long time afterwards, and Christian practice and values continued to define society.

So did Satan. The Reverend MacLeod was a hellfire-and-damnation Highland preacher, and leaning over his open Bible on the pulpit lectern, he thundered weekly about the consequences of sin. The burning pits of eternal fire that waited for the likes of me were scary, so scary that after a time I stopped going to church and to Sunday School. And unlike in earlier times in Kelso (where there was, incidentally, a good deal of fornication in the eighteenth century), there was no societal pressure pushing me through its doors. My parents rarely attended, and our most regular connection with the kirk was Mr Calton. Tall, cadaverously thin and a retired bank manager, I think, who lived in Poynder Place, he was the elder assigned to Inchmead Drive and our council estate. He must have had a heroic bladder. Every Thursday night he would ring the front doorbell, have a brief cup of tea with a McVitie's digestive biscuit in the saucer and pick up a small, stiff, red cardboard envelope that looked like a library ticket. In it was a shilling, our weekly offering. Perhaps my mum saw it as an insurance premium.

Most things about God scared me. I'd seen *Ben Hur* at the Roxy, and it wasn't encouraging for trainee Christians. On his stumbling way to becoming a galley slave, Charlton Heston sinks to his knees as a chunky Roman soldier, who would not have looked out of place next to Ian Hastie in the Kelso front row, lashes him with a whip. Then the holy music plays and a shadow passes over the prone body before it bends down to give the poor soul a cup of water. The chunky soldier intervenes, brandishing his whip, but then is stopped in his tracks with *a look*. We don't see the face of Jesus. Soon after the water incident, in the midst of milling, baying crowds, he is on the *via dolorosa*, head down, dragging a huge wooden cross up some steps. Then the really scary stuff starts. On a huge screen, with loud sound effects, we see Roman soldiers hammering nails through Jesus' hands and feet. There is blood everywhere. Then the cross is pulled up by ropes, juddering as it falls into its slot. Finlay Currie is watching with Charlton who asks why all this is happening; 'He has taken the sins of the world upon him.'

As a 10-year-old, I didn't like any of that. I'd seen *Quo Vadis* with a riotous, camp performance from Peter Ustinov as the emperor Nero, and Christians did not fare well under his thumb in the Colosseum. It was all so brutal and bloody. And then there were the bottomless, fiery pits of Hell with the Devil cackling away somewhere in the background as you were burned to a crisp for eternity. Pain was all around.

The Kirk also seemed to me to be about *no* – about prohibition, about inevitably failing to be good enough and live up to its ideals, and being a sinner. And frankly I didn't warm to the necessary business of abasement, of worshipping an almighty God who, it seemed, had summary power over us all but couldn't prevent death and disaster happening to good people. How almighty was that? Not much of Christianity appealed to me, apart from the youth club in the crypt. And that had been removed by the righteousness of a servant of God.

In the 1960s, the influence of the church seemed to still be omnipresent. At every morning assembly at school, we sang a hymn, and our Queen needed God to save her when the anthem played at the end of films at the Roxy and the Playhouse and when programmes ended on TV. There were six churches in Kelso with spires and bell towers visible from every street corner. The Church of Scotland had three, the Episcopalian Church (always called the English kirk) was close to the ruins of the abbey, the Catholic Chapel near the high school and the Baptist kirk next to Inch Road Infants' School. God was everywhere. God was watching us.

God was also in Govan in 1950. The Boys' Brigade had been founded in Glasgow in 1883 by Sir William Alexander Smith. Its ringing manifesto was unequivocal: 'The advancement of

Christ's Kingdom among Boys and the promotion of habits of Obedience, Reverence, Discipline, Self-respect and all that tends towards a true Christian manliness.' The BB badge was an anchor with 'Sure and Steadfast' engraved on it, and the naval allusions continued with the uniforms and their signature hymn, 'Will Your Anchor Hold?' The new movement was, and remains, very successful, and particularly in Scotland. Despite the obedience bit, there was something about it that appealed. Perhaps it was the military aspect, its organisation into companies and battalions and the ranks of lance corporal, corporal and all that marching about.

In the 1950s and 60s, all we seemed to do in the summer holidays and the light evenings was play war games up in the meadows, dodging bullets behind trees and bushes, with sticks and oral sound effects for rifles. All we read were war comics. *Battler Briton* was a hunky hero. At the Roxy we watched *Reach for the Sky* with Kenneth More's version of Douglas Bader's stiff upper lip and stiff legs and *The Dam Busters* with Richard Todd as Wing Commander Guy Gibson and bouncing bombs. Even on TV, the shadow of the Second World War was long; I remember watching *The Army Game*, a comedy about National Service. So uniforms and marching seemed like a good idea.

I'd joined the junior section, the Life Boys, for about a fortnight and had considered the BBs, fancying their summer camps and seeing myself rise through the ranks. But Kelso's company was affiliated to the Reverend MacLeod's kirk and it met in its hall in Bowmont Street, so that was that.

But in Govan, there was no vengeful reverend or hindrance for the 9-year-old Alex Ferguson. He joined up in 1950, and 57 years later, after spectacular success as a football manager and coach, he gave an interview to *Life and Work*, the Church of Scotland's monthly magazine, in which he recalled how influential the values of the BBs had been:

My Christian upbringing was through the Boys' Brigade. As kids, church is boring but the BB Bible classes were a bit more entertaining. The BB chaplains would make it far more light-hearted and instructive than sitting through a service.

Alex Ferguson recalled Johnny Boreland, who was in charge of the 120 Glasgow Company, and his brother, Jimmy. Both of them ran football teams for the Life Boys and the older BBs.

Johnny was an absolute fanatic for the game. When we went to camp in places like Stonehaven we were given a list of everything we had to bring with us, and at the bottom, in big capital letters, he'd put AND FOOTBALL BOOTS. As soon as we arrived, it would be 'right everybody, get your football boots on'.

Johnny gave us a leg up and developed great enthusiasm in us all. We won the Battalion Cup in a two-leg final in 1950. I still keep in touch with Johnny; he's a marvellous man, absolutely marvellous. I joined the BB team when I was 12, playing in an under-18s league. I remember one time we were losing 5–1 at halftime and Jimmy turned to me and said, 'What's wrong with you? I can normally depend on you.' I got a great surge of belief and confidence, and in the second half I scored a couple. But of course it wasn't just football. We had all the other parts – Bible classes, learning to play the bugle, going for our badges. I did the signalling badge, the camping badge, about nine of ten badges in my time there. As I got to 16 they wanted me to come on as a staff sergeant, but by that time, I had drifted away. But that spell from 9 to 16 was a very important part of my life. It gave us discipline and confidence, and trust in the relationship we developed with officers.

When Alex Ferguson signed for Glasgow Rangers in 1966, he experienced difficulties not related to football. For decades the club had maintained an unstated policy of not employing Catholic players or staff, and it was a matter of concern that Ferguson's wife, Cathy, had been raised as a Catholic. A director asked him if they had been married in a Catholic chapel, and when Ferguson replied that it had been a registry office wedding, the director commented, 'Oh, that's OK.' In a 2021 documentary film about his life and career, the former manager of Manchester United expressed great regret that he had not objected to the question. 'I let myself down there and I let my wife down – that was the most important thing – because she was a devout Catholic.'

In the same documentary, Ferguson observed, 'Glasgow is a city where there is a divide: it's Protestant and Catholic, Rangers and Celtic.' That divide has a long history, and it sprang from tragedy.

Between 1845 and 1852 Ireland was in the grip of *an Gorta Mór*, the Great Hunger, a catastrophe without parallel in nineteenth-century Europe. The potato crop on which ordinary people depended was devastated by blight and more than a million died of starvation. Two million more emigrated, many of them making the short passage across the North Channel to the Firth of Clyde and on to Glasgow. At its peak in 1848, emigration became a flood as a thousand Irish refugees disembarked each week on the Clyde quays, and between January and April that year, a staggering 48,860 came. It was the largest and most rapid influx of new people in Scotland's history, and in the census of 1851, the enumerators counted more than 200,000 who had been born in Ireland. They were desperate, running from the famine in droves, and the new immigrants often priced native Scots out of low-skilled manual work due to their willingness to accept lower wages to put food on the table for their hungry families. It was a demographic shock that drew uncharitable, un-Christian reactions. Here is a report from the 1871 census:

The immigration of such a number of people from the low-est class and with no education will have a bad effect on the population. So far, living amongst the Scots does not seem to have improved the Irish, but the native Scots who live among the Irish have got worse. It is difficult to imagine the effect the Irish immigrants will have upon the morals and habits of the Scottish people.

These seeds of prejudice soon flourished and led to conflict and polarisation, and these became, and continued to be, most visible on winter Saturday afternoons as sectarianism ribboned through the history of Scotland's two greatest football clubs. Celtic FC was founded in 1887 to help raise money for a charity known as Poor Children's Dinner Table. It was the initiative of Brother Walfrid, an Irish priest who had been encouraged by the example of Hibernian FC, who had recruited players from the Irish immigrant community in Edinburgh and the east of Scotland. Celtic played their first fixture against Rangers in 1888, and won 5–2. Support for each club began to polarise around the immigrant Irish Catholic community and native Scottish Protestants. In the middle of the seventeenth century, blue had been adopted as the colour of militant Protestantism when officers in the Covenanter armies began to wear blue sashes to distinguish themselves. Green was forever associated with Ireland, the Emerald Isle.

Sir John Primrose was a wealthy Glasgow merchant who became Lord Provost in 1902, and then Chairman of Rangers Football Club between 1912 and 1923. The same year Primrose took over, the Belfast shipyard, Harland & Wolff, bought three yards on the Clyde at Govan and brought over many skilled workers from Ulster. Almost all of them were Protestants and Unionists, and they began to support their local football club, Glasgow Rangers. The arrival of these immigrants also saw support of a different sort increase. Many joined the Orange Lodges.

These affiliations were made more pointed because of the intro-duction of a Home Rule Bill for Ireland in 1912, which the Ulster Protestants vigorously opposed, and some lodges in the north began to arm themselves. Although the outbreak of the First World War stalled this proposed legislation and diverted all sorts of energies and enmities elsewhere, it had the effect of making the division between Catholics and Protestants in Scotland sharper. At Rangers FC, Sir John Primrose supported the policy of not signing or hiring Catholics.

The equivalent was not adopted by Celtic FC, and throughout the later twentieth century, Protestants were amongst their most distinguished players, the likes of Kenny Dalglish and Danny McGrain. And the club's most successful manager, Jock Stein, was a Protestant.

Since the end of the Second World War, and particularly after the signing in 1998 of the Good Friday Agreement that brought an end to the violence in Northern Ireland, both clubs have come together to stamp out sectarianism, banning inflammatory songs, the waving of the Irish tricolour or the Union Jack and inappro-priate salutes and chants. And with the signing of the Catholic player Mo Johnston by Rangers in 1989, the policy introduced during the chairmanship of Sir John Primrose effectively came to an end.

However, Glasgow's sectarianism and its expression through its football clubs did not take place in a cultural vacuum. In 1929, the Church of Scotland was reunited as the rifts of 1843 were healed, or at least patched over. The United Free Church and its half million adherents gave up their independence and returned to the fold as 90 per cent of Scotland's Protestants came together again, a huge congregation of more than 2 million. But this image of harmony was badly stained by the Kirk's attitude to the Catholic minority. Having lost control of education in 1872, the reunited Church of Scotland was angry at the Education

Act of 1918 that made provision for Catholic schooling and very suspicious of the emerging Labour Party which had begun to attract widespread support from Irish immigrant communities. Suspicion tipped over into racism and expressions of outright hatred, much of it officially sanctioned by the Kirk's leadership. Pamphlets circulated fake scaremongering figures on immigration, and in 1923, 'The Menace of the Irish Race to Our Scottish Nationality' was circulating amongst congregations. Demonised as carriers of the Irish Fever (as typhus became known), as drunks and for being promiscuous, 'breeding like rabbits', the Irish communities in Scotland became the butt of violence and concerted political spite, much of it orchestrated by the recently unified Church of Scotland.

One of the worst episodes erupted in the summer of 1935 in, of all places, the douce, leafy suburb of Morningside in Edinburgh. Violently anti-Catholic and against further Irish immigration, the Protestant Action Society was founded in 1930 by John Cormack. He and several others were elected as councillors to the Edinburgh Corporation, gaining 31 per cent of the vote.

The Eucharistic Conference, the first major event of Catholic worship to be staged in Scotland since the Reformation, was centred on St Peter's Church, in Morningside, and St Benet's, the nearby residence of the Archbishop of St Andrews and Edinburgh. As the date, 25 June, approached, the atmosphere began to darken and rumours spread of a violent Protestant reaction. The conference would attract Catholics from all over Scotland and the Archbishop, Andrew MacDonald, was very concerned for their safety, and with good reason. Here is an extract from his letter to the *Scotsman*:

> The office which I have the honour to hold has been the object of gross insult and of the vilest accusations. For some time it has hardly been possible for a priest to appear in the city without being subjected to unspeakable indignities. They have

been not only the target for vile abuse and most filthy and obscene language, but they have repeatedly been spat upon and molested in public streets. In the factories and public works, Catholic employees, and particularly defenceless girls, have suffered bitter persecution, as contemptible as it is cowardly, and strenuous efforts have been made to induce employers to dismiss Catholics on the grounds of their religion alone.

On the evening of the conference, it became clear that the rumours had not been exaggerated. Crammed into trams arriving from all over the city, encouraged by the ranting prejudices of John Cormack, more than 10,000 supporters of Protestant Action flooded the streets of Morningside. The police had set up a cordon around the outdoor service and the rioters made repeated attempts to charge through. When worshippers attempted to leave, their buses were pelted with stones and, ironically, at a Morningside crossroads known as Holy Corner (where three churches are in close proximity), a bus full of terrified men, women and children was stopped and overturned. Mounted police charged the mob and managed to disperse them. Jim Marin remembered:

I was chased along Canaan Lane by a group of gentlemen [!] when I was just seven years old because I was dressed in the uniform of St Andrews Priory, which is where the Catholic Congress was being held when Cormack's lot turned up. It was a terrifying experience.

Despite this shameful paroxysm of sectarian violence, the Protestant Action councillors continued to serve on Edinburgh Corporation, a statement of widespread, and enduring, support. John Cormack was re-elected for another 30 years by the voters of South Leith, only retiring in 1963. He drove around in a van with 'No Popery' painted on it.

In a limited sense, the major Edinburgh football clubs mirrored the Rangers and Celtic divide described earlier by Alex Ferguson. Heart of Midlothian, named after a novel by Sir Walter Scott, is usually identified as the city's Protestant team, while Hibernian FC's name is clearly linked to Ireland and Catholicism. But in reality religion had a less influential role than geography. Hibernian is based at Easter Road and its hinterland of support was historically from Leith and the surrounding suburbs, while Hearts are in the west of Edinburgh at Tynecastle.

After the end of the Second World War, sectarianism in Scotland seemed to subside. Despite the claims of the propagandists in the Church of Scotland and elsewhere, Catholic Irish immigration had slowed to a trickle in the 1920s and 30s. And in any case Scottish society was changing demographically after the war as the drive for new housing reshaped communities. It must also be a factor that religious conviction, or at least the extent to which religious affiliation shaped identities, was also slackening as new generations grew up in the 1950s and 60s.

At 5.30 p.m. on 31 May 1982, a Polish priest disembarked at Edinburgh airport and walked across the tarmac of the runway in search of a patch of grass he could kiss. Karol Wojtyła, Pope John Paul II, was the first non-Italian to hold the office for more than 500 years, and the first pontiff to visit Scotland. His motorcade took him to scenes of rapture in Murrayfield stadium where 44,000 young Scottish Catholics waited to cheer him, sing and shout their joy that their Holy Father had come. His first words were 'Young Catholics of Scotland, I love you!' The crowd swooned, chanted his name and cheered everything he said. The Pope was said to have been so amazed at his reception that he put aside his prepared speech as the crowd sang 'You'll Never Walk Alone' and, of course, 'Flower of Scotland'.

The motorcade's next destination was St Mary's Catholic Cathedral at the top of Leith Walk where a thousand priests, monks and nuns waited. But en route, the Pope's limousine took a right turn off Princes Street and went up the Mound to the Church of Scotland's Assembly Hall. Waiting on the cobbles outside to greet His Holiness was the Reverend Ian Paisley and 200 demonstrators, who shouted anti-Catholic slogans and threw eggs. But once safely inside, the Pope had a historic encounter with the Moderator of the General Assembly of the Church of Scotland. After 450 years of enmity, it seemed, for a moment, that the religious divide in Scotland was closing at last. Later, John MacIntyre, Professor of Divinity at the University of Edinburgh and Moderator of the Church of Scotland, said that the Pope was a man of peace who had changed the face of the papacy, although he also added that he knew some people would have been unhappy about the meeting. The Reverend Ian Paisley certainly was, and if he had not met his (Protestant) maker in 1978, John Cormack might have thrown more than eggs.

If ancient rifts were appearing to heal between Protestants and Catholics, others were opening elsewhere in Scotland's religious community. Lord James Mackay of Clashfern had been appointed Lord Chancellor by Margaret Thatcher and in 1988, he committed a grievous sin, one that caused his church to excommunicate him. He was an elder of the Free Presbyterian Church, a breakaway sect concentrated in the Highlands and Islands that had doggedly refused to consider union with the Church of Scotland. Mackay's sin was to attend the funeral masses of two former judicial colleagues, Lord Russell of Killowen and Baron Wheatley of Shettleston, who happened to be Catholics. Since the Free Presbyterians held that the Mass was idolatrous (and incidentally that the Pope was the Antichrist), Mackay was suspended from his church in late 1988. Much of Scotland and the rest of the United Kingdom found this incident puzzling. As did some of the members of the Free Presbyterian Church.

Lord Mackay's minister disagreed with the suspension and

the Reverend Angus Morrison declared that 'it is impossible for me to acquiesce the decision . . . and I appeal to the Head of the Church, the Lord Jesus Christ'. He may have been listening, but the hardliners who confirmed Mackay's expulsion were not. The Free Presbyterian Church was riven with dissent and, already very small, it split. The new church became known as the Associated Presbyterian Churches. It was a bizarre episode that few Scots can have understood. The distinguished historian and journalist Kenneth Roy noted that the venerable leader of the hardliners, the Reverend Donald Maclean, 'had begun his long ministry alongside colleagues who had been ordained in the 19th century – the century from which the trial of Lord Mackay of Clashfern had somehow wandered, atavistically, into what passed for a modern Scotland'.

In February 2013, Cardinal Keith O'Brien, the leader of the Catholic Church in Scotland, tendered his resignation. His 75th birthday was approaching, his health occasionally 'indifferent'. That month, the *Observer* published an investigation by Catherine Deveney which uncovered accusations of inappropriate sexual behaviour made by three priests and one former priest against Cardinal O'Brien. These incidents, they claimed, dated back to the 1980s. O'Brien disputed their accounts, but the day after the story appeared, he was a notable absentee from a service at St Mary's Catholic Cathedral to celebrate the eighth year of Pope Benedict XVI's pontificate. The day after that, the Vatican announced that the Cardinal's resignation would take immediate effect. Six days later, the Scottish Catholic Media Office released a statement from O'Brien in which he admitted that 'there have been times that my sexual conduct has fallen below the standards expected of me as a priest, archbishop and cardinal'.

This otherwise standard expression of regret contained a phrase that seemed out of place. Celibate priests are not, or should not be, concerned with 'sexual conduct'. The temporary replacement for O'Brien, Archbishop Philip Tartaglia, produced an understatement when he said that 'the credibility and moral authority' of the Catholic Church had been damaged. At first, the Cardinal planned to retire to a cottage near Dunbar in East Lothian, but he was pressed into leaving Scotland and eventually settled in Newcastle, out of the way and out of sight. No comprehensive investigation was undertaken by the Catholic Church of these cases or others that came to light after 2013. O'Brien was allowed to remain a cardinal and wear his splendid red robes, but only in private, and he died in 2018, having escaped any substantive sanction for his below par 'sexual conduct'.

What did happen was the commission of a report to review the 'Current Safeguarding Policies, Procedures and Practices within the Catholic Church in Scotland'. So that it could be seen as impartial, the Reverend Andrew McLellan, a former Moderator of the General Assembly, was asked to lead the investigation. 'There is no doubt that abuse of the most serious kind has taken place,' he reported, and Catherine Deveney wrote in the *Observer* that 'McLellan had promised a report that was neither timid not deferential. He delivered it.' But the removal of O'Brien and the recommendations of Andrew McLellan did not mark the end of the Catholic Church's woes.

In October 2015, the Scottish Government set up the Scottish Child Abuse Inquiry. Chaired by the retired judge Lady Anne Smith, part of its remit was to investigate residential care establishments for children run by Catholic Orders. A shocking, shameful picture emerged.

In October 2018, the Inquiry reported on what had happened over a long period at Smyllum Park Orphanage, near Lanark. It was run by nuns of the Daughters of Charity of St Vincent de Paul. From the evidence gathered, the Inquiry concluded that the children had experienced 'no love, no compassion, no dignity and no comfort'. The report listed chilling examples of what had gone on behind firmly closed doors:

> Children were sexually abused in Smyllum . . . by priests, a trainee priest, Sisters, members of staff and a volunteer.
>
> There was also problematic sexual behaviour from other children.
>
> Children were physically abused. They were hit with and without implements, either in excess of punishment or for reasons which the child could not fathom.
>
> The implements used included leather straps, the Lochgelly tawse, hairbrushes, sticks, footwear, a dog's lead, wooden crucifixes and rosary beads.
>
> For some children, being hit was a normal aspect of daily life.
>
> The physical punishments meted out to children went beyond what was acceptable at the time whether as punishment in schools or in the home.
>
> Children who were bed wetters were abused physically and emotionally.
>
> They were beaten, put in cold baths and humiliated in ways that included 'wearing' their wet sheets and being subjected to hurtful name-calling by Sisters and other children.
>
> Many children were force-fed.

When Sister Ellen Flynn from the Daughters of Charity was asked about these allegations of abuse, she described them as 'a mystery'. She went on: 'In our records we can find no evidence or anything that substantiates the allegations.' In 2021, the Daughters of Charity agreed to pay £10 million to the survivors of abuse inflicted by their Sisters and others.

Prosecutions continue. In December 2023, three women were found guilty of the gross mistreatment of children at Smyllum

Park between 1969 and 1981. The crown alleged that Sarah McDermott (79), Margaret Hughes (76) and Eileen Igoe (79), committed terrible acts of cruelty. Prosecutors claimed that Hughes forced a girl's hand through a wringer and Igoe put a boy's arm through an electric mangle. McDermott faces six charges of cruel and unnatural treatment. She is said to have beaten a boy with a wooden coat hanger and repeatedly forced food into a girl's mouth. These old women have escaped justice until now, but their victims endured a life sentence of suffering after they were freed from Smyllum Park.

What happened at that institution and elsewhere is beyond appalling. These children, some of them little ones, 5, 6 or 7 years old, were orphans, all alone, incarcerated in this dark, cruel place, living lives of terror and misery. Their future was destroyed by people who purported to be Christians but were in fact vicious sadists, whose inhumane attitudes are symbolised by the discovery of a mass, unmarked grave in nearby St Mary's cemetery. An estimated 400 children are buried there, disposed of, the evidence of decades of abuse, even torture, hidden.

Jesus Christ said, 'Suffer little children, and forbid them not, to come unto me.' And suffer they did.

Between 1966 and 1971 Father Keith O'Brien taught mathematics and science in Catholic secondary schools in Fife before going on to become a parish priest. In April 2022, there were 360 Catholic schools in Scotland, about 15 per cent of all schools in the country, which broadly mirrors the size of the Catholic population. But their survival in an increasingly secular age puzzles some. There are no Protestant schools as such, and there is also a history of public figures questioning why denominational schools should still be supported by the state. In 2019, the former Deputy Chief Constable of Lothian and Borders Police, Tom Wood, wondered what the role of Catholic schools was in fostering sectarianism, and the well-respected sports commentator,

Archie MacPherson, asked: 'What sort of education do we want in a secular society?' But in reality, this is less of a cultural and moral question and more a product of history and, crucially, party politics.

Catholics in Scotland paid a heavy blood price for separate schooling. When the First World War was declared in 1914, many thousands of men of Irish descent volunteered before conscription was introduced, and many Catholic soldiers distinguished themselves in the bitter and murderous trench warfare in Flanders. Six of them were awarded the Victoria Cross, and it was clear to all Scots that the loyalty of this community was not any longer in question. And given what was happening in Ireland at that time, with the Easter Rising of 1916 and the contact between Irish Republicans and the Germans, that loyalty was not necessarily assumed.

In 1918, the British Government agreed to take into the public sector the separate and voluntary Catholic education system that had grown up since the middle of the eighteenth century. The costs would be met out of taxation for what had become a very onerous burden for communities. In the negotiations, three important concessions were won. There was to be full and unfettered access to the schools for parish priests, religious instruction was to be maintained at existing levels and, crucially, no teacher could be appointed unless they were acceptable to the church hierarchy 'in regard to religious faith and character'. When the 1918 bill became an act, there was an outcry. Why should all Scottish taxpayers, the overwhelming majority of them Protestants, fund Catholic education? The Church of Scotland called it 'Rome on the Rates'.

Despite this opposition, vocal and continuing, the creation of these schools did have a longer-term benefit. Instead of being ghettoised as an economically disadvantaged community, with all the combustible dangers that presented (and bearing in mind what happened in Northern Ireland), Scottish Catholics were able to access mainstream further education directly and thereby advance themselves. Like all children with ability, after 1918 they would be in a position to go to universities, and much later benefit from the Anderson and the Robbins Reports of the early 1960s. Arguably, without the 1918 Act, Lord Mackay would not have got into trouble with his church. Catholics like Lords Wheatley and Russell would probably not have been appointed to the bench, or if they had, it would have been after a long process of evolution. By the 1980s, ten of Scotland's 72 MPs were Catholics, as were half of the ruling Labour group on Glasgow Corporation and the (aristocratic) chairman of the Conservative Party, Michael Ancram, although he was descended from Border reivers rather than Irish immigrants.

Even though these examples and many others demonstrate undoubted societal benefits, it is still surprising that these schools have survived in an increasingly secular society. The reality is that their continued existence owes a good deal to the shifting loyalties of Scottish politics. For many decades, until the early twenty-first century, the Labour Party relied on the support of the Catholic minority, especially in the West of Scotland, and that support had a price. Catholic congregations listen to their priests, and if Labour had attempted to assimilate their schools, the hierarchy would not have hesitated to object. And if change was forced through, there would have been political consequences.

In the general election of 2015, a tidal wave of support for the SNP washed through Scottish politics, producing startling results at the polls. The SNP landslide saw Labour lose 40 seats (and an otherwise close general election as a result) and the Liberal Democrats 10. Of 59 seats in Scotland, the SNP won 56. A year after the independence referendum was won by the Unionists with 55 per cent of the vote, the losing 45 per cent voted en bloc for SNP candidates. And later polling showed that a clear majority of the Catholic community had voted for independence in 2014 and then transferred their support to the SNP. In the West of Scotland, previously safe Labour seats tumbled and several senior figures found themselves out of parliament. At Holyrood, the nationalists have formed governments since 2007, and like Labour before them, they needed to retain the Catholic vote. Thus no serious attempt has been made to make Catholic schools non-denominational.

The Church of Scotland had never shied away from involvement in politics. The Church and Nation Committee was set up in 1919, a year after the legislation to support Catholic schools was enacted, and at first it was the fount of anti-Catholic propaganda, including the publication of the aforementioned report on 'The Menace of the Irish Race to Our Scottish Nationality'. In recent years, a far more moderate committee has adopted clear political positions such as campaigning against nuclear weapons and warning of the dangers of climate change. Through the activities of the Church and Nation Committee, the Kirk had long backed the need for a devolved assembly or parliament for Scotland.

On 21 May 1988, a strange event took place that, probably inadvertently, emphasised the Church of Scotland's role in the evolution of the nation's history. For some reason, Prime Minister Margaret Thatcher chose to accept an invitation to address the General Assembly. Perhaps she didn't know that it was the closest thing Scotland had had to a parliament since the Union of 1707. Or perhaps she did. On the day, she made a characteristically blunt and insensitive speech that inevitably became known as 'The Sermon on the Mound'. Misunderstanding one of the letters of St Paul, she declared that 'if a man will not work, he shall not eat', and then moved away from Biblical misquotes to expressing her own beliefs. Towards the end, Mrs Thatcher directly attacked what she saw as the Kirk's meddling in politics, having no idea of its constitution and how different it is from the Church of

England. 'We parliamentarians can legislate for the rule of law. You, the Church, can teach the life of faith.'

In 1988, the Moderator of the General Assembly was the Very Reverend Professor James A. Whyte, Principal of St Mary's College, the divinity faculty of the University of St Andrews. As Mrs Thatcher finished her speech to polite applause and picked up her handbag, he descended from his pulpit to greet and thank her, and to deliver a quintessentially Scottish rebuke for her polarising words. Having shaken her hand, Professor Whyte gave the Prime Minister two pamphlets that he hoped she might find interesting. One dealt with poverty, the other with housing. The latter was particularly poignant since, by 1988, the Conservative Government had sold off vast swathes of council houses and had, it seemed, no plans to replenish the stock. The Moderator went on: 'Prime Minister, I do not think you have ever been in the presence of so many people who pray for you regularly.' It was an exquisitely pointed observation.

I witnessed this remarkable cultural and political collision first hand. My colleagues were there filming for a Channel 4 documentary – *The Rebellion of the Pious* – about the great Disruption of the Church in 1843. When Mrs Thatcher left the Assembly Hall through a wide doorway behind the dais, I saw her throwning the pamphlets to an aide without breaking step and the aide shoving them in a briefcase. Never to be seen again.

The Kirk's support for devolution had intensified into support for the Scottish Constitutional Convention and its deliberations and recommendations. When the Conservatives at last lost power in 1997, events moved quickly. After a referendum and the passing of an enabling act that began with the simple and ringing sentence, 'There shall be a Scottish Parliament', it met after the first election in 1999. Just after 9.30 a.m. on 21 May, Winifred Ewing, the most senior MSP, stood up to speak. 'The Scottish Parliament, adjourned on the 25th day of March 1707, is hereby reconvened.' Memory had made history, and as always, change and loss moved events. For centuries the General Assembly of the Church of Scotland was all there was, the only national gathering that could claim to represent the people, or at least most of them. And so it was fitting, but also ironic, that after 300 years, the Scottish Parliament should reconvene there as work began on its new building. Ironic because just as the nation was reasserting itself and the Kirk had done what it could to represent its concerns and interests, religious faith found itself in a steep, spiralling decline.

In 1957, the Church of Scotland had 1,320,000 members, about 27 per cent of the population. By 2006, the number had collapsed to 504,000, and then it declined even further to 325,695 in 2018, only about 6 per cent of the population. But that statistic was itself deceptive for the Kirk's own census reckoned that only about 137,000 people actually went to church regularly on a Sunday. Since 2018, the collapsing numbers have crashed further. In 2022, there were only 283,600 members of the Kirk, and the numbers who attend regularly on Sundays is now thought to be a pitiful 60,000. The average age of worshippers is 62. One in three parishes has no minister, and only tiny numbers are in training at divinity colleges. The recent pandemic had a devastating impact on elderly congregations, and apparently 45,000 communicants now worship online, 8,275 'in other ways'. The effects of this extraordinarily rapid decline will soon become even more obvious to many more Scots.

In November 2023, the Scottish Churches Trust, a body that attempts to preserve and protect what it calls 'Scotland's ecclesiastical built heritage', released even more bad news. By 2030, as many as 700 churches would be closed, most of them sold and repurposed, wiping out both community and personal histories. One newspaper report quoted Lynette Robertson. She was a member of the congregation of Greenock's Old West Kirk, the first Presbyterian church to be built in Scotland after the Reformation of 1560. It was sold in 2022 to a restaurateur, and people were, said Ms Robertson, 'devastated'. She added: 'This is my fifth church. The one I was christened in is going to be demolished, the one I got married in is already demolished, and another one is now a Carpet Warehouse. It's very hard, it can feel like the break-up of a family.'

These are bald and baleful statistics, and the outcomes will affect more than just the fast-dwindling membership. The Kirk's historic influence used to penetrate almost all facets of Scottish society in institutions such as the Boys' Brigade, the Guild (what used to be known as the Women's Guild) and several others. Churches and church halls are used by Scouts and Brownies, playgroups, lunch clubs for the elderly and as sanctuaries for refugees; their mass disappearance will have deeply damaging effects on communities across Scotland.

From being central, the Kirk has become marginal in the space of only two generations. These institutions mattered because they allowed Scots who joined them to express their Scottishness in a non-political way in distinctive settings that had grown and developed as part of a shared history. Now they are all crumbling, like the empty, boarded-up churches, and feel not like the future, but things of the past, old-fashioned in their values and aspirations. Yesterday's Scotland.

By 2010 it was clear that the Catholic Church in Scotland was also in decline as the number of baptisms, marriages and priests to officiate at them dropped significantly. According to the census of 2011, the situation had stabilised somewhat, and the numbers showed that with a church membership of about 841,000 and 184,283 regularly attending Mass, there had been a radical shift in Scotland's demography. Practising Catholics far outnumbered Protestants for the first time since the Reformation, even when the small congregations of the Free Presbyterians and others were taken into account. It is perhaps too early to tell what the impact of the horrific abuse at Smyllum Park Orphanage (by no means unique) and the hypocrisy and worse of Cardinal Keith O'Brien and others will be. In Ireland, in large part as a result of the exposure of scandal, terrible abuse, criminality and more hypocrisy in the Catholic Church, what had been a near-theocracy became a secular state within a generation. Scotland was not like Ireland, but the census returns in 2031 will be instructive when they measure the strength of the Catholic Church.

An important and welcome positive corollary has been the decline of sectarianism. While incidents still take place, they are less frequent, and attitudes have shifted. In 2008, the *Belfast Telegraph*, a newspaper that had reported the shedding of much blood and many tears in the previous 40 years, took a wry look at what it claimed was Scotland's most Protestant town. Larkhall in South Lanarkshire has a population of about 15,000, and there are seven non-denominational primary schools, one lonely Catholic school and one Catholic church with 1,247 adherents, who probably keep themselves to themselves. The majority in Larkhall are, apparently, ardent Rangers fans, and they hate the colour green with a passion. Retailers who wish to prosper there avoid using it on their frontages, and when the supermarket chain Asda proposed to build in the town and set its green livery above the main entrance, it was discouraged. Asda refused to change. Even traffic lights used to rouse the ire of local Protestants: between 2004 and 2007 the bottom lights were smashed 205 times. Drunken youths have, apparently, been offended by grass and tried to set fire to it. In South Lanarkshire, bigotry has a good look: it looks ridiculous.

In late 2023, I was invited to New College, the divinity faculty of the University of Edinburgh, to talk about a book I'd written on Scotland's early saints and the beginnings of Christian conversion in the sixth century. A former Convenor of the Church and Nation Committee was interviewing me, and towards the end of our session, he remarked that he sensed there was no loss of faith in society, just a loss of faith in churches. Perhaps after its precipitous decline bottoms out – if it bottoms out – there will be a religious revival in Scotland. Meanwhile, it occurs to me that Kelso's Reverend D. M. MacLeod would have much to mourn as he looks down from his place in Heaven, and others much to celebrate with the passing of the twentieth-century's version of the parish state.

6

Shake It Up, Baby

In a dark, cobwebbed corner of my memory lurks the baritone voice of Burl Ives and his big hit, 'The Ugly Bug Ball'. I hated it. I hated its daft lyrics about crawling to the ball and the happy time we'd all have there, and I hate it still. But it's lodged there for ever. *Two-Way Family Favourites* played on our old radio in the kitchen as my mum or my grannie cooked and baked on a Sunday morning. It was a request programme set up by British Forces Posted Overseas (BFPO) to connect families with their relatives serving overseas. It was part of a long hangover from the Second World War when the programme's motto was 'From London, the tunes you asked us to play. From Germany, the tunes that make them think of you'. Most of them were terrible, especially 'The Happy Wanderer' with its 'Val-deri, Val-dera, Val-deri, Val-dera-ha-ha-ha-ha-ha' chorus. Then there was 'She'll Be Coming Round the Mountain'. Really? How exactly do you come round a mountain? All the music sounded the same, one long, cheery, make-the-best-of-it Boy Scout song, and nothing like what any of us wanted to hear. Whatever that was.

Billy Fury and Marty Wilde didn't just sound angry; they were young, and a wee bit dangerous, pouting under their floppy, Brylcreemed quiffs. Instead of 'The Ugly Bug Ball', the sort of dances their music was played at were low-lit, with plenty of dark corners and even darker motives, at least amongst teenage boys. But their music didn't feature much on the Light Programme or the Scottish Home Service, and certainly not on *Two-Way Family Favourites*. The only place I could hear Billy and Marty, and meet girls (or at least be in the same room as them) was the Spinadisc Café in Kelso. They had a jukebox. And stark cultural contradictions in the same building.

Above the café was a room used by the Band of Hope. Originally a Temperance movement, it was very popular in the late nineteenth and early twentieth centuries when the demon drink was thought to be a great social problem, especially amongst working people (although what drove many to drink were terrible living conditions and back-breaking jobs). After the Second World War, its focus was also on providing a meeting place for children where they could watch slide shows and other wholesome entertainments. Their music competed with Billy and Marty on the jukebox. Even more than 'The Ugly Bug Ball', I loathed the Band of Hope's signature tune:

If you're happy and you know it, clap your hands
If you're happy and you know it, clap your hands
If you're happy and you know it, and you really want to show it,
If you're happy and you know it, clap your hands.

I wasn't hearing much that I liked on what my gran persisted in calling the wireless, either. In addition to the BBC's Light Programme and the Scottish Home Service and its accordion music, the dial on our old radio listed longwave stations from goodness knows where such as: Hilversum, Helsinki, Lyons, Budapest, Oslo, Moscow, Brussels, Munich and somewhere called Allouis. We never listened to any of them, though; we stuck to the boring old BBC. But one happy day, all of that changed. One of the valves in the radio in the kitchen popped, and Burl Ives was relegated to history, if not quite out of the reach of my long-term memory.

My dad was an electrician and interested in new-fangled stuff. To our surprise, because money was always tight, he came home one day with a new transistor radio. Compared to the old one, it was small and had a strap so it could be carried. But much more immediately important, my big sister could tune it to Radio Luxembourg. And they played the hit parade. For free. No need to put sixpence in – or more likely wait for one of the big lads to put sixpence in – the jukebox at the Spinadisc. Radio Lux also carried adverts like ITV, and for some reason, perhaps because of his name, I remember Horace Batchelor's 'Famous Infra-Draw Method'. Nothing to do with art, it was his 'foolproof' way of winning money on the football pools. Which my mum and dad did every week during the season, dreaming of riches. Even as a young teenager I remember wondering why Horace had to do adverts on the radio. If the Infra-Draw Method worked, then surely he'd be a millionaire by now – and why tell anybody else about it?

Sometime in October 1962, I heard on Radio Lux the sound that would change the world. And quickly. 'Love Me Do' was the first single recorded by The Beatles. Something about it sounded very different. Although I didn't realise it at the time, it contrasted sharply with the likes of Billy Fury, Marty Wilde, Adam Faith and certainly Cliff Richard. It seemed that these singers were trying to sound like Elvis Presley, Buddy Holly and the other great American names. Paul McCartney and John Lennon weren't imitating anyone. Without rationalising it, but recognising it, what I heard coming out of the trannie was authenticity, something essentially British – and northern English, not southern – a set of voices singing in harmony to perfect melodies. A new sort of music.

What became an enormously powerful global phenomenon began slowly, only gradually gathering momentum. 'Love Me

Do' was a modest hit, only just scraping into the Top 20 at number 17, in October 1962. The next Beatles single was released in mid January 1963, and when I first heard it on Radio Lux, I was amazed, immediately hooked. I had to wait until Saturday morning to go down to Bob Swan's music shop to buy it. The record was expensive at 6s/8d, a third of a pound then, but I remember clutching it in its little multi-coloured Parlophone sleeve like something sacred – even magical, life-changing – as I made my way home. It was not only an expensive purchase, but also a surprising one. I didn't have a record player. I just wanted to be part of whatever it was that was happening. Perhaps if I held the black vinyl close to my ear, I could hear John and Paul.

'Please Please Me' took until early March to climb the charts, but that had nothing to do with quality or popularity. The winter of early 1963 was one of the worst since records of another sort began. Snow began falling in early January and lay on the ground until April. In the interim, we had watched The Beatles perform on ITV's *Thank Your Lucky Stars* as we shivered around the coal fire in the sitting room. They shared billing with Acker Bilk, Alma Cogan, Petula Clark and Frankie Vaughan, a line-up that made the group stand out even more as a break with the past.

New singles followed each other very quickly. Their first official number 1, 'From Me To You', topped the chart in May 1963, within days of its release, and in September, 'She Loves You' (yeah, yeah, yeah) became the first record to sell a million copies. It was followed by the brilliant Christmas number 1, 'I Want To Hold Your Hand', a classic pop song whose originality and power remain undimmed more than half a century on. So many people bought their records – and many more listened on transistor radios that were now carried everywhere by young people – that The Beatles became household names in a very short time. Beatlemania was born, as legions of fans followed them on tour or waited to catch a glimpse of them at airports or sold-out venues. It was said that bandstands in public parks no longer needed bands, for they were filled with music from portable radios. In late 1963, Britain's most popular newspaper, the *Daily Mirror*, recognised that the band were leading a moment of profound cultural change:

> . . . it's plain to see why these four cheeky, energetic lads from Liverpool go down so big.
>
> They're young, new. They're high-spirited, cheerful. What a change from the self-pitying moaners, crooning their love-lorn tunes from the tortured shallows of lukewarm hearts.
>
> The Beatles are wacky. They wear their hair like a mop – but it's WASHED, it's super-clean. So is their fresh young act. They don't have to rely on off-colour jokes about homos for their fun . . .
>
> Youngsters like The Beatles are doing a good turn for show business – and the rest of us – with their new sounds, new looks.
>
> Good luck, Beatles!

On 10 November 1963, we switched on the TV and joined 21.2 million other viewers, the largest television audience to date. We were tuning in to *The Royal Variety Performance*. It was not Charlie Drake or Max Bygraves or Harry Secombe who had attracted such a huge audience, but the fact that The Beatles were due to perform in the presence of the Queen Mother. The *New Musical Express* was rapturous:

> John Lennon announced the last number with cheeky assurance as he asked the audience to join in 'Twist and Shout' by demanding: 'Would the people in the cheaper seats clap your hands, and the rest of you, if you'd just rattle your jewelry' – to get a big laugh.
>
> The Beatles then tore into the excitement-provoking 'Twist

and Shout', and by the end of it the entire audience – Royal Party included – were asking for more!

A clip from the show has survived and can be found online. Unlike most of their concerts, there was no screaming from hordes of apparently hysterical young women in the Prince of Wales Theatre and the music can be clearly heard. What struck me was the group's musicianship, their sheer talent, professionalism and energy. Others were following in their wake, especially from Liverpool and the North. Gerry Marsden of Gerry and the Pacemakers had a fine voice, and they enjoyed tremendous success in 1963, along with the likes of The Searchers and Billy J. Kramer and the Dakotas. But it was The Beatles who led, who made it all possible and shifted the cultural landscape. Author and journalist Hunter Davies observed that their success was not a story solely for the music press: what The Beatles did became front-page news in most mainstream papers.

Muriel Young was a DJ with Radio Luxembourg who hosted recordings in front of large audiences: 'The Beatles changed everything. Before them I used to do all my announcing in cocktail frocks and things, but after The Beatles you could wear any casual outfit you wanted.'

It mattered little to me that most of this was happening outside Scotland, a long way from 42 Inchmead Drive. In part because The Beatles were from ordinary backgrounds, we felt included, even part of what began to feel like a revolution. But there was one very real connection.

On Friday, 5 October 1962, on the same day that 'Love Me Do' was released, the first James Bond film, *Dr No*, was premiered in London. Bond, agent 007, was played by Sean Connery from Edinburgh, who did his best to disguise his working-class Edinburgh accent. I remember seeing the poster: Bond in a dinner jacket, smirking ever so slightly, holding a gun with a very long barrel, and with four women in various states of undress next to him. The (almost) appropriately named Ursula Andress in a white bikini was only the most memorable, and the barrel of Bond's gun dangled very close to her crotch. There was no mistaking the message. *From Russia With Love*, perhaps the best of the whole series, featured Daniela Bianchi as Tatiana Romanova, and there was no mistaking her role, or why she was cast as the femme nearly fatale. What seemed to be different, and seemed to be okay, was that Bond clearly had sex with lots of beautiful women. And he was Scottish. Like us. The cultural weather was changing, and there was nothing the spluttering Reverend MacLeod could do about it.

Wherever The Beatles played, the sound of a sexual revolution rent the air. In concert halls and theatres all over Britain, row upon row of young fans screamed in ecstasy when the Fab Four took the stage. Beatlemania was real. The screaming engulfing the band in unprompted waves was so loud and so persistent that when one of my more enterprising friends went to see them play in Edinburgh, he could hear nothing of the music. And nor could John, Paul, George or Ringo. By 1966, they had given up the punishing touring schedule of live shows not only in Britain but around the world. What was the point of playing music if no one, including the musicians, could hear it? But something that transcended entertainment was at work in those concerts. Perhaps for the first time, women were daring, albeit in large groups, to express their sexuality. In 1963, psychiatrist Dixon Scott observed that the screaming 'would not have taken on the magnitude that it has if there had not been the need to release sexual urges . . . There's no getting away from it – a revolution is taking place under our noses.'

That revolution had an unlikely and inadvertent champion. The deeply ascetic, self-conscious, classically educated Enoch Powell was Minister of Health in 1961, and it fell to him to announce that the contraceptive pill for women could be prescribed on the National Health Service. But not for every woman, only those who were married or whose health might be put at risk by pregnancy. However, a parliamentary question suggested some flexibility, or at least ambiguity. The Labour MP Marcus Lipton asked: 'Is it left to the doctor to decide whether those pills shall be prescribed both for married and single women?' Powell sidestepped: 'It is always for the individual doctor to decide on each case what are the medical requirements.' In the space of two years almost half a million women were 'on the Pill' – always spelled with a capital P – and not all of them were married. Woolworths did a roaring trade in cheap wedding bands that looked like gold.

If what became widely known as the sexual revolution was indeed happening in England, where women were actively taking control of their own fertility, their own bodies, it was a considerably more agonised process in Scotland. A recent oral history project found that in the 1960s, the majority of women who responded experienced outright hostility among doctors, most of them men. 'He made clear his utter contempt of me,' said one respondent. Dr J. C. Murdoch wrote to the *British Medical Journal*: 'There are many doctors who believe that obedience to the moral law of God . . . is more important.' Many of Glasgow's GPs were thought to be particularly antagonistic, in all likelihood because a significant proportion were Catholics. One woman remembered: 'But I did feel in Glasgow that you were a bit of a leper . . . It was just a bit cold, a bit distant, as if you're doing the wrong thing. You would not have wanted to go back there. I mean, you needed to go back, but you would not have wanted to go.'

Some doctors even breached patient confidentiality. Another woman remembered her sister's experience with her GP, a Catholic who had been the family's doctor for years: 'He actually told my parents. I suppose at the time she could have said, "He's not allowed to do that." . . . She got hell from my parents.'

Local newspapers weighed in with headlines like 'Sex on the Rates', an echo of the objection to the public funding of Catholic schooling 50 years before, and 'We Need to Return to the Old Morality'. The Church of Scotland minister Reverend William Still preached that Scotland was in danger of becoming a 'post-Christian and increasingly pagan society'. He would have been horrified to discover that he was not only a moralist but a prophet. Willie Ross MP, Secretary of State for Scotland, received letters that minced no words: 'I deplore deeply that fornication is encouraged among the unmarried' wrote one voter. Only in Scotland's universities and colleges were GPs as liberal as they appear to have been in England. It was not until 1968 that the Health and Public Services Act (Scotland) legalised the prescription of the Pill for unmarried women. In the reaction to that, I was surprised not to find any reference to 'the Jezebels that they are'. Maybe attitudes really were shifting.

In March 1965, I entered politics. We all did, a gang of 14- and 15-year-olds in our council estate. With the death of our Conservative MP, Commander Donaldson, a figure whose name we knew because he had represented Roxburgh, Selkirk and Peebles since 1951, but whom we had never seen, there was to be a by-election. To us teenagers listening to Beatles LPs on my KB Dansette record player (I'd saved up), it looked like a contest between the past and the future. The Conservative candidate was a posh local laird, Robin McEwen, and a 26-year-old Liberal, David Steel, was his principal opponent. There was a palpable sense of excitement around the towns and villages of the large rural constituency as Britain's press descended. The Conservatives sent up former cabinet ministers to support their man, but not all visiting Tories did McEwen a favour. One well-known MP, famous for his splendid handlebar moustache, Sir Gerald Nabarro, helpfully analysed the problem of depopulation in the Borders. Lord Napier and Ettrick, he pointed out, used to have fourteen servants, and was now down to one. It really was them against us, then against now.

I remember one packed meeting for the Conservatives at the Tait Hall in Kelso. The main speaker was Reggie Maudling, a former Chancellor of the Exchequer, and as he asked for questions from the floor, we all turned to hear a motorbike revving loudly outside. In strode the Independent Nationalist candidate, Anthony J. C. Kerr, in a waterproof riding mac and a brown leather helmet with his goggles perched on top of it. He looked like Biggles. Standing in the aisle, he bellowed a statement (about his candidacy and policies) rather than a question to an audience many times the size of any he could attract. Not waiting for an answer, he turned on his heel and left to scattered, bemused applause. Apparently, an envelope containing £150 in used notes had been put through his letterbox a few weeks before (enough for the deposit he would surely lose). The cash probably came from someone who did not support him but thought he might take a few votes from David Steel.

Every evening and weekend for about a fortnight, we flyposted STEELX stickers on every lamppost and telegraph pole we could find. At political meetings we cheered the Liberals and booed the Tories. Change was undoubtedly in the air. We all piled into the Roxy Cinema at 10 p.m., after the film had finished, to hear David Steel make a final, rousing speech. The polls had closed and nothing more could be done, but nevertheless there was real optimism, a conviction that the future might defeat the dowdy, fusty, boring past. The optimism was well founded. The young Liberal candidate soundly defeated the local laird (who had in fact given up campaigning, retired to his stately home with what we would now call stress and left his wife to read out his speeches) and became Britain's youngest MP. 'It's the Boy David!' was the headline the following morning.

David Steel was indeed part of the future, as it turned out.

He had a key role to play in the sexual revolution that was so obviously sweeping across the country in the 1960s. He came top of another poll, that which determined Private Members' bills. These allowed MPs who were not part of the government to put forward new legislation. To his undying credit, Steel chose to champion the cause of abortion, something still illegal in Britain. Sufficiently politically astute to enlist the support of the ruling Labour Government, he piloted the bill through the Houses of Parliament until it became an act in October 1967. It was an immense achievement as women gained more control of their own reproductive rights, of their own bodies. With the widespread prescription of the Pill, the new act reduced the frequency of forced marriages (what used to be called shotgun marriages) and the lifetimes of unhappiness that sometimes followed. The number of children available for adoption also declined, and if there were fewer orphans destined for hellish environments like Smyllum Park, then that was surely a worthwhile side-effect of the sea change in public morality.

Fashion designer Mary Quant had no doubt she had lived through a revolution, recalling 'the perpetual anxiety' about becoming pregnant and the 'real relief' of welcoming the coming of the Pill and the legalisation of abortion.

Like The Beatles, Mary Quant spearheaded profound change in 1960s Britain. She changed the way many young people looked, or wanted to look. There had, of course, been exceptions in the recent past, like the Teddy Boys with their distinctive, long drape jackets, drainpipe trousers and crepe brothel creepers, but at the beginning of the decade most young people dressed much as their parents had done: sensibly and in muted colours. Minor trends came and went, like the dirndl skirt and the Windsor knotting of a tie, but in the 1950s and overlapping into the 60s, young men looked like younger and generally slimmer versions of their fathers when they dressed up to go out on a Saturday evening to the pub or to a party. They didn't wear trousers, but what my dad called flannels, usually grey, with either black brogues or plain-fronted Oxford shoes. The shirt was usually white but could be a Tattersall check with a club or a plain tie worn with what was called a sports jacket. The latter was generally tweed, often with a checked pattern, or sometimes a blazer was preferred, but not many had both. For more formal occasions, it was a suit. And outdoors nearly all men wore hats, either a tweed bonnet (bunnet) or a 'cut' hat made from brown felt, sometimes known as a trilby. For women, it was skirts or dresses, their hems well below the knee, worn with a blouse and a cardigan or a short coat for going out, or a suit more or less modelled on the classic Chanel design. My mum's generation sometimes called these 'costumes'. Twin sets became popular in the 1950s, many of these matching jumpers and cardigans made in the textile mills of Hawick. Women rarely wore trousers, or 'slacks'. And that was more or less it.

In the early 1960s, all of that began to change for young people. After gaining a diploma in art education from Goldsmiths, Mary Quant opened her first shop, Bazaar, in Chelsea in 1955, and its quirky window displays, long opening hours and the fact that music played inside attracted young people. A true entrepreneur, Quant began to have her own designs made up, and by 1963, she had produced the miniskirt – more than any other, a garment emblematic of the new era. Mary Quant named it after her favourite car but credited her customers with how short a skirt it became:

It was the girls on the King's Road who invented the miniskirt. I was making easy, youthful, simple clothes, in which you could move, in which you could run and jump, and we would make them the length the customer wanted. I wore them very short and the customers would say 'Shorter, shorter!' . . . They are curiously feminine, but their femininity lies in their attitude rather than their appearance.

For men, The Beatles were an early exemplar. Their manager, Brian Epstein, smartened them up considerably, persuading them to ditch their rock 'n' roll black leathers for what would become their trademark: identical collarless suits, white shirts and black ties. Mod-style Cuban heels made them – Ringo especially – appear taller. For their groundbreaking concert at the Shea Stadium in New York in 1965, the group wore beige safari-style jackets and black trousers as 55,600 fans screamed their adulation.

It was the Beatles' hair as much as their clothes that defined their look. Long hair was a widespread symbol of change, shockingly different from the military short-back-and-sides that all men, young or old, were given at the barber's. Growing your hair cost nothing, and many teenagers began to imitate their heroes. However, they were often, publicly and sometimes venomously, abused for doing so. The Beatle cut originated in Hamburg in 1960, where the group's original bass player, Stuart Sutcliffe, fell in love with the artist and photographer Astrid Kirchherr. She cut his hair after washing all the grease out of it and combed it down over his forehead. John Lennon and Paul McCartney apparently laughed when they saw the change, but George Harrison asked Astrid to cut his, and in 1961, when Lennon and McCartney were in Paris, they had theirs cut in the same style. For his 21st birthday, John's wealthy Edinburgh aunt had given him £100 and they had gone on a trip abroad. Paul called it 'the Mod style'. It was a significant description.

Mary Quant was also known as 'the Queen of the Mods': she had been inspired by their smart style since the late 1950s. The name came from a small London subculture who loved modern jazz – the Modernists. Mods wore tailor-made suits and ties, and these were kept dry by roomy parkas that could be found in most army surplus shops. These young men and women favoured Italian scooters – Vespas and Lambrettas – and their taste in music covered everything from jazz, soul music and ska to The Who and the Small Faces.

In the summer of 1964, those scooters brought many Mods to seaside resorts in the South of England, most famously Brighton, where they clashed with their antithesis: the motorcycle gangs of Rockers. Wearing biker boots, greasy denim jeans and leather jackets, the Rockers liked their hair swept back off their foreheads, often heavily Brylcreemed and sometimes with a quiff at the front. The back was shaped into a DA, a 'Duck's Arse'. The Rockers harked back to the past – we even had a group in Kelso – and in some senses the clashes that took place reflected not only tribal antipathy between two overlapping generations but also two different lifestyles. Newspaper coverage greatly exaggerated the scale and gravity of the scuffles and running fights at Brighton, Clacton, Margate and elsewhere, and the reporting seemed more anti-youth than anything else. There was an air of middle-aged newspapermen in their braces, puffing on pipes and writing about what they may have seen as a vaguely violent threat, an upending of the social order, to the short-back-and-sides mentality inherited from the Second World War. Some wrote of a 'moral panic' in Britain. But it was really much simpler. When The Who's Roger Daltrey stammered Pete Townshend's lyrics about being put down and hoping to die before he got old, it was an expression of genuine angst and frustration about trying to find a place in society. And it chimed with teenagers: 'My Generation' went to number 2 in the UK in November 1965.

Television, and ITV in particular, had begun to reflect these cultural shifts; in Scotland it was the only way the likes of me and my friends could see what was going on. For most of it was going on in faraway London. On Friday, 9 August 1963, ITV began transmission of a truly innovative series that began with the line: 'The weekend starts here!' *Ready Steady Go!* was live, and it showed bands playing their music as young people danced or milled around them, very close to their heroes and heroines. The cameras were often in shot in what seemed like a small studio, there were lots of big close-ups, of the dancers as well as the musicians, and it felt like a real event: certainly staged, but full of impromptu moments. I remember one couple dancing around during a slow number, and I'm certain the guy had his hand firmly planted on his girl's bum. There were interviews with the performers, and some were hilarious. Another episode featured Lulu singing 'Shout!', and that showed me that Scots could get into all this, whatever *this* was. Lulu could dance, and the cameramen dwelt on her hips in a close-up that is printed on my memory.

This wonderfully energetic and compulsive show was presented by Keith Fordyce (who wore a tie – a slightly discordant note, in my view) and Cathy McGowan. She was only 19 years old, had been a typist and came from Tooting. At the audition, the producer, Elkan Allan, asked McGowan what she thought mattered most to teenagers. Was it sex, music or fashion? She produced the right answer. Fashion. Wearing her black hair long and with a fringe right down to her heavily made-up eyes, this amazingly confident young woman wore the sort of clothes that Mary Quant and others were designing, and her look deeply impressed Lesley Hornby, who would soon become famous as the model known as Twiggy. 'I'd sit and drool over her clothes. She was a heroine to me because she was one of us.'

That sense of involvement was also found on *Thank Your Lucky Stars*, a pre-recorded, more formulaic sort of show, also on ITV, that featured groups and solo artists who usually mimed their songs. It included a section called 'Spin-a-Disc' where young people listened to three new records and judged them. Most memorable was Janice Nicholls. In an unapologetic Birmingham accent, she would pronounce that 'Oi'll geeve eet foive' because 'Oi loiked the backing'. Just like Cathy McGowan, we all thought she was one of us.

In 1967, I became a Mod. My big sister's boyfriend at Edinburgh University was a Londoner and he bought me a shirt with a button-down collar. It was a thing of wonder. Of course, I wore it to school, hoping that girls would swoon as they passed me in the corridor (Rae Smith, Evelyn Johnstone and Isobel Elliot certainly never did: they still weren't talking to me) or at least ask where in Carnaby Street I had found it, when I was last in Swinging London, the other weekend. As my sister's boyfriend said, it was 'Top Mod', but I don't think anyone noticed except Mr Goodall, my Latin and Greek teacher. He was a snappy dresser and knew I couldn't have bought anything like that in Kelso.

Cathy McGowan and her producer were right. Clothes were defining of my generation. Gradually, it became possible to buy Top Mod items in Edinburgh. Levi's, Lee and Wrangler jeans, the top three brands, could be found in Rose Street and also Ben Sherman shirts, some of them button-down. Progress. While I was at school, I had two jobs because Top Mod was not cheap and my mum and dad could only 'kit me out' for everyday clothes, but no more. At various stages, I had a milk delivery job and a Sunday paper round, and in the school holidays I had various sorts of seasonal employment, the most memorable being a few weeks working in a lemonade factory. Middlemas was in the middle of Kelso and wonderfully Heath Robinson, with bottles shoogling and clinking along ancient conveyor belts. But the most lucrative job lasted for about a fortnight in October. And it could not have been further from the urbane world of Mary Quant, Cathy McGowan and The Beatles.

Each autumn, Scottish children were allowed off school for what was known as the 'tattie holidays' – and not only in country towns but also in the cities. They were needed as seasonal labour by farmers to help lift (howk) the year's crop of potatoes. Because of the constant stooping involved, it was thought that children and young women were better suited to the work. Employment at the tattie howking was the epitome of casual labour. At the foot of Inchmead Drive, at 7 a.m., a tractor pulling a flat-bed trailer appeared, and if you wanted a day's work, you jumped aboard and sat on the sides of the trailer. One shudders to think what the modern health and safety industry would make of 20 kids clinging on to a truck bumping up farm tracks with next to nothing to hold on to.

Once a trailer load of workers arrived at a field where a ploughman had made a start on digging up the spuds, each worker was allocated a stent. Marked off by posts and string, these were about 20 yards long (less for smaller children), and as the digger passed, you followed its furrow, putting potatoes in wire baskets for the length of your stent. It was boring and tiring work, but you knew it wouldn't last for ever. Many tattie howkers sang as they worked, like the slaves picking cotton in Georgia. But unlike them, we were well paid, in cash, and although I can't recall exact sums, two weeks' work might have earned £15, enough for more than one button-down shirt.

A new market was created in the 1960s as the baby boomers came of age. Music, clothes, records, radios, scooters, motorbikes and all manner of interrelated merchandise began to sell well, fuelled by programming and advertising on ITV and Radio Luxembourg. There was money jingling in the pockets of young people, and the availability of the Pill meant that many were delaying getting married or avoiding having to get married. That meant more money to spend, and the creative economy kept coming up with new things that seemed more 'with it' than whatever was 'with it' last year.

There was also a new cultural confidence. Popular music in the 1950s in Britain had been derivative, little more than a pale imitation of the work of American artists such as Elvis Presley, Buddy Holly, Bill Haley and many others. But in January 1964, the unthinkable happened. The Beatles' 'I Want To Hold Your Hand' went to number 1 in the American charts and other British artists followed in their wake. And British fashion became popular on the other side of the Atlantic, pulled into the limelight by the success of pop music. While Britain had lost an empire, in the same decade, it was now making sweeping cultural conquests.

In November 2023, a remarkable circle was completed. 'Now And Then' was a ballad written by John Lennon in 1977, three years before he was murdered in New York. The demo was shelved and remained unfinished until electronic wizardry allowed the voices and music of George Harrison, who had died of lung cancer in 2001, Ringo Starr and Paul McCartney to be added. 'Now And Then' (the flip side was a remix of 'Love Me Do' – thus it could be credited with being the first and last Beatles single) rose quickly to number 1 in the charts more than 60 years after 'From Me To You' had done the same. Many of those who bought it will also have spent 6s/8d on 'From Me To You' in that golden, epoch-making year of 1963. Perhaps some of them even owned record players.

7

The Auld Life

In the early 1950s, my mum began to dream. Raised in the crowded body warmth of a tenement in the Borders textile town of Hawick with six sisters and a lone brother, she thought the prefab at Inchmyre was impossibly spacious. No more three to a bed, no more seven to a room, no more using a communal toilet, the little house must have acted on her like a spur, as she began to dream, began to aspire. Our house at 42 Inchmead Drive was a two-storey step up with three bedrooms, a back kitchenette, a sitting room and a bathroom, with a bath. But it wasn't enough – and it wasn't hers. Her aspiration was probably unique in our council estate, and that turned out to be its undoing. Mum wanted to own a house, have a house of her own.

That's why, as soon as it became possible, with my grannie coping as best she could with childcare, she started working night shifts at Inch Hospital in the sometimes grisly business of looking after incontinent geriatrics. She was determined to save up for a deposit for a mortgage so that she and my dad could buy a house. By the late 1950s, they had scraped together enough, perhaps £300 or more. And Mum had heard of a house for sale in Kelso, the perfect place. Known as the Dispensary and built in the later eighteenth century, it stood on Roxburgh Street but looked west with uninterrupted views over the Tweed and the rolling landscape beyond the river. It was a dream that almost came true.

And then my dad used the hard-won deposit to buy a second-hand car. And told someone else about the house, someone who promptly bought it. My mum was devastated, and I'm not sure that she ever got past the disappointment as we stayed on at Inchmead Drive for another 40 years. 'Not for the likes of us' might have been a summary of the reason, or better, the excuse. Outwardly, my dad could be an aggressive, combative man, but I think he lacked an inner self-confidence. 'A millstone round our necks' was how he characterised property ownership. A house that cost a great deal of money and if there was any maintenance or repair needed – and the house was almost two hundred years old, for goodness' sake – then that just added to the weight of the millstone needed to buy it. My dad had lived in rented accommodation all his life, and with a council house, there were none of those worries. It was the council's responsibility. That was the sort of thing he said out loud, and sometimes louder, but I think there were other reasons why he tore down my mum's dream.

His mother, my grannie, Bina, was born in 1890 at Cliftonhill Farm near the old village of Ednam, about two miles north of Kelso. It was the beginning of the long twilight of high farming, the late Victorian zenith of grain and meat production when many hands were needed to plough, plant, weed and harvest. The census of 1891 describes a very busy farm, counting 62 people living in the cottage row and the big house. There were 23 working full-time at Cliftonhill and they raised 25 children, many of whom would have done regular herding jobs, helped with the summer haymaking, banding and stooking, building the hayricks, bringing in the cows for morning and evening milking, finding eggs in the stackyard as well as howking tatties in October.

Bina's mother, Annie Moffat, was a bondager, a 'wumman worker', who was bonded by the contract the farmer had made with her father, my great-great-grandfather, William Moffat. He was First Horseman, the head ploughman, and in the stables at Cliftonhill, the four pairs of Clydesdales were his responsibility. William had brothers and many cousins, and almost all my paternal family worked on the farms of fertile Berwickshire, its red earth grained into their hands.

The bond that bound Annie and all the workers at the farm was made at what were known as hiring fairs, held once or twice a year in Kelso and in market towns all over Lowland Scotland. Families who had not 'been spoken to' by the farmer they were working for, or did not wish to stay on at that farm, sent their principal, usually their father, into town and these men stood in groups in the wide market square as potential employers walked around looking and talking, taking on men and their families for a year's or a six-month term at an agreed fee. It was not many removes from a slave market, and humiliating for those who 'were left standing'. Once a farmer and a father had struck a bargain and hit hands, two weeks later, horse-drawn carts would appear in the town with all the family's possessions piled on them as they moved to work at another farm and another tied cottage. Even though the fee system had almost died out by the beginning of the Second World War, I don't think that sense of servitude and being at the mercy of the judgements of 'your betters' ever left my dad. Like many returning soldiers he voted Labour in 1945 and continued to do so all his life, but his values remained Conservative, and he was always deferential to the landowners, minor aristocrats and wealthy people in whose houses he worked, rewiring and fixing appliances. I remember some of them called him 'Moffat' as though he was a servant. Consequently, he had a sure grasp of 'the likes of us', and we were not the sort of people who owned houses. Even if we didn't – my mum especially – my dad did know our place, and it could never be our own place.

Sometime before the outbreak of the First World War, my

gran left Cliftonhill and moved to Kelso to work as a seamstress. Mum always said she had 'clever fingers'. But in 1915, Bina fell pregnant after a brief love affair with a soldier home on leave from the unimaginable, murderous horrors of the trenches in Flanders. When my dad was born in 1916, my gran became a single mother who had somehow to make ends meet, and no doubt endure the stigma, the stares in the street, the shame of her lover eventually preferring to marry someone else. My dad grew up coping with that in a small town where everyone knew everyone else's business, and it may be that it was a circumstance that gave rise to both his combative nature and his paradoxical lack of self-confidence.

He was the first in my paternal family to be born in a town and not on a farm. Even so, his language, and that of many of his generation, was peppered with memories of the rhythms of the land, the heavy horses and the hard work, outside in all weathers. When his day as an electrician began, it was 'yokin' time' – when the Clydesdales had their harness put on in the stables – and when his work ended, it was 'lowsin' time' – when the buckles were undone, the great peaked collars taken off the big horses, and the salt of their sweat was groomed off them.

With the car paid for by my mum's broken dream, my dad took his mother out for 'hurls', drives around the countryside in the long summer evenings. She had nothing much to say, only staring out of the passenger window across the gently undulating fields of golden barley, the grass parks, and beyond them to the dark heads of the Cheviot Hills. 'Aye,' she murmured quietly when it was time for my dad to move on. If I had been more attentive and less impatient, always asking why we had stopped, sliding about in the back seat, I might have noticed my gran remembering the auld life, the life on the land.

When I am going that way, I always stop at the side of the road above Cliftonhill Farm and get out of the car, no matter the weather or the season. I look out over the south-facing fields running down to the banks of the little Eden Water and blow a kiss to Bina's memory and the auld life that has now vanished. And it was a way of life that vanished within a generation.

As the severe winter of early 1947 bit hard, Scotland's hill farms suffered terribly, sometimes fatally. High in the Lammermuir Hills two shepherds and their collies were moving their sheep flock down to the shelter of the Whiteadder Valley when a blizzard began to billow in from the west. As the dogs arced out on the gather in a wide pincer movement, the swirling snow suddenly engulfed the hillsides. In the blinding, whistling vortex, there was complete whiteout, visibility shrinking to a yard or two. In the roar of the storm, the shepherds could not hear each other, but as night fell and temperatures plummeted, their dogs found them. The following morning, the two men were discovered in the drifts, frozen to death, their bodies crouched, their backs to the west. And beside them were the rigid bodies of their faithful dogs. The collies could have found their way down off the hills, their keen senses showing the way. But they stayed. The dogs stayed.

I heard that story from Bina, one of the few times she talked directly about the auld life. It was harsh, repetitive and often unrewarding, and it could be very dangerous. But compared to the neurotic, centrally heated existence we have now, it could also be a wholesome sort of life: farm workers ate when they were hungry, slept when they were tired and died when they were worn out.

Farming was vital, and during the Second World War Britain had been forced to feed itself as much as was possible, given the dangers to merchant shipping from the German U-boat fleet. Clement Attlee's Labour Government was compelled to continue with rationing for much longer than it wished to, until 1954, and there is no doubt that it was a contributory factor to their defeat in the general election of 1951. Nonetheless, before Labour lost office, the Ministry of Agriculture had managed to lay down the foundations of more productive and more secure farming. And by extension, a very different way of cultivating and cropping the land.

The Agriculture Act of 1947 guaranteed minimum prices for key products in an attempt to insulate British farmers from the wild fluctuations seen in the 1920s and the 1930s. It may be that the terrible damage done in the winter of early 1947 sharpened government thinking. For eighteen months ahead, after full consultation with farmers' organisations, the prices of wheat, barley, oats, rye, potatoes and sugar beet were fixed. And for fatstock, milk and egg producers, prices were guaranteed for between two and four years. A year later, the Agricultural Holdings Act gave lifetime security of tenure to those who rented their farms, often from large estates. Taken together, these pieces of legislation were transformative in that they allowed farmers to plan and encouraged them to invest in modern equipment that would improve yields.

They also brought an end to the auld life, quickly transforming agriculture in Scotland. No longer would 25 children career around the steading of Cliftonhill Farm, whooping and yelling, chasing the hens, helping as well as hindering with morning and evening chores. These busy places would gradually fall silent, and the whinny of horses and the blether in the stables as the Clydesdales were groomed would be replaced by the noise and clatter of machines. Now, Cliftonhill is run, very efficiently, by just two people: Archie and Maggie Stewart. Just as government intervention in the shape of a massive programme of council house building changed the look of Scotland's towns and cities, so these acts of parliament changed the way the countryside looks.

So did Harry Ferguson. In the late 1930s, the Ulsterman revolutionised the way in which tractors worked. Early models had simply pulled farm implements with more power than a pair of heavy horses, and they were expensive and not much used. What Ferguson did was to invent the three-point hydraulic linkage. This allowed the tractor's power to be transferred to whatever implement was attached at the back end: ploughs, harrows, reapers and a host of others. This in turn meant that one man could do a wide range of jobs on a farm much more efficiently, more quickly and without a great deal of help. After 1946, the Standard Motor Company of Coventry adapted an empty, redundant aircraft factory and began to turn out these little grey tractors in huge numbers. Between 1946 and 1956, when production ceased, they manufactured 517,651 models, and they were not expensive at £325. More than half of Standard's output went for export, but nevertheless, in a ten-year period, a quarter of a million tractors were bought by British farmers. Known as the Wee Grey Fergies, they transformed the landscape of Scotland almost overnight.

The centuries-old rhythms of horse working faded very quickly. No longer would the Clydesdales be lowsed in the stable yard, the mud and little stones picked out of their great hooves, their manes combed out and the salt-sweat brushed off their flanks. No longer would hard feed be ladled out of the corn kists into their bowls, water buckets topped up and hay stuffed into the mangers at the back of the loose boxes. And no longer would the First Horseman and the other ploughmen sit on the kists, listening to the contented munching of the heavy horses while they smoked their pipes in the long summer evenings, talking of the day's work, the day to come, the weather and anything that they had heard from the farms round about. When the little grey tractors came, the horses were put out to pasture and the men who cared for them and often loved them for their hard work and constancy, were forced to learn new skills or move away into the towns and cities, as most of them did, leaving behind the auld life as it faded into the darkness of the past.

Cruickshank of Denny was a principal manufacturer of horse ploughs in Scotland, and the last of them were made in 1958, a date that marks the end of a way of life. As the Clydesdales vanished from farm steadings, these seismic changes had a wider effect. At the foot of Cliftonhill, in the tiny village of Ednam, was the smiddy. Most villages had blacksmith's shops so that when the horses needed to be shod, they did not have to walk too far. In 2002, Dave Welsh remembered how history shifted:

The smiddy [at Sprouston, near Kelso] was hard work, and pretty constant. Maybe 120 to 150 horses from the farm places around would be shod and when they were being worked, that would be every six weeks or so. Some of them were not very cooperative: they leaned on you. At times when there wasn't so much on the go, we'd make shoes and hang them on hooks around the wall. I mind the smiddy elders, the old men who came in to blether and sit smoking their pipes. Likely the daughter-in-law or the wife wanted rid of them [from] in front of their fire. They argued all the time. 'Aye, that would be when oo was at Kersknowe, no, Kersquarter, or no, maybe Redden.' Argued about bloody anything.

The smiddy began to tail off. And it was a question of did we want to adapt to machinery, maintenance, that sort of thing. Eventually we stopped altogether in the 1960s.

Important facets of community life were lost in villages and towns all over Scotland as argumentative old men lost their seats by the warmth of the forges and had either to stay at home in the winter or seek other ways to meet their friends. Paradoxically, horse working lingered a little longer in towns. A horse-drawn float delivering milk or coal needed to stop often, every few yards, and a vehicle would waste fuel to little purpose if it only had to move short distances every few minutes.

Something less tangible was also lost, and that was empathy. The heavy horses were not machines: they had likes and dislikes, foibles that could not be explained, and particular talents. If ploughing or carting was to be done well, horsemen needed to understand the language of these creatures that could not talk. This was not a matter of kindness but of professionalism. If a furrow was to be straight and a Clydesdale responsive to a flick of the long reins, then the horse needed to be fit and content. More than that, its compliance had to be earned by good husbandry. These powerful animals were immeasurably stronger than any human being and they worked by consent and through patient training from a young age. Good horsemen were careful to create relationships with their Clydesdales not because they liked them, although few did not, but because that was the best, indeed the only, way to do good, consistent work. Although these were little practised by the outbreak of the Second World War, the rituals of the Horseman's Word understood this. The secret word young men were given at nighttime meetings in the stables was ENO, ONE said backwards. For oneness, harmony between man and animal, was at the heart of farm work for centuries.

The wee grey Fergies were liked for different reasons. They made life easier and often much less harsh. It is important not to romanticise the auld life for it could be miserable to depend entirely on muscle power, both human and animal. Out in bad weather in an age before waterproofs, men and women often wore sacking over their shoulders to keep the rain off, at least for a time. I remember an old ploughman telling me: 'If it was looking like rain, you hoped it would come in the afternoon, and not the morning. If it did, you would be wet all day.'

In the 1951 census, the landward areas of Scotland were defined as not the cities, or large and small burghs, but rather the countryside with its villages, farms and crofts. Its population then was substantial at 1,532,610, roughly 30 per cent of the nation's total population. Now described as rural areas, both remote and more accessible, the number of people who lived there had almost halved by the 2011 census to 889,366, very few of them working on the land, most of them commuters or retired. Now only 67,000 people work on Scotland's farms, crofts and smallholdings. Over my lifetime, it has been a seismic shift, not only changing the way the countryside looks, but also how it feels and sounds.

Mechanisation not only emptied farm cottages, it also saw productivity soar as new methods were adopted. Farms consolidated, and in Lowland Scotland became larger with one or two workers able to cope with more acreage and more stock. Across the arable sector fields were made bigger and hedges grubbed up and trees cut down to allow more land to be ploughed. Yields have tripled in 70 years as more fertilisers and pesticides were used. Stock rearing changed. Not all animals are now free range, and the battery farming of laying hens has become common. Most beef cattle are brought in, complaining loudly for the first few weeks of confinement in the byres, to be fed the year's crop of silage so that they don't have to suffer the worst of the winter weather and risk losing valuable condition. Only Scotland's sheep stay out all year.

The wider costs of soaring productivity are now becoming clear. According to the chairman of NatureScot, Professor Colin Galbraith, 'Scotland's nature is in crisis.' A *State of Nature* report published in 2023 found that one in nine species is threatened with extinction. Some of the most fragile include birds that were once common: swifts, lapwings, kestrels, curlews and greenfinches. Several species of moths are under severe threat, and lichens, mosses and wild flowering plants have suffered catastrophically. Half of the population of native seabirds has disappeared since 1986, and that had happened before the outbreak of bird flu in 2019. Clearly by no means all of this has been caused by changes in farming methods, but there is no doubt that the countryside has been severely damaged and depleted as hedgerows disappeared and pesticides and fertilisers were sprayed across the big fields. Policies and practices need to change, and quickly, before the last curlew falls silent.

The demand for timber during the Second World War greatly increased and saw widespread felling of Scotland's forests, and after 1945 the Forestry Commission began a comprehensive programme of replanting. Its effects can be seen everywhere in the countryside, and especially in the vast acreage of woodland in the Highlands. By 2019, 18.5 per cent of the land area of Scotland had been afforested, and a cycle of harvesting and replanting has gone on for decades. When hillsides are clear-felled, the effect can be ugly, unnatural, a scar on the landscape that can be made to look even worse when neighbouring woodland not yet mature is left standing. It can also be very damaging in the fight to combat climate change. Trees are vital in the process of carbon capture and in slowing down global warming. But when forests are clear-felled, these virtues are compromised. Once the trees are harvested, huge machinery is brought in to plough the naked forest floor before new trees can be planted, and that process emits a great deal of carbon dioxide.

In November 2023, more warnings were aired. The policy of the Scottish Government is to increase the total acreage of forestry from 18.5 per cent of the land to 21 per cent. Grants are offered for planting and tax advantages offered to those who want to buy up land and turn it over to forestry. The *Eskdale and Liddesdale Advertiser*, based in Langholm, ran a story that three farms had been sold for tree planting. Instead of grazing for sheep and cattle, their fields would disappear under many thousands of pine trees. The newspaper's editorial called the development 'modern day clearance and nothing short of rural political crime'. And this was not an isolated case. Between 2021 and 2022, the number of farms sold for tree planting doubled. The effect of this can already be seen. The same newspaper featured a telling photograph. It was a picture of the pupils at Newcastleton Primary School in Liddesdale. There were only four of them.

The look of these forests can be like a vast green blanket, covering and hiding the contours of the land. This effect of uniformity comes in part from the preference for one species. Sitka spruce is native to Alaska and therefore hardy as well as fast-growing. Within 30 or 40 years of planting, a forest of sitka can be harvested. But these vast acreages can be sterile, the dark forest floor barren because the regiments of trees are routinely planted very close together to maximise yield. Nevertheless, forestry can animate the landscape when it is not converting farms into forest in that it provides 25,000 permanent jobs in Scotland, and this workforce can bring life to remote places as families settle there and services and facilities have to be provided.

In many places, the great woods have been developed to attract visitors with walking routes and mountain bike tracks laid out. Great rewilding projects are underway in the Highlands with one at Glen Affric stretching over a vast acreage as it attempts to revive native woodland and to create an environment for all fauna to thrive by excluding deer so that the young trees can establish themselves. Farms too are diversifying to attract visitors, and some are setting up their own specialist retail outlets to try to mitigate the stranglehold of the supermarkets. Tesco, Asda, Sainsbury's, Waitrose and Morrison's sell 80 per cent of all groceries and their power keeps prices low.

Archie and Maggie Stewart have converted Cliftonhill into an organic farm, and they grow and sell their own oats. Once it is milled, it makes excellent porridge and oatcakes. Three old cottages have been converted into holiday lets, and their website mentions attractive walks with the chance of seeing wildlife like otters and herons. It is a welcome rebirth that sees people come back and the everyday glories of the landscape enjoyed once more. I'm sure that when I stop by the side of the road above the fields, I can hear Bina sigh and shake her head. But perhaps on the edge of that disapproval there is a smile.

8

Paper Papers

Every Sunday morning, at about 9 a.m., Jimmy Davidson's mum used to open the front door of her flat, winter or summer, wearing a transparent pink negligee. She had to pay me for her newspaper, and she'd sorely test my powers of concentration as I counted out her change. Jimmy's mum never said a word, and neither did I as I handed over her *Sunday Post*.

Published by D. C. Thomson of Dundee, it was a cultural phenomenon. In 1968 its readership peaked at almost 3 million, more than 80 per cent of the entire population of Scotland. Almost every house on my Sunday paper round took the *Sunday Post* (except Miss McHarg at the Woodside Stud – she read the *Sunday Telegraph*) and another paper, usually the *Sunday Mail* or the *Sunday Express,* and for the more cosmopolitan, the *News of the World.* As well as being the world's most read newspaper, it was enormously influential in Scotland. For the eight regions of the country, the news section was editionised; our sports pages carried exhaustive coverage of Borders rugby, even occasionally reporting on Second XV matches and listing the final scores of many games from the day before, sometimes including schools. In the cities, the Second and Third XI teams of amateur football clubs I'd never heard of had scores listed and sometimes match reports. They probably reported on shinty matches in the northern edition, but I never saw that.

The Fun Section contained icons that endure to this day. Oor Wullie, a spikey-haired, dungaree-wearing cheeky chappie had inconsequential, undangerous adventures. Strangest of all, he was pictured each week sitting on an upturned bucket, something that must have been very uncomfortable since these tend to have a thin, raised metal rim. The other full-page strip cartoon featured the Broons of Glebe Street, the comforting epitome of the Scottish nuclear family and the embodiment of its moral code. Paw and Maw Broon presided over a large family who appeared to cram into a tenement up a close in Glebe Street. Lanky Hen (Henry) Broon was the eldest and he had two sisters, Daphne and Maggie, one beautiful, the other less so, and a hunky brother, Joe, and another, speccy Horace, and also the twins and the bairn. Granpaw Broon, a widower, was a frequent visitor to Glebe Street, puffing his pipe, offering opinions. How they all fitted into a small flat was never explained. The world of this cartoon strip seemed ageless, a working-class Brigadoon with no unpleasantness that common sense could not dismiss and a strange sense of enduring comfort. Perhaps the cartoon represented a kind, upright, certainly idealised version of Scottish, urban, working-class culture epitomised by the solidity of the family, the ageless Broons.

The rest of the *Sunday Post* carried local as well as national news stories, further enhancing its appeal across Scotland. In the middle of the paper were regular features 'The Doc Replies' and 'The HON Man' (this was baffling because HON was not short for Honourable but stood for Holidays on Nothing), but perhaps the most significant feature was 'My Week' by Francis Gay. It was a nom de plume given to a fictional columnist who held very socially conservative views, and each week, he recounted in diary form what had been happening in his world. A member of the Church of Scotland, Francis often delivered improving homilies salted with a great deal of reassurance. His wife was known as the Lady of the House. She was just as conservative but much less outgoing than Mr Gay, only putting on her hat and her good coat to attend church and meetings of the Scottish Women's Rural Institute. Despite the revolutions of the 1960s, the doings of the Lady of the House and her husband were much read and, I suspect, closely identified with. Behind the novelty and sparkle of pop music, fashion and the changes in sexual mores, respectability still mattered to Scots. And it was an old-fashioned sort of respectability, one that my mum would have recognised.

*

The National Library of Scotland is in every sense an adornment to the cultural life of the nation. Completed in 1956, the main building on Edinburgh's George IV Bridge is adorned by Hew Lorimer's slender allegorical figures representing history, law, medicine, music, poetry, science and theology. Behind the façade lies treasure, a huge archive that tells Scotland's story from many perspectives. On a dreich Thursday in December, the NLS's excellent staff had excavated what looked like a huge building block of that story: all the editions of the *Sunday Post* for 1967, when the paper was in its pomp. That year, it happened that the calendar included 53 Sundays. Heaving the huge block of bound copies onto a foam-cushioned lectern, and perched on a high seat, I began in January and several hours later closed the volume at the end of December. It was like a journey in a cultural time machine.

The *Sunday Post* was published in a tabloid format, and my first impression was that it was absolutely jam-packed with stories; the printed columns almost reached the edge of the page, and there was very little white space. It was a dense read and an extraordinary breadth of coverage. And it was by no means all Scottish news. On 12 March 1967, the front-page photo was of a happy couple in a high society wedding at St Mary's Cathedral in Glasgow, with the bride's veil blowing in a gusting wind. But with one exception, all the other seven main stories were foreign news, and the splash was a pungent whiff of the rapid passing of the British Empire: '400 Children Will Fly to Aden for Easter'. These were the families of servicemen fighting nationalists in an attempt to maintain a garrison thought to be a crucial strategic link with Far East Land Forces. Only a few months later, the British were forced to withdraw and Aden became Yemen. The other front-page stories were from Malta and Rhodesia (also former colonies), Mexico, Switzerland and in the bottom left-hand corner, beneath a story about the suspension of the star Celtic footballer, Jimmy Johnstone, there were five lines about the politics of West Berlin. Couthy, borderline obsessive about Scottish sports reporting and constantly upholding what might have been seen as the values of the Kirk – the *Sunday Post* was all of those things. But parochial it was not. The paper even covered events in England. Readers expected and got a good long read on a Sunday morning, and there was no need to buy another newspaper to stay informed. The *Post* had it all.

Generally between 32 and 36 pages, the paper had a consistently huge story count. News occupied the first six or seven pages, and then, in addition to Francis Gay and the other regular features, it was striking to read so much interaction with the huge readership. People communicated with and confided in the *Post* in large numbers. 'Wife Is Shocked By What Husband Said In His Sleep' is the lead on page 17 and under it is the story:

In his job my husband has to be away at intervals to attend sales. He was away at one last month for a few days at a place he goes to regularly. Unfortunately for him, my husband talks in his sleep. I'm sure he has been having an affair with his landlady. What should I do as I've two young children? – H

Hard-headed advice followed.

If you have ideas of separation or divorce, Mrs H, you wouldn't get very far in a court of law merely on what your husband says in his sleep. In fact, unless you've got something more positive (or negative) against your husband, you should just ignore the sleep-talk which may well have no basis in reality. Think twice before you make any move you might regret.

Occasionally, the page leads seem eye-watering when read through a more modern lens. 'The Doc' writes:

Why So Many Women Go Fat in their Forties
I've seen it happen so often, and I'm sure you have too.
Women, who up to the age of 40, keep their figures trim and neat, and take pride in doing so.
Then they let themselves go.
They begin to develop a double chin. Their weight creeps up.
Why do so many women get fat in their forties?
Firstly, because nature, in her wisdom, has arranged things so women get more value from their food than men.
That's because, in nature's eyes, women are more important than men!
Because they're on the go all the time, women need this extra value from their food.
So long as a woman's chasing after her bairns, doing big washings, cooking for a large family . . .

And so it goes on.
The *Sunday Post* could also be politically acute, if not always politically correct. On 29 October 1967, the Sunday before the sensational Hamilton by-election won by the SNP, a page lead read 'Women Are in Revolt'. Below it was an analysis that judged, from vox pop interviews with female voters and others, that

something was brewing in this safe Labour seat. The sub-head was 'They May Be the Surprise Packet in Hamilton on Thursday'. They certainly were.

As I used to do in 1967, I quickly turned to the back pages to read the rugby results and reports. These were as detailed as I remembered, and they listed results with teams I'd forgotten existed: Grangemouth 6 Old Spierians 3; Edinburgh Northern 6 Seapoint 9. Having been sufficiently intrigued to look them up, I discovered that Old Spierians were from Beith in Northern Ayrshire. The pitch at Marshalland was apparently notorious for its muddy conditions. In the 1960s, the club could field four XVs and one player, David Shedden, became a Scottish internationalist. But, in 1972, they ceased to exist when they were forced to merge with Dalry HSFP to form Garnock RFC. *Sic transit gloria mundi*, but at least the glory was memorialised in the encyclopaedia that was the *Sunday Post*. The inside back pages were packed with football coverage from all over Scotland with match reports offering much comment and analysis. Some of it was scathing.

I had forgotten that the Fun Section with Oor Wullie and the Broons was bound differently into the middle of the paper. It had to be turned through 90 degrees to be read, not a problem with a 32-page tabloid, and was probably presented in that way so that it could fold to an A4 size for younger readers. But I did have difficulty with a bound volume of 53 copies, nearly 1,800 pages, and I had the impression from one or two raised eyebrows that my exertions disturbed the sepulchral peace of the reading room.

What struck me was the sheer quality of the artwork in the Fun Section, the precision of the drawing. From 1936 onwards, with the writer, R. D. Low, Dudley D. Watkins drew the two cartoons and, unusually, was allowed to sign them. The economy of line and the variety of expressions on the characters' faces is extraordinary, especially considering the speed with which Watkins must have worked. In addition to the Broons and Oor Wullie, he drew Desperate Dan for the *Dandy* and Lord Snooty and His Pals for the *Beano*. There exists a slightly surreal cartoon strip from the *Beano* where Lord Snooty emerges from his castle. 'Ah! There's Mr Watkins,' he says to his pals, 'the man who draws us for the *Beano*. Let's ask him to teach us how to draw.' Mr Watkins is not keen. 'I'm sorry, kids, but I'm too busy just now. Tell you what, I'll give you this book on drawing to study.' Very sadly, this gifted man died young at 62 of a heart attack, a half-finished Desperate Dan cartoon strip on his drawing table.

The speed with which newspapers were produced was amazing, none more so than the Saturday evening sports editions known as the *Pink* (the different colour was used to avoid confusion with the daily papers). These were published all over Britain and consumed avidly when bundles were heaved out of vans and rushed onto the counters of newsagents who stayed open late to sell them. In Kelso, we were sent the *Edinburgh Evening News Pink*, and even though it had to travel 45 miles by road (Dr Beeching having closed the railway), there were copies in John Menzies in the Square by about 6.30 p.m. I can remember the van arriving, and the fact that the newsprint came off on your fingers. The *Pink* carried virtually every sports result, football and rugby mainly, but also, in the summer, golf and cricket, and there were match reports for the big games. My dad did the football pools (another, much more remote dream for my mum) and the *Pink* would tell him how many millions he had won, or would one day. When we began to rent a TV, my weekly trip to join the Saturday evening queue outside the paper shop ceased. Instead of the smudgy, slightly grubby *Pink*, we listened to the dull monotone of the man reading out the football results like the eulogy at a funeral before my dad threw his pools coupon on the fire.

Reporters at football and rugby matches that finished only an hour or less before the publication of the *Pink* were always rushing. At intervals during the matches or stoppages in play they telephoned their newsrooms, where copytakers who had excellent shorthand took down their words. When the final whistle blew at about 4.30 to 4.45 p.m., the report was completed and the results confirmed. The reporter's nightmare was a last-minute score that would change the result: a new introduction and final paragraph would be needed, using up precious time and holding up production.

Minutes after final whistles echoed around Scotland's sports grounds, the great presses under the editorial offices of the *Edinburgh Evening News* would rumble into action, spitting out perfectly folded pink newspapers, which would be quickly bundled up, tied with string and rushed across Market Street to Waverley Station. The rail network took the newspapers all over south-eastern Scotland and up into Fife, and as a grizzled old veteran of shouting his copy down the phone in a freezing press box once said: 'By the time the crowd at Stark's Park in Kirkcaldy had got to the pub, they had a copy of the *Pink* and a report on the Raith Rovers match they had just seen before they had started on their second post-match pint.'

The availability of sports results on TV and later on the internet saw the decline of the *Pink*, and in 2002 the *Edinburgh Evening News* ceased publication of their Saturday sports paper. (Although a football nostalgia pullout insert, printed in the familiar pink, was rebooted in 2020.) Rupert Murdoch's Sky TV also had a hand in the decline of these logistical miracles when the kick-off times in the Premier League began to move away from the standard 3 p.m. start on a Saturday. Teams played on different days as well as at different times so that viewing figures were spread over a longer period for live matches in order to maximise revenue. But the *Pink* edition and all of Scotland's newspapers were the nation's prime source of sports news for many decades before those changes began to take effect.

Until the end of the twentieth century, more Scots read more newspapers than the English, the Welsh or the Irish. A survey undertaken in 1982 by Stirling University offered a snapshot of the strikingly different cultural habits north of the Border. It was found that 84.6 per cent of all adults read a morning paper compared to 75 per cent in England and Wales. The difference was shown to be even more emphatic when circulation figures were taken into account. The sales of morning papers in Scotland were 451 copies per 1,000 people aged 16 or over against a figure of only 271 per 1,000 in England and Wales. The four main Scottish daily papers are all regional as well as national in their coverage and are read by just over 30 per cent of all adults while only 5 per cent read the twelve English regional titles. The two main Scottish Sunday papers, the *Sunday Post* and the *Sunday Mail*, were read by 82 per cent of Scots. I remember that the most popular partner for the *Sunday Post* on my paper round was the much more tabloid *Sunday Mail*. It must also be significant that Glasgow had three evening papers. Only London had the same number.

The reasons why the Scots consumed so much newsprint are likely historical. In the mid nineteenth century, proportionately more Scottish children went to school for longer than in England, and literacy was significantly more widespread. The regional nature of Scottish newspapers also made them more popular. They carried national British and foreign news, as they do now, but also a great deal of local coverage. This brought papers closer to their readership, and what appeared in their columns was not distant but could have a direct effect on readers' lives.

Since the end of the twentieth century, the world of print journalism has shifted, and shrivelled dramatically, with circulation figures collapsing not only across Scotland but in Britain and in the United States. Here are some examples: in 1980 the Aberdeen *Press and Journal* sold 113,038 copies each day, and by 2020, that figure had fallen to 30,330; also in 1980, the *Dundee Courier* sold

135,566, but 40 years later the circulation was 23,889. Since the paralysis and devastation of the pandemic from 2020 onwards, these numbers have fallen even more sharply and now the *Scotsman* sells only an average of 8,762 copies each day. Circulation figures are so bad that several papers no longer publish them.

The reasons for this rapid decline are not difficult to discover. Between 1990 and 2010 online news feeds of various sorts proliferated rapidly and were updated 24/7. Instead of being frozen on a page, the changing news and new events could be reported much more quickly online than any newspaper could manage. And as mobile phones became smarter and ubiquitous, 24-hour news could be accessed virtually anywhere and at any time. As with TV, the internet thrives on images, many of them moving, and research shows consistently that consumers of online news prefer to watch and listen rather than read. And mobile phones and their excellent cameras provided high-quality pictures, often filmed at an incident by witnesses. All of which was bad news for newspapers as pixels quickly replaced print.

As circulations decline, an unwelcome and inevitable concomitant factor is the drying up of advertising revenue: what made newspapers profitable. Advertisers also usually prefer pictures, and with ever more sophisticated techniques, they can target their market online much more accurately. And it is cheaper. Newspaper production entails massive overheads with office, staff, production and distribution costs, while online content, disseminated through the ether, can be generated by fewer contributors – by no means all of whom are journalists. In fact, increasingly, online sites cannibalise what already appears in print without attribution. Newspapers have responded by creating their own websites and the *Scotsman* was one of the first to do this. But access to the internet is free, whereas newspapers have become expensive, with some online versions sheltering behind paywalls. Unable to alter a lifelong habit, I buy paper newspapers and it is expensive. Taking three on a Saturday and one on every other day, the bill comes to £28 a week. What appeals to me is not that a newspaper is a user-friendly object, like a book (and not like a Kindle), but that rather than focusing so heavily on news, there is now much more comment than there used to be. In the past, editorials made the political slant of a paper, or its support for a particular cause, clear. But now the middle pages of the nine I buy are full of analysis and comment from public figures or experts, and that can be very illuminating. The same can be true of sports reporting. Rather than the raw information supplied in the *Pink*, correspondents often spot things when Scotland play rugby that I miss when watching on TV.

As with many aspects of Scotland's cultural life since 1950, these changes have been rapid and profound – and in the case of the collapse of newspaper circulation, to be regretted. Despite the scandalous behaviour of the tabloids with the likes of phone hacking and the hounding of well-known people by photographers, I believe that a vigorous, interrogative press plays a vital role in society. In a democracy, voters should be informed, but as budgets shrivel, there is less and less investigative reporting, less and less exposure of political stories and coverage of local affairs, and far too much sensationalism (to stem the tide of falling circulation). And unlike the vast tracts of the internet, unreachable on virtual clouds, what appears in print stays in print and is subject to legal sanction if the reporting is untruthful, inaccurate or illegitimately gathered. Because of the findings of a parliamentary inquiry into phone hacking, Rupert Murdoch was forced to close the *News of the World*. Because the internet is evanescent and often untraceable, malpractice and untruth often go unchecked and unpunished.

For younger readers, the 1950s and 1960s was a golden age for published print, but not what appeared in newspapers. A newsagent in Kelso known as Jock the Box (his shop was more of a kiosk) was a tiny wonderland of colour, of excitement, of wham, bang, zap and kapow – the best place to buy comics. The range seemed vast, from war comics like the *Commando* series, or space travel with Dan Dare in the *Eagle*. I liked Battler Britton in the *Valiant* and Alf Tupper, the Tough of the Track, in the *Victor*. Jock the Box also sold second-hand American comics for older children called *Classic Illustrated*. Having read *Ivanhoe*, *The Count of Monte Cristo* and *The Man in the Iron Mask* in this series, I could pretend in later life that I had actually read the novels. What made me really want to read Robert Louis Stevenson in the original were the illustrated versions of *Kidnapped* and *Treasure Island*. When I was younger, I was allowed one of the weeklies. There were almost certainly more on sale, but I can remember the *Topper*, the *Dandy* and my undying favourite, the *Beano*.

Most of the comics stocked by Jock the Box have long ago folded, their readership growing up and drying up. But, in 2023, the *Beano* bucked a dismal trend: its circulation has been climbing. The exploits of the Bash Street Kids, Dennis the Menace and Gnasher and Lord Snooty and his Gang are now bought every week by more than 58,000 readers, a gain of about 4,000 on 2022, which was higher than 2021. Perhaps not all of the expanding readership are youngsters and the bulk of the sales are through annual subscription. A survey recently estimated that a cumulative 28 million people had at some point in their lives read the *Beano* and knew instantly who Minnie the Minx and Little Plum were and what they got up to. Perhaps Bash Street is leading the way to a revival in the reading of paper papers rather than staring at screens. Or, more likely, it's a whizz-bang flash in the pan.

9

The Imperial Cheddar

Every weekday, morning lorries inched their way around the tight bend into Crawford Street to the back of the Tweeddale Co-operative Society and its unloading bay. Off the lorries came several three-foot-square wooden crates, tea cartons from India, large, heavy cardboard boxes from New Zealand and sacks from the West Indies. All were stamped *Produce of the Commonwealth*.

In the summer of 1964, my mum, who worked in the ledger department, had a word with Bill Taylor. The head grocer gave me a summer holiday job so that I could earn a few shillings and, equally important, stay out of trouble with Ernie Woodhead and his gang.

Once Jocky Sinclair and I had unloaded the morning deliveries, I spent the start of the day with a white plastic board and a length of wire secured to the top edge. Inside the heavy boxes from New Zealand was Anchor Cheddar Cheese. Huge blocks of it were sealed inside a thick, clear plastic casing, and the first and worst job was to get them out and onto the counter in the back shop. On the long sea journey, a foul-smelling, greasy liquor had collected at the bottom of the sealed plastic, and as I poured it down the sink, the stink was vile, sick-making.

Once I'd heaved the slippery yellow block up onto the counter and wiped it down, I started to slice it up with the wire cheese cutter. Pinned to the wall was the number of 1lb, ½lb and ¼lb (for childless cat ladies) pieces that were needed. Once these had been weighed, I wrapped them in crinkly greaseproof paper, wrote the weight on them in pencil and loaded them onto long wooden trays. The tea cartons were jemmied open, the glittering silver foil peeled off, and the Indian tea weighed out and ladled into little standing packets with a scoop; the same was done with the sacks of Demerara sugar. Once the trays were full, they were slid onto shelves in the small fleet of Co-op grocery vans that did the country rounds, visiting farms and villages where housewives and grannies climbed up the back step to buy what was needed to feed hungry mouths and get all the gossip of the morning.

The vans and milk delivery vehicles of Kelso's Co-op sat at the centre of a web, a wider community beyond the town, of what were called the country rounds. When I helped Tommy Pontin with the country milk on summer Saturday mornings (when I wasn't playing rugby), I saw firsthand how it all worked. Most people who lived in farm cottage rows did not have a car, and Tommy acted like an informal link, where trust seemed both unspoken and absolute. Old ladies would give him their pension books, which he would later take into the post office where the teller would, unquestioningly, fold in the notes and slide over the coins. The following day, Tommie handed over the cash. He would also shop for things that the Co-op vans didn't stock. I remember him buying a set of fire dogs for one put-upon house-wife stranded in her remote cottage with a young family. This was, I see now, a community at work, a set of guileless transactions that made life much easier but seem to have long faded into obscurity.

As has another facet of our identity. Every morning, Tommy wore his black beret and his battle-dress jacket from his time in the army, fighting alongside not only British troops, but also Canadians, Indians, Australians, New Zealanders and many other units from the vast British Empire, the places that in peacetime supplied not soldiers but cheese, tea and sugar.

It has all gone now. In a dizzyingly short period, the pink patches of empire on my primary classroom wall maps faded, shrivelled and then disappeared almost entirely.

Too young to take note of the detail, able only to pick up on atmospheres and remember snapshots, I had no idea that the passing of the British Empire was a momentous, cathartic process whose effects would reverberate decades later amidst the recent Brexit referendum and all its associated travails. In retrospect, when I was young, I can see that references to the empire – and the attitudes that went with it – were everywhere, and not just when lorries came into the Co-op depot. They were on the kitchen table and in our cupboards. Labels on Robertson's Golden Shred marmalade carried the image known as a Golliwog. According to company history, the idea for a company mascot came from John Robertson, the son of the business owner, who had witnessed children playing with black-and-white rag dolls, called gollies, in the States. Golliwogs could also be dolls, but the connotations were unmissable, especially when the word was shortened to 'wog'. (The Robertson's Golly was retired in 2002.)

My dad liked Camp Coffee. Created in Glasgow in 1876, the syrupy liquid consisted of sugar, water, dried coffee and chicory extract. I thought it was disgusting, like treacle, but it was the label more than the smell that stuck in my memory. Beneath the line 'Ready, Aye Ready', sitting on a stool outside his tent, a Highland soldier in a kilt, spats and plaid daintily sips a cup of the stuff while, standing to attention beside him, is a uniformed Sikh servant, complete with striped turban and neatly trimmed beard.

The other memorable image from the 1950s was from the front page of the *Scotsman*. The post-imperial humiliation of the Suez conflict, and being told what to do with the remains of our empire by the Americans, had passed me by, despite dark murmurings from my parents. But I do distinctly remember references to lots of little wars concerning the formerly peaceful pink patches on the map of the world. The Mau Mau in Kenya definitely sounded sinister and apparently communists were threatening to prise Malaya out of our hands. But a photo in the *Scotsman* baffled me. A bearded man in long, flowing black robes and a mitre like a top hat without the brim was labelled as the leader of terrorists. Archbishop Makarios III was the Primate of the Greek Orthodox Church on Cyprus and de facto leader of the island's Greek-speaking community. Could he really be a terrorist? It seemed very unlikely to me.

In 1960, we went on a brief holiday to London, by far the furthest from home I had ever been. My dad drove all the way in a day because we didn't know any relatives we could stay with en route. In those days, the A1 went under medieval gateways in Berwick and Alnwick and through the middle of towns. No one had thought of bypasses. When we finally got there, to the great city, we were to stay with my uncle David in his house in Colindale. A sergeant in the Metropolitan Police, he took some days off to show us around London, and he certainly knew how best to do it. I was awestruck. It was not only that the city was so vast, it was the scale of its monuments. Leicester Square and Nelson's Column, Admiralty Arch and the Mall aiming arrow-straight and wide to the Albert Memorial and Buckingham Palace beyond it. Then across Horse Guards Parade to a set of steps up through a narrow alleyway to Downing Street where only a single policeman stood outside Number 10. Down Whitehall to Parliament Square to Big Ben, the Commons, the Lords and Westminster Abbey. All so familiar from the TV, and all so strange. I didn't know the phrase at the time, or even think it, but we were walking around an imperial, processional city, the capital place of much more than Britain. I didn't realise it until much later but it was a grandeur out of scale with a developing reality.

My gran took little interest in history, or the news, except for one protracted and ultimately bloody episode in the loss of empire, and it was a series of unfolding events I was old enough to remember. In 1965, the Prime Minister of Southern Rhodesia, Ian Smith, declared a UDI, an acronym that quickly entered popular parlance. His unilateral declaration of independence was the outcome of frustration. Despite protracted negotiations, the British and Rhodesian Governments had been unable to agree the terms of independence for the former colony, and Smith took matters into his own hands. When the BBC reported the momentous news, I clearly remember my grannie saying something like 'Oh, my goodness, me' and exchanging glances with my dad. My mum shook her head. That moment had nothing to do with constitutional arguments or political self-determination, and it brought the murky politics of central Africa into our living room.

Between 1947 and 1970, Southern Rhodesia saw huge waves of immigration from Britain. More than 200,000 came to settle, many of them working-class people seeking a better life in the African sunshine, far away from grey, foggy, austerity Britain. This influx tripled the white population and piled pressure on Smith in his negotiations. Black Rhodesians outnumbered white settlers by twenty to one: what proved to be an ultimately unsustainable ratio.

Many years later, I discovered the meaning of that moment glimpsed between my gran and my dad. He was very concerned for the safety of his half-brother. Bina's lover, my dad's dad, was Robert Charters, who after being gassed in the trenches in 1915, never fully recovered his health and died in the 1930s. But not before he had fathered a legitimate family. His son, Sandy Charters, had emigrated to Southern Rhodesia in the early 1950s and made a successful new life for himself there. The white population owned most of the land, and after the failure of the UDI, it would only be a matter of time before that changed, most likely as a result of violence. The loss of the British Empire was not a distant shifting of geopolitical plates, or simply emblematic: it was something personal for many families. And it was closely linked to the social evolution of post-war Britain.

In all sorts of unspoken, unfocused ways, the experiences of wartime bonded my parents' generation. Privation, rationing, fear of a common enemy and personal loss had pulled my mum, her peers and their families together as they constantly made do and mended, and tried to ignore the perpetual uncertainties on the home front. If your name was on it, your number was up; a bomb could end it all in a moment. These dark thoughts were especially prevalent in large towns and cities, and people learned to live with them. While war tore across North Africa and Europe and erupted in the Far East, they tried – as far as censorship and a lack of hard information allowed – to follow its ebb and flow, and prayed it would not engulf their families. And when Hitler's bombers did bring the war to them, they coped – as a community – as well as they could with the destruction and the suffering.

For my dad and many thousands of other Scots serving in the armed forces, jeopardy could be much more immediate. Because he was an electrician, Private Jack Moffat served in the Royal Engineers. For years I thought that, unlike brave Battler Britton, he operated well behind the lines, that he didn't kill any Germans, that all he did was to keep the lights on. I didn't know, and he didn't tell me, but that image of a bespectacled electrician in a uniform, clutching a toolbox, was very distant from the reality.

Crinkly-edged black-and-white photographs kept in the old yellow cigar box in the sideboard next to the bottle of Harvey's Bristol Cream had little to add. Most were group shots of men in shirtsleeves, long khaki shorts and forage caps, all smiling, blinking in some desert sun somewhere. I'd been told they were taken in Palestine and Transjordan, now Jordan. Because he had brought back a small piece of greenish glass shaped like a lion's head from Petra, I knew my dad had been to the ancient city. But I had no idea what he and his company of Royal Engineers had been doing. Fixing stuff? Replacing plugs and light bulbs? No idea.

Not until my big sister Barbara accessed my dad's war records did I begin to piece together what it was he and his comrades had been doing when they were on active service. Private (later Corporal) Jack Moffat was mentioned in dispatches – twice, and each time given a medal with an oak leaf to signify that. Twice, an official report from an officer described his 'gallant action in the face of the enemy'. Twice, it seems, he had risked his life. In warfare, engineers build things and are often associated with the essential business of throwing temporary bridges across rivers and canals, keeping armies moving, that sort of thing. But as an electrician who knew how circuitry worked even when any helpful documentation was absent or inaccessible in a foreign language, my dad had a more specialised, more dangerous role. As an NCO, he led a small team who followed front-line troops and, as quickly as they could, reconnected electrical supplies destroyed by retreating Germans or Italians. This work was considered essential but very dangerous because transformers and other installations were often booby-trapped. I don't know this for certain, but in this tricky business, I suspect my dad took a big risk – twice.

His company of Royal Engineers was assigned to the British Eighth Army as they fought their way up the Italian peninsula after the 1943 landings. German resistance was dogged, determined and well-planned, a brilliant fighting retreat that greatly slowed the Allies' advance and prolonged the war. I only ever heard scrappy bits and pieces of the detail, but my dad served alongside two Londoners, a man from Kent and another electrician from Elgin on the Moray Firth. I wish I knew more for certain about this little team. But with postcards and, I think,

Christmas cards (although both petered out), he did try to keep up a correspondence with them. I do remember one summer we went on a Highland camping holiday, when it rained most of the time, and there was a brief, awkward reunion. We parked outside a council house in Elgin, and while the rest of the family sat in the car, my dad went inside to talk to his old comrade. Stuart was his name, Stuart from Elgin. One can only guess at the intensity of that wartime relationship, of taking your own life and those of others in your hands over many months. Perhaps that's why my dad didn't want the distraction of introducing this man to his family. Perhaps they owed each other a great deal and needed to talk about wartime incidents they did not want to share, or forget, but did not want to intrude on their post-war life. How I wish my dad had been less reticent, for much of what I have discovered is incomplete or surmised.

In the yellow cigar box was another photograph, not one taken in the desert. In a square with a large church behind them stand a couple. The man wears a raincoat and a black cut hat while his wife (I assumed) stood close in a long, waisted coat, holding a clutch bag. My gran told me they were Italians (actually, she said 'Eyeties'), two people dad had met near the end of the war when he was working in the cities of the north: maybe Milan, she wasn't sure. Perhaps the man was a civilian involved in some way with the local electricity supply and knew how it was all laid out, or should be.

Many years later, after my dad had been felled and half-paralysed by two severe strokes, I took him and Mum on holiday to Italy. For her it was an adventure, the first time she had been abroad, and for him it was a return. As I drove out of Pisa airport and was cut up on the roundabout by two Vespas, my dad was furious. He rolled down the passenger window and roared a torrent of abuse at the riders, in fluent Italian. '*Hey, paesani! E molto pericoloso! Abbiamo bambini nella machina!*' – 'Hey, peasants! That's really dangerous! We have children in the car!' Perhaps *pericoloso* was a word he used often in Italy at the end of the war.

When he was in Palestine or Egypt, my dad did not trouble himself to learn Arabic and instead talked disparagingly about 'the wogs'. He remembered the children begging, constantly holding out their hands for *backsheesh* – some coins. After the war, the word was absorbed into Scots as 'buckshee', meaning something free or of little value. My dad's racism was nothing if not even-handed. In Palestine, he came across Jewish settlers, or men he called 'Jew boys'. I am certain his attitudes were not unusual, more that they were an ugly, characteristic hangover from the British Empire. In different ways, both Palestine, as a mandated territory, and Egypt, as a colony, were part of the empire, and my dad was a British soldier in the imperial army which held it all together. Just. They were there to keep 'the wogs' under control. And there was also, without doubt, the sense of an afterglow of great power, perhaps an inherited swagger, a power that was soon to fade very rapidly. For that generation, the image on the Camp Coffee label was no metaphor: it was a memory.

By 1979, when Ian Smith was forced to concede power to the African majority in the independent nation that was soon to become Zimbabwe, what Victorians and Edwardians called 'the Great Game' was almost played out. By then, all that remained was Hong Kong, the Falkland Islands and a scatter of small islands in the Caribbean. The first two were soon contested and one of them lost. But while the political realities were undeniable, the attitudes of my parents' generation had already been formed. To them, the loss of the empire cannot have represented anything other than decline, a Britain that had fallen from Great. No more would The Mall see troops of prancing Bengal Lancers, the red tunics of the Royal Canadian Mounted Police or platoons of Gurkhas following a royal carriage. Queen Elizabeth II's father had been crowned Emperor of India and was head of state over vast territories, power that was more than symbolic. His daughter eventually ruled over only Great Britain and Northern Ireland and was Head of the Commonwealth, a pale legacy held together by tradition, sentiment and consent.

In the 1950s and the 1960s, all us kids played were war games, and much of what we saw in the cinema and on TV was drawn in various ways from the Second World War, the moment before the empire fell and ultimately the main catalyst for its precipitous loss. All that sacrifice and raw patriotism was celebrated in films such as *The Dam Busters*, about the bouncing bombs that destroyed German dams in the Ruhr Valley, and *Reach for the Sky*, about the amputee pilot Douglas Bader.

It was on TV that the after-effects, rather than the afterglow, of victory made their mark on my generation's idea of Britain. In 1957, a series called *The Army Game* began on ITV. With an entirely male cast, of course, it was a sitcom based at an army camp full of national servicemen and the small group of regulars who trained them. It was a world everyone understood. Some episodes survive, and the comedy is, unsurprisingly, laughable for the wrong reasons, but they depict a world that was central to Britain's – and Scotland's – sense of itself. A daffy commissioned officer, a barking, dictatorial sergeant and a platoon of devious, wide-boy privates dodge around shaky sets trying to foil or outdo each other's plans. It is a male-dominated world built on clearly understood gradations of status and formality, and one that felt familiar and comfortable. The officers spoke received pronunciation, the NCOs had worked themselves up from the ranks (but no further), and those other ranks were no better than they should have been. The title of the first of the *Carry On* films came not from a 'carry-on', meaning a fuss or a shambles, but from an officer's order: 'Carry on, Sergeant!' As its empire dissolved and its structure was revealed, British society was built on place and position and everyone knowing theirs. Social class was what divided 1950s and 1960s Britain – and Scotland.

Despite the disappearance of the empire, its successor, the Commonwealth, presented opportunities. At the end of his illustrious rugby career, and after his last lecture from my grannie, Ian Hastie and his family emigrated to New Zealand (where, surprisingly, he became national darts champion), and others left our town to settle in Australia and Canada. Between 1950 and 1960, more than 500,000 emigrated from Scotland. Most simply crossed the border rather than the ocean to find jobs in the more prosperous south, and especially the south-east, like my uncle David did when he joined the Met. Later, my cousin, Jock, followed him. Corby in Northamptonshire was known as Little Scotland because its busy steelworks attracted skilled workers from the declining heavy industries in and around Glasgow. The Scottish economy was in decline and people were forced to seek brighter prospects elsewhere.

*

Shivering in a couple of draughty, unheated Ford Anglias, four young people made their way from Glasgow to London in the week before Christmas, 1950. Led by a fervent young nationalist, Ian Hamilton, they were determined to right a historical wrong. Almost seven centuries before, Edward I of England, the Hammer of the Scots, had stolen the Stone of Destiny. Since the ninth century, the block of red sandstone had sat beneath the throne of every king's crowning, and it was more than a grave affront that it was kept in Westminster Abbey. The Stone had to come home.

Hamilton and his fellow conspirators had only the most rudimentary notion of a plan, but despite a series of comic, almost farcical incidents, it would eventually succeed. As the abbey closed for the day, Hamilton hid under a cleaner's trolley and pulled his overcoat over his head – and was discovered almost immediately.

But instead of raising the alarm and detaining the young student, the policeman merely threw him out. When the conspirators later forced their way into the abbey, with alarming ease, more farce was played out. Built into a wide and deep shelf under the seat of the throne of Edward the Confessor, the positioning of the stone was awkward, and it turned out to be very heavy (135kg). When finally extracted, this piece of ancient history fell hard on the floor and became plural, breaking into two pieces – suddenly the Stones of Destiny.

One of the students, Kay Matheson, drove away from the abbey with the smaller piece in the boot of her car, but when she braked suddenly at traffic lights in Knightsbridge, the catch sprang open and the stone fell out onto the road. It was very late at night, and it seemed that no one saw the young woman manage, somehow, to heave it back in and drive away unnoticed. Meanwhile, Ian Hamilton was going nowhere. He had lost his car keys outside the abbey. It was pitch black, but after many lit matches, he found them and drove off with the larger fragment. After more adventures, the conspirators finally repatriated the Stone of Destiny to Scotland. Where it belonged. And then, after negotiation, it was meekly given back. No prosecutions were ever brought. Hamilton later described the incident: 'I've defended a lot of daft people during thirty years as a criminal lawyer, but I doubt very much if I've defended anyone who was as daft as we were then.'

Behind all this shambolic, patriotic chaos was a charismatic man, a lawyer called John MacCormick. In 1950, he was Rector of Glasgow University, and his election campaign had been run by Ian Hamilton. Before the outbreak of war, MacCormick had been central to the evolution of the Scottish National Party, negotiating with other nationalist groups to form the National Party of Scotland in 1928 and, six years later, merge it with the Scottish Party to create the SNP. MacCormick was formidably effective but mercurial in his loyalties. Seeing home rule for Scotland as an unwon cause, he was prepared to back more established political parties if he thought they were more likely to achieve it. Despite having had a hand in creating it, MacCormick left the SNP in 1942 and stood for the Liberal Party in the general election of 1945. His last outing in the polls was in 1959 when he stood against Commander Donaldson in Roxburgh, Selkirk and Peebles, coming a very creditable second and helping to set up the seat for the young David Steel.

John MacCormick was replaced as the leading figure of the SNP by Robert McIntyre, a doctor who worked in Stirling. On 13 April 1945, there was a by-election in Motherwell, and the GP stunned other parties by taking the seat from Labour by 617 votes. There had been a truce between the parties during the war that by-elections would be uncontested and only the sitting party would put up a candidate. The SNP was too small to have been party to this arrangement, and so McIntyre made history, becoming the first ever SNP MP. However, his tenure lasted only three months, and at the 1945 general election, Labour regained the seat.

John MacCormick had begun to work up other, non-parliamentary initiatives. Remembering the Church of Scotland's historic commitment to home rule, or devolution, as it became known, the Scottish Covenant was drafted at the Assembly Halls in Edinburgh in 1949. This was, in essence, a petition. It pledged 'to do everything in our power to secure for Scotland a Parliament with adequate legislative authority in Scottish affairs'. Circulated widely, the Scottish Covenant was signed by a staggering 2 million people, 40 per cent of the whole population. But it had little political impact: other parties ignored it, and at the 1950 general election, the SNP polled a negligible 0.3 per cent of the vote.

When George VI died in February 1952, Prime Minister Winston Churchill summarily announced that the King's heir would be styled as Queen Elizabeth II in Scotland despite the indisputable fact that no Elizabeth had ever sat on the Scottish throne and that it was separate and distinct from the throne of England. There was a public outcry at this apparently offhand denial of history, and when post boxes with the device of EIIR were erected, many were promptly defaced, some even blown up. John MacCormick led a campaign to show that Churchill's decision was more than culturally insensitive: it was illegal.

The disjunction between support for the Scottish Covenant, emotive issues like the Stone of Destiny and the regnal number of the new queen, and what failed to happen at the ballot box, is difficult to fathom. Perhaps simple factors were at work. After the great upheavals of the war and its aftermath, it may be that few had the appetite for more, unnecessary, seismic change. Or maybe it was something that could wait. Housing, the NHS, the persistence of rationing, for goodness' sake, and other more mundane matters all took precedence. Or perhaps it was a lack of confidence. After the firework of Dr Robert McIntyre's victory at Motherwell, the SNP had to wait more than 20 years to taste electoral success. In the 1959 general election, the party fielded only five candidates who polled a miserable total of 21,738 votes.

By the early 1960s change was in the air as the SNP's base began to move away from the romantic, historical nationalism of John MacCormick, Ian Hamilton and the middle-class academics and lawyers who shared their views. A farmer from Killin, Ian Macdonald, stood in the 1961 by-election at Glasgow Bridgeton and was delighted with 18.7 per cent of the vote. So delighted that he sold his farm and became the first National Organiser of the SNP. Realising that the party had no solid foundation and only a tiny membership, Macdonald travelled the country setting up local branches and recruiting. By the time he stood down in 1968, there were 484 branches and 120,000 members, the basis of what would seem like a startling series of successes that apparently sprang from nowhere.

The first inklings of change came in 1962. Tam Dalyell won the rock-solid Labour seat of West Lothian in a by-election, but Billy Wolfe of the SNP came out of the blue to poll 9,750 votes and push the Conservatives into third place with only 4,784 votes and the loss of their deposit. Ian Macdonald had flooded the constituency with activists, and they were not the sort of supporters familiar to John MacCormick, but young people who, as a recent historian has observed, 'were more sober types less interested in poetry than in digging out figures on the Scottish economy'. Five years later, and after a great deal of work from Ian Macdonald, these tectonic rumblings exploded. In the 1966 general election, the SNP had not even contested the Hamilton seat, but when the sitting Labour MP resigned a year later, Winnie Ewing won a spectacular victory, sending the first SNP MP to Westminster since Dr Robert McIntyre's brief sojourn in 1945. To the exultant crowd outside the count, she declared with characteristic brio, parodying the title of a hit musical: 'Stop the world! Scotland wants to get on.' Even though the seat was lost in 1970, Hamilton was a turning moment. Since 1967, SNP MPs have sat at Westminster and the party finally came to power in the Scottish Parliament when it formed a government at Holyrood in 2007.

The rise of the Scottish National Party is by far the most striking and significant change in the political history of Scotland since 1950; and it is a development that has profoundly affected the whole of the United Kingdom. The cultural divide between the Conservative and Labour parties broadly, although by no means always, reflected the existing fault lines of social class. All sorts of affinities and alignments have traditionally followed the parties' leads and shaped their policies: working class and middle class, trade unions and professional associations, Catholic and Protestant and many more. After the Labour Government's creation of the Welfare State after 1945, the party was seen as one that advocated more state control and that was likely to nationalise industries and tax more heavily those who earned more. The Conservatives were broadly seen to be on the side of the individual and of free enterprise, more attuned to the realities of 'human nature' and the instinct to compete and seek material gain. These are familiar, sweeping generalisations but nonetheless a rapid pencil sketch many might recognise.

The SNP changed this picture radically in Scotland, cutting across old fault lines, gathering support widely, especially amongst Catholic voters in the West of Scotland. Although the party has had to acquire the necessary suite of policies to compete with the Conservatives, Labour and the Liberals, and has placed itself broadly on the centre-left, there is really only one issue at the core of its existence. Independence, withdrawal from the union of 1707, is what brought the SNP into being; it is their principal objective and the reason so many people joined. The power of the concept of independence consists in the fact that it can mean so many different things to different people, many of those very emotive. 'Freedom!' roared a woad-covered Mel Gibson as William Wallace in *Braveheart* as he confronted the English army. Despite some controversy around the film's depiction of Wallace, the image has a powerful emotional pull and an historical attraction. In 1320, only fifteen years after Wallace's horrific death, Bernard, Abbot of Arbroath, wrote to the Pope. In a surviving letter, he asserts, in perhaps Scotland's most quoted quote, that 'for, as long as but a hundred of us remain alive, never will we on any conditions be brought under English rule. It is in truth not for glory, nor riches, nor honours that we are fighting, but for freedom for that alone, which no honest man gives up but with life itself.'

Other supporters of independence see different benefits. Scotland's own distinctive culture can at last begin to disentangle itself from England's. Some believe that the Scottish economy will thrive, others that it can more easily become green without waiting for the rest of the UK to catch up. But playing quietly but insistently under this debate about the prospects for an independent Scotland is a clearly audible and constant drumbeat, an unwillingness to be associated any longer with England and the English. Nationalist movements always require 'the other', those who are not 'us' to be clearly identified. And, overwhelmingly, that means the English.

Had they lived to see it, my parents' generation would have found that anti-English sentiment baffling and probably distasteful. They fought and lived through one of the bloodiest wars in history as part of a united kingdom, not just on behalf of specific bits of it but standing together, shoulder to shoulder, against a manifestly wicked enemy. My dad's team was from London, Kent and Scotland, and they risked their lives together. They fought for each other as well as for themselves and their families, making no distinction between Scots, Irish, Welsh or English. And my dad never saw himself as anything other than Scottish *and* British. There seemed to be no contradiction or unease. We lived four miles from the border, many crossed it most days to go to work or to shop, and the idea of it becoming a frontier would have horrified that generation who risked their lives to defend a united kingdom.

A study of wedding photographs taken between 1950 and the end of the first quarter of the twenty-first century might be seen to offer an unlikely but interesting gloss on Scotland's recent political history. As a child I seemed to suffer having my face scrubbed every second Saturday morning to go to family weddings in Kelso and Hawick. The children of my mum's surviving five sisters, her brother and some of her cousins were beginning to 'settle down', as people then said, and start families. But not until the standard group shot was taken of smiling relatives standing on either side of a bride and bridesmaids in white and a groom and a best man in suits of sober colour sporting a carnation buttonhole. These line-ups all looked very similar at least until the late 1960s when my big sister got married. My own wedding was in 1976 at St Salvator's Chapel at the University of St Andrews and as the setting implies, it looked posh. My wife was demurely beautiful in a white dress while my best man and I wore hired morning suits of black tail jackets and stripy grey trousers.

At around that time, there was an unheralded, certainly unrecorded in any forensic sense, set of changes quietly in motion. Scottish men began to wear kilts at weddings. That trend accelerated quickly, and soon most of the bridegrooms and best men, as well as the majority of their younger male guests, were buckling on their kilts and positioning their sporrans correctly (important to get that right) before turning up at the church or the registry office. And in time it came to be not only a kilt. Many wore tailored, formal dress jackets. There are fifteen types available for hire, the most popular being the Prince Charlie, made from wool with silk lapels, decorated with (usually) impractical, redundant, lozenge-shaped metal buttons on the sleeves – history tells us they were put there to stop soldiers from wiping their noses – as well as on the front and also on a small tail at the back, and a fly-plaid over the shoulder pinned with a large and very masculine brooch. By the time of my daughter Beth's wedding in 2017, I had transitioned from Top Mod to Rob Roy, and the whole affair resembled a Highland Games more than a wedding.

At least I didn't look like George IV. In 1822, Walter Scott organised the King's state visit to Scotland, the first of a reigning monarch since Charles II, and, following the worldwide success of the Waverley Novels, he decided to clothe the whole occasion in tartan, including the King himself. And this despite tartan having been the uniform of rebellion since the late seventeenth century until the Battle of Culloden in 1746. At a royal levee at Holyrood

Palace, King George IV made a spectacular entrance. Swathed from head to foot in tartan, wearing two belts (to restrain his belly – he tipped the scales at 20 stones, but was only just over five feet tall), dirks and a bonnet, his kilt sat well above the knee over flesh-coloured tights, essential to hide his varicose veins. On the first state visit since the Jacobite Rebellion in 1745, he was in Edinburgh for only a week. Watching the entrance of this tartan dumpling was Lady Dalrymple. 'Since he is here for such a short time,' she sniffed, 'it is as well we see so much of him.'

Queen Victoria carried on the royal family's keen interest in all things Highland when they bought and rebuilt Balmoral Castle and got into the habit of spending the early autumn there. High society saw the Queen and her Prince Consort as the acme of taste and fashion, and many wealthy courtiers acquired shooting lodges and sporting estates and began to deck themselves out in tartan as they lairded it around the heather and turned up at social events. But even though kilts, plaids, dirks in the tops of socks, brogues and fancy jackets became more than acceptable, the gear of the Gaels, the Highland clans, was not adopted by ordinary Scots until much later – until wedding photographs began to look different towards the end of the twentieth century.

It cannot be a coincidence that these sartorial shifts occurred at the same time as the rise of the SNP, and indeed they may be linked in the most general sense. What could look more Scottish, more un-English, than a man in a skirt? A tartan skirt? The rising flood of tartanry long ago engulfed the tourist traps of Edinburgh's Royal Mile, but by the close of the last century, it had trickled into the wardrobes of hundreds of thousands of Scotsmen. Many felt that their identity had become both more Scottish and less British, and what better way to state that than by looking different.

10

Last Orders

In a small town where everyone knows everyone else, and in some detail, under-age drinking is impossible. However, in 1967, the breathalyser had yet to be invented and in Scotland it was possible to pass a driving test at 17, before you could legally order a pint of beer. These two factors allowed a unique set of circumstances to connect with a happy accident of geography. Jock Bell had not only passed his driving test, but he also had access to his dad's three-wheeler, a Reliant Regal he called 'the barrow'. On a memorable summer Saturday night, four thirsty teenagers piled into this tiny car, and Jock drove us to Coldstream, where not everyone knew us. At 10 p.m., the landlord of the Besom rang a bell for 'last orders, please!' But by that time at least half of his clientele had left for a brisk walk. Across the Tweed Bridge and a mile to the south, there were no last orders, at least not for a while. The Collingwood Arms lay in the village of Cornhill, which lay in England, which was another country. It did not close until 11 p.m. After a welcome extra hour drinking bitter instead of 'pints of heavy', we crammed into the Reliant Regal and took the quiet country roads south of the river back to Kelso, having visited a much more civilised part of the world.

The 10 p.m. closing time for Scottish pubs produced a much less welcome effect than a bracing, sobering walk to Cornhill and back. In Scotland, the mostly male clientele knew the bell would toll and the pace of drinking would accelerate with pints and whisky chasers lined up to delay eviction as long as the landlord would dare to allow. That stoked up consumption towards levels of drunkenness and worse, and frequently provoked a scramble for a carry-out. This in turn led to noisy, Rabelaisian scenes on the pavements outside pubs where drunks lurched around, knocking back what they had carried out and sometimes regurgitating it as they leaned against a supportive wall. They crowded into chip shops to allay a false, beer-induced hunger and chucked away what they did not eat or just dropped it on the street. And petty squabbles could turn nasty. None of this was attractive, and in 1973 Dr Christopher Clayson agreed that it had to change.

He was an unusual and courageous man. Educated at George Heriot's School in Edinburgh, he trained in the university's prestigious medical school. But when Clayson took his finals, it was clear that he was very ill. Spitting blood, the young man feared he had contracted tuberculosis, a disease that used to kill half of those who had it. But history intervened, and the university brought forward the date of his exams so that they could take place before the General Strike of 1926, when students would be used as strike-breakers – and, crucially, before Clayson's symptoms could rule him out of sitting them. Having qualified, he spent his first three years not as a doctor but as a patient. Once he had recovered from TB, he eventually became the Superintendent at the Lochmaben Sanatorium, where he introduced much higher standards of food and hygiene. These were effective but it was not until the development of streptomycin coupled with other treatments in the late 1950s that TB was eventually conquered.

In 1966, Christopher Clayson was elected President of the Royal College of Physicians in Edinburgh. After retiring in 1970, this eminent and compassionate doctor received a letter that would allow him the opportunity to effect great change in

Scotland's cultural life, change that would in turn promote better health. The Conservative Secretary of State for Scotland Gordon Campbell MP asked Clayson to chair the Scottish Licensing Law Committee and consider potential changes in the legislation, particularly issues related to the opening and closing times of public houses.

Clayson and his committee took a liberal and forensic view of these issues. They agreed that alcohol consumption was not a taboo or something to be repressed; rather, it was an acceptable part of life in Scotland and should be normalised as much as possible. The committee's goals were to eliminate as far as possible the macho, male-dominated drinking culture. In the opening lines of his 'A Drunk Man Looks at the Thistle', Hugh MacDiarmid gives a powerful sense of this and how competitive drinking could be:

> I amna fou' sae muckle as tired – deid dune.
> It's gey and hard work coupin' gless for gless
> Wi' Cruivie and Gilsanquhar and the like,
> And I'm no' juist as bauld as aince I wes.

The committee sought to encourage moderation and believed that what was known as 'the ten o'clock swill' was bad for men's health, and that the carry-out stampede spilled drunkenness onto the streets of towns and cities, especially at weekends. Not good or welcome images. Clayson was keen to mitigate extremes, the wide spectrum between teetotal abstention and regular inebriation, and to counter the main point of going into pubs to become 'fou'.

Four units of alcohol a day was thought to be moderate, and sensing that there might be press interest, he was very open, saying, 'I have my four units every day – a sherry and a couple of glasses of claret with a meal . . . The problems start when you take the whole week's allocation in one day or over a weekend. The liver can't cope.' While four units a day might now be thought by some as excessive (medical advice since 1976 has varied), Dr Christopher Clayson died in 2005 at the age of 101.

His committee called for radical change in Scotland's licensing laws. Pubs should be permitted to increase their opening hours by a third, they should be open on a Sunday, and if standards were met, families with young children should be able to use them. By the time the Clayson Report was complete, the government had changed, and it landed on the desk of the Labour Secretary of State. Willie Ross MP was teetotal and not in favour of change. There was also predictable opposition from the Church of Scotland and other groups. But in the event, pubs were allowed to stay open until 11 p.m. from December 1976 onwards and, from late 1977, to begin opening on Sundays. There was also a gradual extension of all-day licences for Scotland's 4,350 pubs and 10,651 other licensed premises. But what Clayson saw as a central recommendation was rejected, and later he wondered if the hand of Willie Ross was behind it. The admission of children to licensed premises was denied. 'What we said was that the introduction of children to alcohol should just be part of normal family life,' Clayson later wrote.

Despite this initial disappointment, the changes that did pass into legislation were both welcome and effective. Surveys showed that the rate of consumption of alcohol in pubs slowed and that their male-dominated culture began to change as more women used them. Alcohol-related public order offences declined, and in 1977 there were fewer drink-driving convictions. This decline may have been affected by policing issues because most stations changed shifts at 11 p.m. and some offences might have been missed; nevertheless, by 1984 it was clear that the cultural atmosphere around drinking was changing. In an article in the *British Medical Journal*, another survey found that 73 per cent of respondents agreed that 'the present licensing laws were an improvement on the old ones', and 51 per cent agreed that 'these days you don't see as many drunks around as you used to'. Christopher Clayson should have taken comfort from these positive perceptions. Scotland's licensing laws were more liberal that in England and Wales and, contrary to what opponents feared, they set a new and different tone.

In Edinburgh, I lived in a tenement block which had a pub on the ground floor, and I noticed an immediate change: much less noise at closing time and much less litter and worse on the pavements in the morning after. We were slowly beginning to move towards a European model. While the Portuguese, Italians and the French drink almost twice as much as the Scots, wine is an integral and accepted part of their culture, usually accompanying a meal, and public drunkenness is rare.

After some legislative tinkering in 2005, licensing laws in Scotland have been standardised. Pubs are only allowed to open after 10 a.m. (although there can be exceptions for local events such as the Border common ridings which often begin very early in the morning) and they generally close at 11 p.m. Clubs and other bars can stay open until 2 a.m. and sometimes later. Hotels and pubs can open on Sundays, and what would have greatly pleased Christopher Clayson, some now admit families. In shops and supermarkets, alcohol can be bought between 10 a.m. and 10 p.m.

I saw these changes take effect in 1977 in spectacular fashion. By that time I was running the Edinburgh Festival Fringe and grappling each year with Scotland's licensing laws. We argued that in August, thousands of performers whose shows came down at 10 p.m. and often later had nowhere to go for food and drink since pubs (and most restaurants) closed too early. Edinburgh City Council were finally persuaded to allow us to use the Royal Mile Centre, a sprawling, cellular function suite on four floors with several bars and places to eat, and to give us a temporary licence until 2 a.m. for a month. But only if it was a club. We therefore offered membership to all performers and a restricted number of members of the public. At £1, the cost was intentionally nominal because of our wish to look after all our hungry and thirsty performers. But such cards as were available to the public changed hands for much more than £1. Some nights, it felt as if the Fringe Club was under siege. The lack of a membership card did not discourage attempts to gatecrash. I had to employ bouncers not only at the door on the High Street but also to keep watch around the back of the cliff-like building. Having come up the closes from the Cowgate, desperadoes took to climbing up the rone pipes to windows they hoped to prise open on the upper floors. It was crazy, for most of these we caught had had a skinful. I like to think they would have bounced.

In August 1976, when the old licensing laws were still in force, the Fringe Club turned out to be attractive to more than inebriated rock-climbers. Early on a Saturday, my private line rang with a surprising call. Would I be happy to invite Princess Margaret and her party to the Fringe Club after they had seen a show at the festival? When the royal party arrived, strangely, in a minibus, I waited outside to greet the Queen's sister and her entourage. Two of our bouncers were standing on either side of me. Huge men who worked at Bilston Glen Colliery, James and John wore white shirts so large that they seemed like sails on which tiny black bowties were fixed. They only had to glare at any members of the public or the few press who had got wind of the visit. And then, just as I was about to shake hands with the Princess, James and John stepped in front of me, virtually shouldering me out of the way, bowed deeply and said, 'Good evening, your Worship.'

Once safely inside and seated at their table (James and John were now in tow, having decided to become protection officers), the royal party were offered drinks, and I remember almost all of them immediately lit cigarettes. The air in the Fringe Club was always a thick fug of smoke, something no one remarked on at

the time. But looking back now, it occurs to me that on the eve
of radical changes to the culture of an important social compo-
nent of Scottish life, there were no discernible stirrings to see
tobacco consumption banned from public places, even though it
was becoming ever clearer to the medical profession that smoking
was killing many more people than alcohol.

In 1950, Dr Richard Doll designed a study of lung cancer
patients in 20 London hospitals. There was a suspicion that the
rising rate of cancer of this sort may have been caused by car
fumes, or perhaps asphalt as London's roads were gradually being
repaired after the devastation of wartime bombing. But it quickly
became clear that cigarette smoking was the cause: it was something that was common to all the patients in the study. Doll's
findings persuaded him to give up smoking immediately. When
the details of the study were published in the *British Medical
Journal*, the conclusions were stark and unambiguous:

> The risk of developing the disease increases in proportion to the
> amount smoked. It may be 50 times as great among those who
> smoke 25 or more cigarettes a day as amongst non-smokers.

Subsequent research in different parts of Britain confirmed Doll's
conclusions. Yet, despite these clear health warnings and the unequivocal links with lung cancer in particular (the incidence of
which had been rising steeply in the 1940s, and especially during
the war years when smoking may have been at its highest), little
public attention was at first paid to Doll's work. The culture of
cigarette smoking was too deeply embedded to be affected by a
single piece of research: in 1950, 80 per cent of men and 40 per
cent of women smoked. It was seen as glamorous. In his many
classic Hollywood films, Humphrey Bogart seemed never to be
without a cigarette (a 60-a-day man, he died an early death, aged
57, of oesophageal cancer); likewise, Audrey Hepburn, with Holly

Golightly's elegant cigarette holder in *Breakfast at Tiffany's*, and Marlene Dietrich and James Dean in everything they did. Slim, strikingly beautiful and sophisticated, they seemed to inhabit a world where blue-grey clouds wreathed almost every scene. In addition, tobacco companies promoted smoking as an appetite suppressant, particularly to women who believed that their slender figures stayed that way because of cigarettes. There is strong evidence that nicotine does suppress hunger; however, the risk of contracting fatal respiratory or circulatory illness is acute.

I remember watching *The Third Man* with Joseph Cotten and Orson Welles. Set in bleak, post-war Vienna and soundtracked with an unforgettably distinctive theme tune, it had a sinister atmosphere. The empty streets and ruined buildings were shadowy and menacing, although, I confess, half the time I had no idea what was happening. The film was directed by Carol Reed, and in 1959, he translated some of its cinematic language to make a very noirish TV advertisement for a new brand of cigarettes. Just as in the rain-washed, midnight streets of Vienna, a man in a trench coat and a cut hat pauses under a streetlight. After looking around, seeing no one, he lights a cigarette. As the moody music dips and the match flares, a voiceover intones: 'You're never alone with a Strand.' The advert is memorable and has survived as a powerful example of how glamour and mystery seemed to swirl around the act of smoking, but the cigarette brand did not endure: Strand lasted only a year before being withdrawn.

What made the culture of smoking so widespread and so accessible was an invention. In 1880, James Bonsack patented a revolutionary design for a cigarette-making machine. Until then, hand rolling (which still goes on) was how cigarettes were made, but Bonsack's contraption with its small conveyor belts, pulleys and hoppers could turn out 200 in a minute. With fine-tuning, the output rose to between 500 and 600 a minute. In 1888, thirteen British tobacco companies, headed by W. D. & H. O. Wills, bought the right to use Bonsack's machine, and they brought out a new brand, one that would last for generations. Wills' Wild Woodbines were an instant success.

The mechanisation and speed of production made cigarettes cheap, but it also altered how people (almost all of them men in the late nineteenth and early twentieth centuries) smoked. Pipe and cigar smokers did not necessarily inhale the tobacco, taking the smoke down into their lungs. But cigarette smokers did, and the physiological stimulus, the hit this gave, made them more addictive. By 1914 and the onset of the First World War, cigarettes had become known as 'the soldiers' smokes', and it was estimated that more than 90 per cent of all men on active service smoked. In the trenches, it was much easier to light a cigarette (always being careful to conceal the flame and not give away position and invite the attention of enemy snipers) than it was to fiddle about filling and tamping the bowl of a pipe. And cigars were too expensive and lasted too long. The Red Cross and other voluntary organisations raised money to buy cigarettes for soldiers, with some included in rations for both the army and the navy. The latter would greatly influence the names of brands as well as the design of packets. In 1915 alone, British soldiers and sailors consumed 1,000 tons of cigarettes and 700 tons of pipe tobacco. Cigarettes were thought to help settle nerves before fighting began and relieve the tedium of life in the trenches. Perhaps the smoke also masked unwelcome smells.

For a long time afterwards, branding reflected the importance of cigarettes to British troops in the First World War, associating them with victory, patriotism and sacrifice. Senior Service, Player's Navy Cut, Nelson, Admiral, Capstan and many others remembered Britain's glorious naval history, the exploits of the Grand Fleet in the First World War and the blockade of Germany. On packets of Player's Navy Cut there is a portrait of a bearded sailor, encircled by a lifebelt, with 'Hero' on his cap. In the background are symbols of Britain's maritime greatness: a three-masted warship that might have fired broadsides at Trafalgar and a much more modern destroyer. Player's Navy Cut cigarettes were only discontinued in 2016, but Capstan Full Strength are still going strong.

During the Second World War cigarettes were part of servicemen's rations. My dad remembered round and rectangular tins of 50 cigarettes; he said that supplies were irregular and often ran out. In Italy, his unit was in frequent contact with American forces, and he recalled that 'the Yanks always had fags', and records show that the big tobacco companies like Philip Morris and others sent hundreds of millions of cigarettes across the Atlantic. Instead of tins, my dad watched GIs opening cartons of ten packs of twenty cigarettes 'each!'. British military rations of tobacco did not cease in 1945. When the RAF was stationed in West Berlin in the 1980s and 1990s, men continued to be entitled to cigarettes.

Even though Richard Doll's research was largely ignored at first, people knew anecdotally and indeed instinctively that cigarette smoking was unhealthy. Heavy and long-time smokers with wheezing chests and persistent coughs were not uncommon and 'fags' were often called 'coffin nails'. The tobacco companies responded with marketing initiatives. Cigarette cards had been introduced by Player's at the turn of the century. 'Castles and Abbeys' was the first collection, and these cards became more common; they changed and expanded to include football players, vintage cars and other themes. In 1956, the Kensitas brand pioneered coupons. When enough had been collected, they could be exchanged for items in the annual gift catalogue. When Embassy supplanted Wills' Wild Woodbine and Player's Medium Cut as market leaders in the 1960s, it was in part because they offered more coupons and what appeared to be a range of quality gifts.

By 1962, views on smoking seemed to be changing. That year, the Independent Television Authority agreed with the ITV companies that cigarette advertising should not be shown before 9 p.m. By 1966, it was banned, although, strangely, only for cigarettes and not for cigars. 'Happiness is a cigar called Hamlet' was a tag line that continued to be broadcast as late as 1991. Twenty years earlier, a government health warning had become mandatory on all packets of cigarettes.

In the 1960s, the tobacco companies had started to produce more brands of tipped cigarettes, and these somehow persuaded smokers that many of the worst elements, such as tar, were being filtered out. On the end of the filter tip, it was possible to see brown smudges, but few seemed to wonder what was not being filtered out. Fags also grew longer. Rothman's King Size was a bestseller before being supplanted by Benson & Hedges and its distinctive gold packet.

Pipe smoking seemed more acceptable for a while, and the Labour Prime Minister Harold Wilson was often seen with a metal-stemmed pipe in his mouth. Perhaps he thought it made him appear more avuncular, more solid, dependable. In the enormously popular *Morecambe and Wise* comedy series, Eric and Ernie were sometimes seen in bed together, wearing pyjamas, reading the paper. This strange set-up (reminiscent of Laurel and Hardy's short film *Early to Bed*) often featured Eric smoking a pipe similar to Harold Wilson's, perhaps to emphasise his masculinity. Pipe smoking did not have the racy glamour of cigarettes, and in any case was a much older and more traditional way of consuming tobacco.

Attitudes to smoking and old habits were slow in changing. A Scottish woman who took part in a study of the relationship between heart disease and smoking remarked to a researcher that when, in 1965, she went into hospital for her first heart operation, there was an ashtray in the locker beside her bed.

In 2005, the Smoking, Health and Social Care (Scotland) Act made it illegal to smoke in enclosed public spaces such as pubs, cinemas, restaurants and shops. Smoking in cars was also banned if any passengers were under 18. In the face of all this regulation and its implicit discouragement, numbers declined steadily; in 2022, 12.9 per cent of adults identified as smokers in Britain, compared to 60 per cent in 1950. In Scotland, the 2022 average was slightly lower with 11.5 per cent of those over 16 smoking regularly. But in some deprived areas, the percentage could be much higher. In north and eastern Glasgow 37.5 per cent smoked, in south-west Glasgow, 34 per cent, and in West Dunbartonshire, 33 per cent. Hotspots tended to concentrate in the huge council housing schemes. However, the average number of cigarettes consumed each day had declined from 15.3 in 2003, when the number of smokers was much higher at 28.5 per cent of the adult population, to 10.5 per cent in 2022.

Despite the stubbornly high numbers around the West Coast, a huge, tectonic, social and public health shift has taken place since 1950. Cigarette smoking was long seen as an integral part of Scottish culture, associated with nights out, celebrations and also more quotidian contact in communities. Cigarettes were offered around, lit for each other and enjoyed while relaxing with a drink in a pub or with a cup of tea in a back kitchen. Now, smoking is often a solitary activity, as those who remain addicted are forced to leave a pub or restaurant and stand outside for the few minutes it takes to smoke a cigarette. That can sometimes mean a disjointed conversation as a chair is suddenly vacated, followed by the unwelcome odour of stale smoke when the smoker returns. Social pressure will surely mean a continuing decline in the sale of cigarettes and a corresponding rise in Scots' lifespans.

Many of my parents' generation killed themselves, more or less knowingly, through smoking. Both my mum and dad were active, slim, and in common with many who went through the war, they ate sparingly, generally avoiding rich foods. But they smoked all their lives. My dad suffered two strokes in his late fifties and then a fatal heart attack when he was 70. After his death, my mum seemed to smoke more, perhaps finding consolation or some stress relief in cigarettes, and she too died of a heart attack only four years after my dad. Like many of my own generation, I was attracted by the grown-up glamour of smoking and its association with film stars and pop musicians. All four Beatles smoked what they called 'ciggies', and before he died at 58, George Harrison said that years of heavy smoking had probably given him cancer. In 2000, Keith Richards of the Rolling Stones finally managed to stop, and also gave up alcohol. It's never too late.

This change occurred within the span of one generation. Many of the baby boomers and their cultural icons followed their parents into a smoking habit, but as the evidence of the harm it did mounted, many millions of people stopped. Smoking is now almost entirely absent from social occasions, even those that are private and not subject to the law. Only in the evenings or at lunchtime, outside workplaces or the entrances to pubs, are smokers regularly seen, shivering pariahs driven there by an addiction they find hard to overcome.

11

Never Up to It, Then Past It

University in the late 1960s and early 70s was so much fun that no one wanted to leave. The trick was to do just enough work to avoid being chucked out after your first year and then at the end of second year con your way into an honours course. At St Andrews that meant four years of fun instead of three and no exams until your finals. I used to believe that it was native wit and charm (it certainly had nothing to do with hard work) that got me exemptions from sitting exams at the end of second year and, with little more than a well-timed hop and a skip around assorted tutors, into junior honours and a third year of relative idleness.

In fact, it was sheer luck, of the right time, right place sort. Recently, I made the shocking discovery that the separation of Queen's College and its reinvention as Dundee University had left St Andrews critically short of students, only 1,900 in 1967. (For comparison, in the academic year 2023–24 they had 10,234 students.) So that's why I got in with only three Highers (and nothing great either, only an A, a B and a C) and why they were so keen to hang on to me and any other second-year student. Still, I managed 40 years of mileage out of delusions about native wit and charm.

At the end of the summer term in 1971, at a party in an orchard near Kingsbarns – the scent of apple blossom, Laura Ashley frocks, linen shirts, Pimm's and a definite feeling that the world was turning more slowly on a warm, balmy evening – I sat down next to my chum, Lennie Taylor. Together we had played rugby for the First XV for three years. Despite having some good players, we never did particularly well. And the problems were perennial. Our pack of forwards was mostly a bunch of skinny boys whose closest acquaintance with manual work was carrying a pile of books to the library. Each week we came up against big, strong men who had the added motivation of playing against '*fung* students', who they considered a bunch of expensive burdens on the taxpayer; that is, on them, personally. And the sodden Scottish winter didn't help. Endless scrummages in the mud, lineouts in the rain and countless casual opportunities for the opposition forwards to put the boot in. I played in the front row and bore the brunt of much of the taxpayers' malice.

'I'm not playing next year,' said Lennie, 'at least not in the First XV.' Explaining that it wasn't the prospect of another season of miserable, muddy defeats but the need to get down to some serious work meant that he felt he couldn't spare the time for training during the week. Final exams beckoned. I was in the same boat. Shame not to play at all, though.

I spent the summer working in the Borders, living at home, listening to my mum telling me to *stick in* and do well in my final exams. And without explicitly saying it, *stop messing about and do some work*. Like everyone else's, my mum knew everything even when she couldn't possibly. I paid off my overdraft and even saved a bit. If loads of hours in the library reading all the set books I hadn't got around to over the previous three years, and catching up so that I didn't sound like a clueless idiot in front of the rest of my chums in senior honours tutorials, then a pint or two at the Criterion Bar would surely be in order. Occasionally.

You couldn't miss Lennox Arlington Mercurius Taylor. He was one of the few black guys at St Andrews in the early 1970s and when I met him in South Street at the beginning of our final year, he had news. 'A few of our team mates from the First XV are giving up as well.' We were walking under the archway into the library quad and a sign that said: *In principio erat Verbum*. The irony was not lost on me. 'Maybe we could have a few beach games? A bit of seven-a-side?' I said. 'Maybe,' smiled Len, and I trailed off to find a warm corner in the stacks where I could catch up on three years of *Verbum*. That was how it began, a season of playing sport for fun in a team we dubbed Lennie's Lions.

*

'The next time I hear a profanity, I shall be awarding a penalty against.' The Right Reverend Robin Buchanan-Smith's moustache bristled. And our prop-forward Steve Stone's narrow forehead furrowed. 'What the fuck's a profanity, ref?' Marching back ten yards, we explained, very quietly, to this idiot medic what a pro-fuckingfanity was, dickhead!

Time was agonisingly short, less than five minutes to go. The match hung in the balance. Rosyth Civil Service Second XV had the ball and were wasting precious seconds discussing what to do with it. It was a puzzle – because it was the first time they had had possession for the whole of the match, except for a moment or two after we kicked off to start the second half. We were leading 96–0 with less than five minutes to score a try and add the conversion to make it 101. Three figures. Unheard of in the annals, et cetera, et cetera. And certainly unheard of in the far-off days when it was only three points for a try. A record beckoned. And it was the last game of the season.

Our inspiration, our beloved captain, Lennox Arlington Mercurius Taylor, exhorted us to one last, supreme effort. We were Lennie's Lions after all, and at this level, rugby was another game entirely. All the refugees from the muddy trials of the First XV were fit, young but experienced and intent on having a good time. We swept aside every team on the Fourth XV fixture list. Waid Academy FP second team, Madras College FP 4ths: all the giants of Fife rugby fell before us. Our only hiccup came in the match against Dundee Elephants, a team of senior medics. Led by Dolph Onsteiner, an 18-stone colossus who had played American college football and thought he was still wearing the helmet and body armour, they restricted us to 30 points. Almost felt like a defeat. Dolph left his footprints on my chest and ran around tackling people who didn't have the ball. The Right Reverend's mouth was too often agape for him to blow the whistle for penalties and clouds of profuckingfanities blew on the sea breeze over the leafy suburbs of St Andrews.

After what seemed like a departmental meeting, the Rosyth Civil Service Second XV came to a decision. Somehow positioning the ball under his pot belly where he could still see it, their balding scrum half hoofed it into touch. The Right Reverend looked at his watch, looked up at the pleading faces of the civil servants and decided that there would be just enough time left for a lineout.

And then everything went into slow motion. From the touchline Lennie threw the ball high in the air. It spun end over end. Lindsay Doig rose, unaided – honest, ref – in the middle of the lines of forwards to catch it cleanly. Passed back to Chris O'Donnell, the only known weightlifter ever to play scrum half, the ball went out to Mickey Stanley who made a half break before passing to me. I burst through the flailing civil service defence into the clear and their full-back suddenly remembered a previous appointment. The April drizzle seemed to stop immediately. The sun came out and bathed the scene in a yellow glow as I floated towards the posts. And when I touched down, the orchestra reached a crescendo: cymbals clashed, timpani crashed and a heavenly choir soared. Ninety-nine to nothing! Trails of glory streaked through the pale blue sky. Lennie's Lions in excelsis!

I had been taking the goal kicks all afternoon, converting about half of the 25 tries we had scored. As the string section swelled and the waves crashed, and thoughts turned to a deeply impressed queue of gorgeous women already forming outside the Criterion Bar to greet their heroes, I made the usual nonchalant mark in the ground with my heel. Smack in front of the posts. Having trudged down the pitch, the Rosyth Civil Service Second XV stood in front of me, wondering how to explain a scoreline of 101–0 on Monday morning. I smiled a generous, consoling smile, half-inclining my head in sympathy and took three paces backwards. Rose petals floated on the balmy wind, drums rolled. I ran up, kicked. And missed. Or, rather, I hit. The crossbar. The ball shot back over my head and bounced somewhere behind me. Waves of relief washed over the civil servants' faces. Some of them managed a gloating smile, even a chuckle.

I turned to face my teammates. They were standing on the centre-line, hands on hips, thunderstruck, glaring at me as if we had lost. The deathly silence was shattered by the Right Reverend's shrill whistle for full time. For a clergyman, the university chaplain, he managed a passably evil grin. 'I expect you'll be paying for quite a few pints of beer this evening.'

There were consolations. After our exertions for the St Andrews University Fourth XV on Saturdays, some of us turned out for Neasden United, our Sunday League homage to the legacy of *Private Eye*'s ashen-faced Ron Knee. It too was tremendous fun, and during the week I played basketball for the university with a bunch of Americans. We beat almost everyone, except USAF Edzell, the base having a terrific team of huge black guys, most of them way over six foot tall. And in the summer term, I played a few games of cricket. Sport, amateur sport, was ingrained in my life, something I, and many of my friends at university (where the facilities were excellent), did almost without thinking, virtually every weekend. And we did it not because we wanted to stay fit or encourage physical and mental wellbeing, but because as team games, the rugby, football, basketball and cricket matches were a lot of fun.

Team sport forged memories and enduring relationships in a way few other pursuits do. Of course these recollections become gilded, and that is part of the attraction. Each year, recently interrupted only by COVID, I go to a reunion of a schools rugby team that played against Wales schoolboys in 1966 (we lost 6–3) and we laugh as the realities are sifted out from the exaggerations and the flat-out lies routinely told by grey-haired men who cherish increasingly vivid recollections of events that never actually took place. The fictions about who really did what to whom, where and what the score was or might have been, if the wind hadn't turned around at half-time, and almost everything else had been different, instead of how it actually was – all of that imparts a richness, great amusement and also a sense of life's passage. But I think the fact of having played in teams was a valuable, precious experience that is probably not available outside sport. And by sport, I mean amateur sport.

Until very recently rugby was truly popular and populist in the Scottish Borders, an integral part of local identities. When a young man said he 'played for Kelso', no one was in any doubt which sport he meant. A survey carried out in 1992 showed that on each winter Saturday in Scotland, weather permitting, no fewer than 167 teams of fifteen players turned out. This included schools as well as club games. And that added up to more than 2,500 participants, to say nothing of match officials, club committee members, helpers, ballboys and groundsmen. On the terracing of the Border grounds stood an estimated 10,000 supporters, many of them, especially from Hawick, willing to travel to away games. When all this involvement was added together, it produced a surprisingly high quotient. One in eight Borderers regularly watched, played or otherwise enabled rugby. It was part of life, deeply embedded.

After the inaugural Rugby World Cup in 1987, the game quickly became professional at the very top level and the subtraction of star players from their traditional clubs did result in a falling-off of support. Although some teams, like Walkerburn RFC, did struggle, these trends were largely counterbalanced by the surge in women's rugby, the extension of the fixture list and the increasing use of substitutes which allowed more people to play and be involved.

Elsewhere in Scotland, there was also a great deal of regular sporting activity. In 1999, it was estimated that there were almost 2,000 amateur football clubs, many of them fielding more than one team each weekend. Cup and local league competitions were keenly contested, and the game seemed to be flourishing in schools, despite the occasional effects of industrial disputes between teachers and local authorities. Girls' and boys' teams competed in area leagues, and national finals were often played at famous grounds such as Hampden Park in Glasgow.

The 1999 survey also showed that team sport reached right across the age spectrum. In Scotland, after football, the next most popular sport, played by many thousands of men and women, was lawn bowls. There were around 1,900 clubs, and it seemed that every town and suburb had at least one of those immaculate squares of gleaming turf where perhaps the most sedate team game of all is played.

However, this sunny, positive picture of mass participation was to change rapidly in the opening decades of the twenty-first century. By 2017, the number of amateur football clubs had declined dramatically, halved, to 1,050, and player numbers fell from 35,000 to 33,000 between 2013 and 2017. Several venerable clubs such as Campsie Black Watch, Clark Drive and Knockentiber ceased to exist, and many others were finding it increasingly difficult to recruit committee members as well as players. The research indicated that the greatest losses occurred in football's traditional heartland, the Central Belt.

Iain Milne, the former Scotland and British Lions player, wrote in 2018 that from his own count, he believed that there were fewer than 5,000 adult male players who turned out regularly for their clubs, and in a report published in 2020, 'Has Rugby Become a Sport for the Viewer rather than the Player?', researcher Tom Rowe published a set of surprising figures. Scottish Rugby (formerly the Scottish Rugby Union) reckoned that in 2016 there were 49,625 registered players, including women and children. Three years later, that number had declined sharply by 27 per cent to 36,207.

Tom Rowe contrasted this rapid decline in participation with the growing popularity of professional rugby on TV. In 2023, the Rugby World Cup had staggering viewing figures of more than 800 million worldwide, making it a hugely lucrative commercial property, very attractive to advertisers and sponsors. Annual international matches, especially those in the Six Nations Championship held at Murrayfield in Edinburgh, are regularly sold out – and ticket prices are steep, most seats at £100 and over – and some rugby players have become global celebrities, with many retired players finding roles as pundits.

So why are fewer and fewer people playing? It seems to me that the answer is relatively straightforward, and it is one that also explains the decline of amateur football. Enormous television rights revenue has created two different games, two different cultures. The Scotland rugby team is currently ranked fifth in the world, its highest-ever placing, while the domestic amateur game is dying. The one used to feed the other as talented players rose through the ranks of their local team, the district sides and then on to the international team. But huge amounts of money and the need for instant success have all but blocked that well-worn path. There are only two professional sides in Scotland (far fewer than in England, Ireland and Wales), one based in Glasgow and one in Edinburgh, and the old clubs who used to supply players for the international team are rapidly becoming irrelevant. At the beginning of my own rugby career, playing for Kelso when I was 17 and still at school, I dreamed of playing for Scotland. Many Kelso players had achieved that, and so why not? But, sadly, that possibility has become more and more unlikely for today's players.

Professional rugby is now coming to resemble professional football in that it matters little that a Scotland player is Scottish. Out of the recent match-day squad of 23 that faced Italy in the last game of the Six Nations Championship of 2023, thirteen were born overseas. Scotland has more players from South Africa, Australia, England, New Zealand and elsewhere than England, Ireland or Wales, and they come to play for their adopted nation because they are offered lucrative contracts. The longer-term difficulty this presents is clear. The pipeline of young Scottish players is all but blocked, and the Under-20 team is regularly soundly beaten. In their last match of 2023, they lost by 40–17 to Italy. Their senior team is regularly bottom of the Six Nations Championship, but to improve their standing, the Italians have invested not in signing expensive foreign-born players but in rugby academies and the amateur domestic game, so that, eventually, home-grown talent will emerge. Scottish Rugby has failed, so far, to put in place a similarly far-sighted policy. Because there is such a gulf between amateur rugby and football and their professional versions, ambition is much restricted. There is now no path to glory, and it seems to me that many young people would rather watch Scotland and the professional teams on TV than try to become good enough to play in one of them. Why bother? It looks like another world – because it is.

All of which means that the grassroots game is dwindling, and a great deal more than international matches is being lost. Team sport, of whatever standard, is healthy in all senses, fostering mental as well as physical wellbeing. Statistics released by the Scottish Government and other agencies point to an increase in healthy outdoor pursuits such as walking, and that is welcome. But there is nothing like team games and all the relationships, obligations, shared memories and laughs that go with it. They need to be fostered urgently because they can raise a barrier against a new and increasingly deadly epidemic.

In the executive summary of his survey of participation in sport undertaken in 2018, Nick Rowe wrote: 'The picture of a nation that is too inactive for its own good is stark, as are the consequences. Scotland is currently near the top of the league table of countries that are overweight or obese.'

Rowe's statistics are alarming. Almost one in three Scots, 29 per cent, is obese, compared with a global average of 13 per cent. Our obesity levels are the second highest in the world, second only to the USA. And 66 per cent of Scots are either overweight or clinically obese. The increased risks to health are huge, diabetes and kidney disease being the most common.

Since 1950, Scotland has looked different, and recently Scots themselves have begun to look very different. In the early twenty-first century, these malign trends suddenly seemed to accelerate. Between 2012 and 2022, the number of overweight adults rocketed by a staggering 46 per cent. By 2021/2022, obesity had become an epidemic in Britain with 1.2 million hospital admissions with illnesses closely linked to or directly caused by excess weight, having doubled since 2016 to 2017. By 2023, more than 3,300 obese people were being admitted each day. That huge figure is three times the number who have smoking-related diseases.

What has happened to amateur team sport in Scotland is not only a matter for nostalgic regret, the mournful loss of heroes who no longer walk down our street. The decline is part of the cause of the explosion of overweight and obesity. More and more Scots are failing to get off their backsides, appearing to prefer watching sport on TV to playing it. Not only are they seriously damaging their health, they are missing out on a great deal. Are we becoming viewers rather than doers?

12

A Woman's Place?

It can be tempting to read history backwards, to believe it is possible to see the seeds of the present planted at specific times in specific places and then flourish as agents of change. Most of the time, that sort of rationalisation is misleading, a knowing reinterpretation of the past to help make more sense of the here and now. But sometimes, a series of related moments turned out not to be coincidences and did send a clear message, the beginnings of one of the most profound changes to affect Scotland since 1950.

At the University of St Andrews, one of the highlights of the year was the election of the Charities Queen. I can recall the 1970 contest very clearly. It was open to first-year female students who were interviewed by a panel of men. Each candidate, and there were plenty who applied, had to answer personal questions, sing a song and generally acquit themselves with some wit as well as show a degree of self-confidence. A shortlist of six Charities Princesses was selected, and money was raised for charities because everyone who voted had to pay for the privilege.

At the same time (I think it must have been the winter term), I saw a group of women standing at the corner of Market Street and Greyfriars Gardens, a busy crossroads at the west end of the town. When I passed them, they all wolf-whistled at me, and there may have been one or two comments. I remember being surprised, amused – and cheered. The group was led by Sue Innes, and I later discovered that she had entered the competition to become Charities Queen, having submitted a decidedly unflattering photograph. If Sue Innes had won, she promised to campaign for the abolition of beauty contests. She didn't, but eventually they were.

Sometime after the wolf-whistling incident, she became editor of the student newspaper, *Aien*, and in one week's edition there appeared a list of the top ten men. Each entry carried a description and a note of what had impressed the judges. Somewhat disappointed to be ranked seventh, I was said to be cuddly and, oddly, fond of wearing a tartan scarf. Rugged, intelligent and charming were not adjectives that appeared next to my name. Just cuddly. Needless to note, I never lived it down, especially at rugby training.

In a small university, Sue Innes's initiative in turning the tables made an impact. It was clever, brave and ahead of its time. And it was for me the beginning of a change in attitude, a gradual and often faltering process of regarding women as natural equals, and trying, and often failing, not to objectify them, not to think like a judge at a beauty contest. I was young, not shy, and I liked the company of women, three impediments that often tripped me up. In the summer of 1971, I bought a paperback copy of *The Female Eunuch* by Germaine Greer. The cover was striking and brilliant: a headless and legless female torso with handles attached. The content made a huge impact as it dismissed evolutionary change in attitudes to women and instead preached revolution. The language was robust and the ideas startling. Five years later, I met Germaine Greer in Edinburgh (when I was running the Festival Fringe) and as I offered to shake hands, she hugged me. Maybe I really was cuddly.

These incidents in St Andrews, and reading *The Female Eunuch*, were not agents of any sort of personal conversion. Their impact had more to do with awareness. Until then I hadn't given the status of women much thought and had few fixed views. If anything, it seemed to me to be an issue of fairness: why should women not have the same rights and opportunities as men? But, of course, it was not as simple as that.

These moments, and no doubt others like them elsewhere, did not happen without context. Significant demographic shifts had been taking place in Scotland for decades. In the 1951 census, the total population was 5,095,969 and this comprised 2,661,220 females and 2,434,749 males, a slightly lop-sided pattern that would persist. In 2022, Scotland's highest-ever total was recorded at 5,436,600, and this divided into 2,794,800 females and 2,641,800 males. These numbers can be mined to show how the status – and prospects – of women in Scotland have changed since 1950.

Of those aged over 16 in 1950, 76 per cent were married, but in 2021 that number had fallen dramatically to 45.2 per cent. Figures for those in long-term relationships who are not married are more difficult to come by, but there is no doubt that over that period fewer and fewer people have exchanged formal vows and rings. In 2021, 35.4 per cent of people over 16 identified themselves as single, and 19.2 per cent were either divorced or widowed. In simple terms, that means that almost 55 per cent of Scots, a clear majority, are unmarried, a radical change since 1950.

With the population of women outnumbering men, and considering that the life expectancy of the latter has long been lower, spinsterhood was not uncommon. Across Scotland, the picture could be patchy. In the Highlands and Islands, poor economic prospects persuaded more young men than women to leave, usually to go south in search of jobs. The same was true in Orkney and Shetland, and to some extent in Dumfries and Galloway and the Borders. This meant something straightforward: a gender imbalance that resulted in a high number of unmarried women in these regions. In the Central Belt, the picture was more balanced.

Other economic factors also played an important role. The traditional stigma of a wife going out to work (it implied to some that a husband was unable to earn enough to support his family) began to erode after the Second World War. In munitions and other wartime industries, women had shown themselves to be highly capable, able to do jobs that had been thought too arduous. In some sectors, such as the jute mills of Dundee and the textile manufacturers in the Borders and elsewhere, a female workforce was preferred. Before the term had been invented, there were house-husbands in Dundee, disparagingly known as 'kettle-bilers'.

After the 1960s and the increasing availability of the contraceptive pill (although rates of childbirth had been falling steadily before then), women stayed in work, and were often unmarried, for longer. The Equal Pay Act of 1970 was the combination of the Labour Party's manifesto pledge of 1964 that women had a right to 'equal pay for equal work' and the need to conform with the laws of the European Common Market. This legislation applied not only to wages and salaries but also the entitlement to holiday pay and pension rights. For many women, the act held out the promise of a different way of life, or a progressive career, one that might last a lifetime and not be interrupted by marriage or childbearing. By 2019, slightly more than 1.35 million women in Scotland were in permanent employment, a radically different picture from 1950.

Changes on this scale would have been impossible without political activism and the courage of a few women who could see a different future not only for themselves but also for their daughters.

In 1921, the Football Association pronounced that 'the game of football is quite unsuitable for females and ought not to be encouraged'. The Scottish Football Association agreed, and even though women had been playing the game since the 1880s, their teams were banned from using official pitches and had no access to accredited referees, funding or equipment. A century later, the Lionesses, England's women's football team, won not only the European Champions Cup but also the hearts of football and sports audiences the world over. Their flair, their supportive and sporting attitudes were a refreshing change from the sulky, over-paid prima donnas playing the men's game. Watched by packed stadia and enormous TV audiences, the Lionesses seemed to have rediscovered the spirit of football, reinstated it as a team game, as they clearly played for each other, did not throw tantrums or commit cynical fouls like the men and expressed real joy at their achievements. And they showed that they could survive failure with dignity. When the Lionesses lost the World Cup final to Spain in 2023, there was disappointment but none of the sour recriminations that often follow defeat in the men's game. But that same year, another milestone was reached when Mary Earps, the Lionesses' goalkeeper, was voted the BBC Sports Personality of the Year by the viewing public and made an MBE in the New Year's honours list.

England's great successes warmed the heart of a pioneering Scotswoman. Elsie Cook helped it all happen, having had a hand in the creation of the women's game. Born in Stewarton, a small town to the east of Glasgow, Elsie became involved almost by accident. In 1961, her mother, a netball coach, was asked to recruit a girls' football team to play in a charity match. There were no strips, no boots and no money. And so Elsie put up posters to attract players, asked for donations of old football boots (and rugby boots), found a set of jerseys (and sewed on the badges and numbers) and also discovered a star player. More than 500 spectators watched Susan Ferries score seven goals:

You could hear people muttering around the pitch, 'Have you ever seen a goal like that? And it was a lassie!' Susan had all the attributes of a top male player and I thought, there must be other lassies in Scotland with that same talent. So, at age 15, I took over the team.

So that, despite the SFA ban, Stewarton Thistle could operate, Elsie borrowed strips from men's teams, used a pitch on Sunday mornings when most people were in church and asked spectators if they could be touch judges or even referees.

Women's football was growing in popularity all over Europe in the 1960s, and in 1971 UEFA voted to lift the ban. It was almost unanimous with 31 associations voting for the motion and only one against – that was Scotland. Elsie Cook went to see Willie Allan, the Secretary of the SFA, to attempt to win his support. 'Football is not for women, it's far too physical,' he pronounced. Elsie remembered that 'he couldn't quite bring himself to say the words, but he patted his chest area and looked me straight in the eye'. Newspapers were even more disparaging when reporting on games: '22 crackpot females running around a football pitch, bouncing boobs all over the place.' A headline from the *Weekly News* read: 'Hey Ref, Stop the Game! The Left-Back Has Broken a Bra Strap.'

Despite all this, and much worse, Elsie Cook was determined. By 1972, she was the manager of the Scotland Women's football team and organised the first international match with England, where the game was no longer banned. By holding it in Scotland, the English women agreed with Elsie that a statement should be made. On 18 November, at Ravenscraig Stadium in Greenock, history was also made as England narrowly defeated the Scots by three goals to two. Elsie Cook recalled the occasion, immediately setting a different tone:

. . . it was a great honour. The score didn't matter. What was more important was just playing with women, it was absolutely amazing. We felt we were now recognised . . .

If we won, we won. If we lost, we lost. It was about growing the game and opening up football for everybody. Opposing teams were our rivals, but we befriended them and that's how we kept expanding the game.

While the SFA ban was still in place, Stewarton Thistle were allowed to compete in the English Cup competition and reached the final. Managed by Elsie Cook, they played Southampton Ladies. Fifty years later, with Pamela Lloyd, the Southampton captain, Elsie carried the cup out onto the pitch at Wembley before the Cup Final match of 2022. Overcome by emotion, she remembered her dreams all that time ago: 'While people were trying to stop us from playing, all I could see was the World Cup, the Olympics, Professional Leagues, European Cups all stretching out in front of us in time, and I knew it was the goal.'

*

Nightmares as well as dreams were the experience of too many women in Scotland. In 2023, Mary Sinclair spoke of her experiences as a married women 50 years before. Like Elsie Cook, she was battling for recognition, but of a very different sort:

It was accepted that there might be violence in the marriage, but it was seen as domestic . . . The door went and I was just an absolute mess, strangle marks on my neck, bruises inside my hair, my lip was burst, my eye was burst, my hair was everywhere, legs were bruised, hands were bruised. I was in a state. I opened the door and she [the social worker] took one look and said, 'What is going on here?' I just broke down. I told her what was happening, and she said, 'A dog wouldn't get treated like this. Mary, you need help. I know of an organisation that can help,' and she told me about Edinburgh Women's Aid.

In 1973, Marion Blythman and a colleague from the Glasgow Women's Liberation group had gone to London to visit the Chiswick Women's Refuge. Established in 1971 by the uncompromising activist, Erin Pizzey, it was the first of its kind in Britain. 'We drove home to Glasgow, I remember. Actually, we were both weeping from the sorts of things she told us and this realisation that we had that there really was a big problem here and that nobody was doing anything about it.'

Marion Blythman was a founding member of Edinburgh Women's Aid, which opened its first refuge in Scotland in December 1973. Mary Sinclair recalled a dark, three-bedroom council house with cold linoleum flooring that was somehow welcoming, a place where she was believed, where she felt, 'I'm OK, I'm safe'.

A central difficulty for campaigners and activists was that domestic abuse was not recognised as a crime, and it was largely ignored by the police who saw it as a private matter between spouses. Linda Okroj, a worker at Edinburgh Women's Aid and, later, at Scottish Women's Aid, remembered:

> I'll always say that the agency that . . . had the biggest sea change have been the police. When I started, the police were just unbelievable. The first police talk I ever did, a police sergeant said, 'Och, come on now, hen, you know yourself, his team gets beat on a Saturday, he's no' very happy, he beats up his wife. She knows he doesnae really mean to do it and by the Monday they've sorted it oot. Now, what's the point of us having a whole load of paperwork?' Seriously . . . and, I mean, you often think people make that up. I was there. It was just like 'Oh God'.

By the mid 1970s there were fifteen Women's Aid groups in Scotland, and they were expanding the network of refuges as the scale of the problem became more and more apparent. Academic research at Stirling University was producing startling and indisputable statistics. A painstaking, case-by-case examination of police records revealed an epidemic on a scale that few expected. Of all violent incidents reported and investigated, a staggering 25 per cent were committed by men against their wives or partners, usually at home.

Legislative change began at last to reflect changing views. In 1981, the Matrimonial Homes Act gave important protection to abused women. Even if their husband or partner was the tenant or the owner of the home where the family lived, women gained the right, with their children, to stay there if there were problems. They could not be simply thrown out any longer. If there was violence – and that would always have to be proved beyond a reasonable doubt – then an abusive partner or husband could be excluded by interim interdict. In 1989, rape in marriage was recognised as a crime in Scotland, and in the 1990s and 2000s further legislation dealt with stalking, housing rights, harassment, forced marriage and certain forms of domestic and sexual abuse.

The establishment of the Scottish Parliament in 1999 helped highlight women's issues in general, not least by recognising that many of then related to the whole of society, not just women. A former Strathkelvin Women's Aid volunteer, Jackie Baillie, was elected as an MSP:

And very much from early on, there were debates and things they never really found time for on the agenda at Westminster. So domestic abuse was up there in the early days of the Parliament. Poverty, you know, children, all of the things that some people would describe as women's issues that . . . I think they are society's issues. But suddenly there was the space and the time to talk about these things. And the space and the time . . . to then do something about it . . . I was encouraged by the fact that at the very beginning and right the way through women across [parties] have actually all come together on this agenda and have put politics to one side . . . They've used that powerful grouping to do what they can on service delivery, on increased staffing and resources, and on improved legislation, you know, and things like the domestic abuse courts wouldn't have happened otherwise. So that's a powerful thing to have. And I think it's only there, not because we have right-on men, but because there is a critical capacity of women in the Scottish Parliament and that's stayed that way.

It took longer than anyone wished, but finally, in 2018, the Domestic Abuse (Scotland) Bill came before the Scottish Parliament. For the first time, domestic abuse – and all its variants, such as coercive behaviour – was defined. Instead of a breach of the peace, or assault, or even attempted murder, domestic abuse was about to become a crime. When the bill was enacted into law, a small group of campaigners in the public gallery of the Parliament wept and hugged each other. And, memorably, all the MSPs in the chamber got to their feet and turned to applaud them. It was indeed a turning point. Scotland had set an example for the world to follow.

*

On Niddrie Mains Road, in the centre of Craigmillar, a large council housing estate on the eastern periphery of Edinburgh, stands an unusual, eloquent sculpture. On one side of an open doorway sits a bespectacled woman who offers a bow to a young boy with a violin tucked under his chin. It commemorates an incident that took place in 1962 and the achievements that flowed from it. When Helen Crummy, a resident of Craigmillar, went to Peffermill Primary School to see her son's head teacher, Angus Lyall, she asked him a question that eventually sparked many answers. Helen's father had been a talented fiddler: was it possible for her son, Philip, to have violin lessons at his primary school? Angus Lyall shook his head: 'It takes us all our time to teach the children the 3Rs far less music.' This dusty reply was not something Helen Crummy could accept.

Instead of acquiescing to what Lyall said, or complaining, she and others in Craigmillar took action. The Peffermill Mothers group became a fundraising organisation whose efforts helped the school secure more and better equipment and facilities for the children from the estate. Such was their tenacity, they became known as the Dangerous Mothers. Craigmillar was at that time a sprawling estate like those on the edges of Glasgow and Dundee and elsewhere. Council housing had been built since the late 1920s before accelerating after the Second World War, and there were several fourteen-storey tower blocks, a lack of local amenities and many of the familiar attendant difficulties. At one point, unemployment in Craigmillar soared to 40 per cent. Despite this backdrop, Helen Crummy and her group decided to bring music and drama to the windswept, grey-harled streets of the estate. They mounted community musicals and encouraged participation at all levels. A neighbour of Helen Crummy, Jack Kane, became a local councillor (and eventually Edinburgh's first Labour Lord Provost), and he helped as much as he could with resources and arm-twisting.

Throughout the 1960s, the musicals became more and more popular and more ambitious. Yet the work of what became the Craigmillar Festival Society was largely ignored by the Scottish Office and the UK Government. So Helen Crummy applied to the European Economic Community's anti-poverty programme and travelled to Brussels to make her case. Funding of more than £200,000 was awarded, and in 1976 a Comprehensive Plan for Action was produced. A model of its kind and much imitated, it promoted the central notion that arts and cultural activities are not peripheral or the preserve of elites but integral to the regeneration of communities. On the lintel above the open doorway where the sculpture of Helen Crummy sits is an inscription, 'Let the People Sing', and on the door itself: 'History will be made when the people play their part.' And that is what happened.

In 1976, around 600 people were employed, most of them part-time; 1,700 more were volunteers and 17,000 took part in the work of the Craigmillar Festival Society in some way. Large numbers attended the events, and it was an enormous and surprising success. Helen Crummy was adept at recruiting celebrity help and secured endorsements from Billy Connolly, Sean Connery, Bill Paterson and others. At that time, I was running the Edinburgh Festival Fringe and I met Helen several times to talk about how our two organisations could cooperate. She knew that August and the Edinburgh Festivals was the only time when the cultural focus in Britain shifted decisively away from London. The Craigmillar Festival Society should be involved in the Fringe, use it as a showcase, and there was no argument from me.

When Helen died in July 2011, at the age of 91, there appeared an eloquent obituary in the *Scotsman* which began:

> Helen Crummy was one of those rare individuals whose innate modesty concealed an iron determination to change the world for the better, above all for the poor and the marginalised. Where some might see the victims of poverty as part of an endemic social problem, she saw the unfulfilled potential of people who, given the opportunity, could overcome disadvantage and find self-esteem.
>
> For her, every child, no matter how poor, was a precious gift; every adult, regardless of circumstances, was worthy of respect, and deserved to be listened to.

*

In 2015, a glass ceiling appeared to shatter. All the leaders of the three largest political parties in the Scottish Parliament were women. Ruth Davidson led the Conservatives, Kezia Dugdale was the Labour Leader, and Nicola Sturgeon was both Leader of the SNP and the first woman to be First Minister. It had been a halting journey to reach that point, one that saw the numbers of female MSPs stall and sometimes dip. In 1999, a bright future seemed to dawn when out of a total of 129 elected members, 48 were women, a number that grew to 51 in the 2003 election. But fewer women won seats at the two subsequent elections, and it was not until 2021 that there was real growth when 58 female MSPs were elected, 45 per cent of the total. The gender balance had at last entered what statisticians call 'the parity zone'.

Of course none of this happened by accident, but the distance travelled in less than 40 years has been spectacular. In the 1987 general election for the UK Parliament, only three female MPs out of 72 won seats in Scotland, 4 per cent of the total. In 2019, 18 out of 59 were elected, meaning that women made up 30 per cent of all Scottish MPs. In Holyrood, parties took action before the election in 2021 to improve the sluggish numbers of women who represented constituencies and were high on the regional lists. In places where a sitting MSP had stood down, the SNP introduced all-women shortlists of candidates, and Labour alternated men with women in the lists. For example, in the Glasgow list, that meant Pauline McNeill was top and most likely to be elected and the Labour Leader, Anas Sarwar, was second. These measures resulted in the election of more women and also had the effect of promoting diversity of other sorts. In 2021, Pam Gosal, a Conservative, was the first MSP from an Indian Sikh background, the SNP's Kaukab Stewart was the first female Muslim MSP and Labour's Pam Duncan-Glancy was the first permanent wheelchair user elected to Holyrood.

On a superficial level, the Scottish Parliament of 2021 also looked different. Amongst the grey and navy suits, women MSPs brought splashes of colour as well as different sensitivities and attitudes. But more than that, they also brought the promise of a different future for all of Scotland's women. The journey from the miseries of Mary Sinclair and the many hundreds of thousands of women who have been oppressed in the recent past is by no means over. But by the third decade of the twenty-first century, women at last have achieved positions of power, if not yet parity. After millennia of patriarchy, their influences are just beginning to be felt. Of all the seismic changes, both subtle and obvious, recorded in previous chapters, the full participation of women in the life of Scotland may yet prove to be the most radical, the most far-reaching change of all.

13

Permacrisis

On 7 October 2008, the Labour MP for Edinburgh South West arrived in Luxembourg. As Chancellor of the Exchequer, Alistair Darling was attending a monthly meeting of European finance ministers. In the middle of the morning, an aide came into the conference room with a note. Would the Chancellor take an urgent phone call from Sir Tom McKillop, the chairman of the board of the Royal Bank of Scotland?

Alistair Darling described the conversation some years later when I interviewed him. 'He said that the bank was haemorrhaging money. I asked him, "How long can you last?" And what he then said shook me to the core. "Well, we're going to run out of money by early this afternoon." I just closed my eyes and thought, what if they close the doors and shut down the cash machines? He then said, "What are you going to do about it?", which I thought was quite a remarkable thing to say – "What are *you* going to do about it?" What was in my mind at that point is that if people thought the biggest bank in the world had failed, there would not be a bank in the western world that was safe.

'The risk I have always seen is that people forget how close we came to a complete collapse . . . and it wouldn't just have been the banks in ruins, it would have been complete economic, and therefore social, collapse. People without money can do nothing – you can't buy your petrol, you can't buy your food, anything.'

At the end of another interview, with a characteristically wry smile, Alistair Darling said, 'You shouldn't really panic unless it's absolutely necessary.'

On the same morning as the Chancellor was talking to the chairman of the Royal Bank, the chief executive, Fred Goodwin, was addressing a large meeting of bank investors in central London. After his upbeat, optimistic assessment of the bank's prospects, a member of the audience looked up from his Blackberry and asked a question: 'Do you realise that while you've been speaking, telling us how well the bank will do in the future, the share price has crashed with 35 per cent wiped off its value?' Goodwin was said to have been shocked, and he immediately left the meeting.

Founded in 1727 in Edinburgh, 32 years after its great rival, the Bank of Scotland, the Royal Bank was not only part of Scotland's history but also a byword for solidity and respectability. Its senior executives were seen as pillars of the community. Along with others, it had the right to issue its own notes and was headquartered in a splendid neoclassical building in St Andrew's Square. After a century-long agreement with English banks that neither would open branches or seek customers in each other's country had lapsed in the mid 1960s, the larger English banks began to take a predatory interest. By 1986, the board realised that unless RBS changed and began to take initiatives, it would sooner or later be taken over. George Matthewson was appointed as director of strategic planning and development in 1987, later becoming chief executive. Not trained or experienced as a banker but as a businessman, he introduced innovations such as telephone banking and orchestrated the bank's takeover of the much larger National Westminster Bank (NatWest) in February 2000. At that point, Matthewson stepped down, became chairman, and appointed Fred Goodwin as chief executive.

Under his leadership, RBS began to expand rapidly by engineering a series of takeover bids. By 2005, it was the fifth-largest bank in the world and had moved its headquarters from the Georgian splendour of St Andrew's Square to a vast, new, modernist complex at Gogarburn, not far from Edinburgh airport. By that time knighted, Sir Fred Goodwin was now ensconced in a vast office with spectacular views, and he entertained even bigger ambitions. But it was said by colleagues that the chief executive was a ruthless manager (his morning meetings became known as 'morning beatings'), and that his ego began to outrun good sense and caution. In 2007, RBS reported record profits of £9 billion, and its assets were said to amount to £2.2 trillion, larger than Britain's GDP. About 25 per cent of those huge profits were generated by its American banks: along with many others, one of them, Greenwich Capital, had been especially active in what was known as the sub-prime market. Driven by generous bonuses and the need for ever-rising profits, Greenwich had begun to lend money to people who, in the past, would not have been viewed as a good risk. But so long as property prices continued to rise and the value of the assets exceeded the size of the loan, the bubble of sub-prime would not burst.

In 2007, the banking sector was astounded when Northern Rock – a building society before it morphed into a bank – collapsed. As customers queued outside branches, it was the first run on a British bank for 150 years. Confidence was beginning to crumble. In September 2008, Lehman Brothers, a huge American bank, crashed and shock waves reverberated around the world. It had been brought down by the toxic loans agreed in the sub-prime market, vast amounts of debt that would never be repaid.

In April 2007, the Royal Bank of Scotland bought the Dutch bank ABN-AMRO and briefly became the largest bank in the world. But it too was riddled with sub-prime debt that would never be redeemed. What made the situation terminal for RBS was not only the failure of due diligence to uncover the high degree of risk, but the fact that they overpaid for ABN-AMRO. The price of €71 billion was mostly in cash, rather than shares, and that severely depleted RBS's reserves, forcing them to borrow, which caused a vicious downward spiral.

As the scale of sub-prime lending became clear and the lending packages around it so complex that it was impossible to unravel, banks stopped lending to each other. RBS was then compelled to undertake a rights issue to raise cash, offering more shares to existing shareholders at a discount. While this was successful and many took up the offer (unaware of what was happening in the debt market), not enough cash was raised, and the share price continued to fall. Many investors lost a great deal of money, many of them in Scotland. RBS was forced to the brink of bankruptcy. And, on 7 October 2008, Sir Tom McKillop was forced to call Alistair Darling.

All the major British banks were in difficulty, and on the evening of 8 October, their chief executives met the Chancellor at the Treasury in London. After the collapse of Northern Rock and then Lehman Brothers, the Labour Government had moved to stabilise the British banks by offering guarantees that would prevent any from closing their doors. Those plans were fast-tracked in a day and presented to the chief executives that evening. An agreement had to be reached before the markets opened the following morning at 7 a.m. Even though there was no real alternative, Goodwin and the others railed against the central tenet of the plan, that the government would take a majority stake in each bank, effectively nationalising them. Knowing that they had no choice, Alistair Darling went to bed at 11 p.m. By the time he got up at 5 a.m., the chief executives had of course agreed. A statement was agreed, communicated to the markets, and collapse was averted. One of the Treasury team, Shriti Vadera, commented that the rescue package was not about saving the banks but saving the British economy from the banks. It was no less than the truth.

The whole bailout probably cost the British taxpayer £1 trillion, much of which will never be repaid. The behaviour of the banks, especially RBS, was widely condemned. Fuelled by greed and ego, encouraged by huge salaries and bonuses, bankers had become gamblers with other people's money and cost everyone but themselves dear. The reputation of Scottish banks for probity and steadiness was shredded. Trust evaporated.

Even though he was forced to resign at the age of 50, Fred Goodwin was entitled to an index-linked annual pension of £704,000. After an outcry, this was reduced to £342,500 a year, but was allowed to take a tax-free lump sum of £2.7 million out of his pension fund. In 2012, Goodwin's knighthood was 'cancelled and annulled'. Questioned by a House of Commons committee in 2009, he admitted he had had no technical banking training and held no formal banking qualifications. Sir Tom McKillop said that he was also completely unqualified, but he did at least apologise for his bank's behaviour.

A year after the banking collapse of 2008, the ground shifted under Scotland's political parties. Cracks began to widen into chasms. Since the first elections to the Scottish Parliament in 1999, Labour had been the largest party but, as the constitutional arrangements had intended, it had always governed in coalition. Led at first by Jim Wallace, the Liberal Democrat Party had been Labour's partners until the polls opened on Thursday, 3 May 2007. When they closed, the votes were for the first time counted electronically, a new approach that should have produced quicker results. Instead, it produced the wrong result.

At 5 a.m., inside the main hall of the vast Inverness Sports Centre, the returning officer, Arthur McCourt, was about to mount the podium to announce the results of the list seats: how voters had exercised their second preferences. The piece of paper in McCourt's hand noted that Labour had won four seats in the Highlands, the Conservatives two, the Greens one and the SNP none. That result would have made Labour the largest party and returned them to government at Holyrood.

Dave Thompson, an SNP candidate, was suspicious. For someone who had been out campaigning and canvassing, that result seemed at best counterintuitive. And so he vigorously challenged the calculations before it was announced. It turned out that tired officials had made a catastrophic mistake. Some had been awake for 35 hours because local council elections had been held on the same day. When the printouts of an Excel spreadsheet that listed all the vote totals from the e-count were re-examined, it was found that the clerks had failed to scroll over the file properly and had left out all the SNP votes. The result was recast. Labour had won three, not four, seats, the Conservatives two and the SNP two. By the smallest of margins, by one seat, the SNP was the largest party with 47 MSPs and Labour was second with 46. For the first time in their history, the SNP found themselves in government, and Alex Salmond replaced Jack MacConnell as First Minister. It was a historic moment, but one that took its time to happen.

Although the SNP gained 20 seats, they did not come from the outgoing parties, from Labour or the Liberal Democrats, so much as two smaller parties. The Greens lost all of their list MSPs and the Scottish Socialist Party was also wiped out, losing six MSPs. Their charismatic leader, Tommy Sheridan, was mired in legal proceedings around the *News of the World's* claims that he had attended 'swingers' clubs' in Manchester and taken drugs (he later served a prison sentence for perjury), and he had, with others, left the party. Two independents also lost their seats. Despite the dramatic result, the constituency vote, the first preferences, showed a relatively stable picture with the SNP on 664,227, only marginally ahead of Labour with 648,374, while the Liberal Democrats had 326,743 and the Conservatives 334,743. As the largest party, the SNP could only govern with the compliance of the Conservatives under Annabel Goldie.

When Gordon Brown's Labour Government stood for re-election in 2010, it lost more than 90 seats in England and Wales but did relatively well in Scotland. North of the border, there was a 2.5 per cent swing to Labour, and the party increased its representation to 41 seats. Prior polling and the results of the 2007 Scottish election had encouraged the SNP to believe they might play a role in supporting a minority Labour Government, but in the event, they won only six seats. No party gained any of their target seats and the popular vote – Labour on 1,035,528, the Liberal Democrats on 465,471, the SNP with 491,386 and the Conservatives on 412,855 – looked very much like business as usual. There was no warning of the sea change that was about to wash over Scottish politics.

At Westminster, the Conservatives were the largest party but had fallen some way short of an overall majority. After a deal of negotiation, a coalition agreement was hammered out with the Liberal Democrats. It came at a price, one paid mainly by Nick Clegg's party. They were forced to accede to a programme of severe austerity in the wake of the banking crash, an eye-watering £6 billion worth of cuts to public services in 2010–11. These included the abandonment of a key Liberal Democrat election pledge: a refusal to increase higher education tuition fees. There was agreement on a referendum to change the first-past-the-post system for electing MPs, but the Conservatives campaigned vigorously against it and the Alternative Vote System was duly rejected by two thirds of the few who voted.

A year after the general election of 2010, a landslide engulfed the Scottish political landscape. In the Scottish Parliament elections, Labour was swept away, and Alex Salmond led his party to a victory no one had predicted and no one had thought possible. The SNP won an overall majority of seats, 69 out of a possible

129 with Labour losing sixteen overall, and some major figures were forced out of parliament. When Alex Salmond was told that the SNP had taken the Labour heartland seat of Clydebank and Milngavie in Glasgow, his biographer David Torrance reported that his reaction was 'Fuck me!', and when he was later told that his party would form a majority government, he said, 'That's not possible.' But it was. The Liberal Democrats were routed, losing twelve of their seventeen seats and 25 candidates polled so poorly that they lost their deposits. It was a stunning, unexpected victory that only began to seem possible as the opinion polls shifted in the last few weeks of the campaign. It forced a clean sweep of opposition resignations as three Party Leaders left their posts: Iain Gray (Labour), Tavish Scott (Liberal Democrats) and Annabel Goldie (Conservatives).

The constituency votes showed something of the causes of this remarkable result. Labour had hung on to 630,461 compared to 648,374 in 2007. The SNP had soared from 664,227 to 902,915. The Liberal Democrats had lost 169,029 votes, falling steeply from 326,742 in 2007 to 157,714 in 2011. Contrary to expectations, their votes had not migrated to Labour but instead to the SNP, and others had joined them. It was an unwelcome variant on a quote from Shakespeare's *Romeo and Juliet* that was often used by Liberal leaders. 'A plague on both your houses' was meant to rally support for a real alternative to the predictable cycle of Tory and Labour. But in 2011, Liberal voters turned on their own party as well as the Conservatives and Labour and supported what they saw as something different from the old politics.

Several new factors seemed to be at play. Clearly, the Liberal Democrats' coalition agreement with the Conservatives had cost them dear in Scotland, as it would do in the rest of the United Kingdom in 2015. In return for five years in government, something no Liberals had tasted for generations, they lost a great deal of support and achieved very little of any substance. It seemed to many that the lure of the ministerial cars and the red boxes were more important than Liberal Democrat values. The SNP victory of 2007 and the landslide of 2011 also confirmed that politics in Scotland was now very different from England. Since 1945, Labour and the Conservatives had alternated in office, a pattern that lasted for the first nine years of the Scottish Parliament. The Conservatives' Scottish representation at Westminster had disappeared in the 1990s, prompting one commentator to point out that there were more giant pandas north of the border than Tory MPs. Paradoxically, it was the Scottish Parliament, something they had opposed, that kept the party alive in Scotland.

As it was designed to do, in contrast to the first-past-the-post system, the lists had ensured that Conservative views were represented at Holyrood, and in time they would become the largest opposition party in the Scottish Parliament. But it was the lack of Scottish Conservative MPs that caused an illogical dissonance. Why, in terms of matters that were not devolved, such as foreign affairs and defence, should Scotland be governed by a party its people did not vote for? Even though that made no sense (because a substantial group did support the Conservatives), many people believed something was out of kilter. 'Conservative' became at least partly synonymous with 'English', but not necessarily with Geordies from the North East, or Yorkshiremen and women, or indeed any of England's strong regional identities. The Old Etonians who seemed permanently in charge of the Conservative Party – they were very English, and they seemed to care little about Scotland, apart from grouse-shooting or visiting the Queen when she was at Balmoral.

This sense of disconnection was not much helped by the Labour Party's inclinations and focus. Gordon Brown had been popular in Scotland, winning a general election there in 2010 while losing it in England and Wales. With his departure, another sort of London elite seemed to take over when Ed Miliband defeated his brother to become Labour Leader in 2010. That sense of remoteness and irrelevance was greatly exacerbated when Jeremy Corbyn succeeded Miliband in 2015, and the Labour Party seemed to be involved in issues and governed by attitudes that baffled many Scots, driving even more into the arms of the SNP.

Events began to move quickly. In 2010, the minority SNP Government had been forced to drop a bill that called for a referendum on independence. All that hesitation disappeared after the 2011 election. Their overall majority made a new call for a vote irresistible. The Edinburgh Agreement was agreed and signed on 15 October 2012. It empowered the Scottish Parliament to bring forward a new bill that would 'deliver a fair test and a decisive expression of the views of the people of Scotland and a result everyone will respect'.

The Edinburgh Agreement conceded a vital point to the SNP Government. They would be allowed to determine the wording on the ballot paper, and their preferred wording shaped the long campaign that led up to the independence referendum. The favoured version was 'Do you agree that Scotland should be an independent country?' It was rejected by the Electoral Commission because its opening three words were thought to make it a leading question, one that expected the answer 'yes'. It was therefore modified to 'Should Scotland be an independent country?' What this form of words enabled was a pro-independence campaign that sounded positive, while the anti-independence groupings would inevitably sound negative since they sought the answer 'no'. Somehow this could be – and was – intuited as a vote against Scotland.

With characteristic canniness, Alex Salmond wanted to hold the referendum in the early autumn of 2014. That was to be Scotland's year, when the nation would take centre stage as the host of two great sporting events. In the summer, the Commonwealth Games was to be held in Glasgow and golf's Ryder Cup at Gleneagles in Perthshire. And 2014 was also the 700th anniversary of the Battle of Bannockburn, Scotland's greatest military victory over England. No one needed to labour the analogies. Alex Salmond hoped that the summer of Scotland would be positive, setting an encouraging tone for those who wanted a different future. And that the celebrations at Bannockburn would somehow show that Scotland could win out against overwhelming odds.

Since the signing of the Edinburgh Agreement and the advantages it handed to the SNP, it seemed to me that there was every chance that the Yes campaign would prevail, that Scotland would leave the United Kingdom and that a very uncertain, perilous future would unfold. I found it vexing, and I couldn't work out the question that independence would be the answer to. Scotland's problems with health, education, low productivity and a host of other pressing issues would surely only get worse if we withdrew from the British union. To solve our difficulties, we needed co-operation not separation. The most dangerous impact of all, one that had not been addressed by the SNP, was the inevitable necessity for a new Scottish currency. To protect it against speculation in the money markets, something that would happen instantly, the Scottish pound, or whatever it was to be called, would need a huge fund, probably in US dollars, to back it. And where would $100 billion come from? It all seemed utterly reckless.

And, as a Borderer, I found the idea of a formal frontier, perhaps even a hard border, impossible to contemplate. The English, the Northumbrians and Cumbrians are my neighbours and friends, not foreigners, and both my sisters and their families live in Newcastle. Would there be long queues on the A1 at Berwick-upon-Tweed or at the Carter Bar in the Cheviots? More than that, I had a powerful revulsion to a persistent and clearly audible base note that rumbled under much of the debate. Nationalism requires there to be 'the other', those who are 'not us', and leading to the referendum in 2014, the other were undoubtedly the English, my friends, my family, my nephews and their children.

Many years before, I had been active in Labour Party politics on a local level, campaigning in Edinburgh South for a charismatic, brilliant young candidate. Gordon Brown and I became, and have remained, close friends, and after the signature of the Edinburgh Agreement, I went up to Fife to talk to him about the coming referendum. In the months leading up to the vote on 18 September 2014, we campaigned, gathered support, held events in big theatres and halls, doing as much as we could, believing that the outcome was by no means clear. On 6 September, a YouGov poll indicated that, for the first time, the Yes campaign were leading with 47 per cent supporting them and 45 per cent for No. Other polls showed narrow leads in the opposite direction, all within the margin of error. It was going to be very close indeed.

Apparently, this was not a view shared by Prime Minister David Cameron, who seemed unconcerned. More worrying was the fact that initially he refused to discuss the referendum with his predecessor, Gordon Brown. It was a serious difficulty. Two years before, I had met the Conservative MP Rory Stewart. We shared an interest in the history of the South of Scotland, and in a quirky response to the referendum (he was MP for Penrith and the Border), Stewart had formed a group called Hands Across the Border. I also knew that he was friendly with David Cameron, a fellow Old Etonian. It took me several days and scores of mobile phone calls, but I eventually tracked him down (he was walking in the Alps). He agreed to communicate our anxieties to Cameron immediately, and the blockage was quickly removed.

Centrally important at that moment was 'The Vow'. We realised that in order to persuade most people to vote No, there could be no return to the status quo. There had to be a vision for a new Scotland that included guarantees and new powers for the

Scottish Parliament. And a timetable for their implementation should be attached. On 16 September 2014, the *Daily Record* ran 'The Vow' on its front page – signed by the three party leaders, David Cameron, Nick Clegg and Ed Miliband. On the eve of the poll, Gordon Brown made a powerful speech stating that 'the silent majority will be silent no more'. The emotion in his voice was clear as he exhorted No voters 'to hold [their] heads high and have confidence' as they went to the polling booths.

On 18 September, there was a huge turnout, the largest ever seen in a British election or referendum. Passions ran high as 84.59 per cent of the electorate (which included 16–18-year-olds for the first and only time) went to the polls or voted by post.

There was no exit poll on the night, but YouGov was predicting a 54 per cent to 46 per cent win for the No campaign. And so it came to pass. At 1.30 a.m., tiny Clackmannanshire, formerly a Westminster seat held by the SNP, was the first to declare. The final count was 55.3 per cent for No and 44.7 per cent for Yes. It set the pattern for the night. A total of 2,001,926 voted to remain in the United Kingdom and 1,617,989 voted for independence. And the massive turnout made the result seem like 'the decisive expression of the views of the people of Scotland' enshrined in the Edinburgh Agreement.

It was an emphatic result, one that would draw a line under what had been a divisive, bad-tempered campaign peppered with online abuse and occasional scuffles in the streets. At times there seemed to be no political opponents, only allies or enemies. But within hours, David Cameron appeared determined to prolong division. To the dismay of No campaigners, at 7 a.m. on the morning after the vote, he walked out of Downing Street to announce a series of measures that would curtail the voting rights of Scottish MPs in the House of Commons. Wrapped up in an acronym known as EVEL – English Votes for English Laws – these would exclude Scots from voting on England-only matters.

After a bitter campaign fought to keep Britain united, here was a prime minister actively promoting continuing division. Scottish Liberal Democrat MP and Chief Secretary of the Treasury, Danny Alexander, was furious: 'Talk about trying to snatch defeat from the jaws of victory. What it did was just give the nationalists a whole grievance agenda from a minute after a result was declared. It was just dreadful.'

The referendum of 2014 was not the full stop that Unionists wanted to see and that Alex Salmond had said it would be when he talked of a 'once in a generation' event. The Prime Minister had made sure of that, and the SNP was about to make another seismic statement. Only eight months later, a UK general election was held. And on 7 May 2015, the political map of Scotland turned almost completely yellow; the red of Labour, the blue of the Conservatives and the orange of the Liberal Democrats almost disappeared.

The 45 per cent who had voted Yes, 1,617,989 disappointed voters, took their revenge on the Unionist parties when they turned out en masse in support of SNP candidates. Only three failed to win a seat, and 56 men and women, 50 of them new to Westminster, out of a Scottish total of 59, would join the new UK Parliament. They ranged from 20-year-old Mhairi Black, the youngest MP for more than three centuries, who defeated Douglas Alexander, a former Labour minister, to George Kerevan, a newspaper columnist and author, as well as a large cohort of very surprised SNP local councillors.

After the tsunami hit, the political landscape was devastated as Labour lost all but one seat and the Liberal Democrats were routed, down from eleven MPs to one. This only reflected their savage fate across Britain as the electorate punished them for five years of coalition. Scotland's political map was changed utterly on 7 May with few certainties left standing as the wave swept across former Labour heartlands.

There was more surprise throughout the rest of the United Kingdom. Opinion polls had predicted a close result, but in the event failed to pick up a late surge in support for the Conservatives. They won 330 seats, and Labour was reduced to 232. It was enough for a slim majority over all other parties. But it was clear that the loss of 40 seats to the SNP had not only badly depleted Labour's representation, it had delivered a Conservative majority in the United Kingdom. This was something that suited Nicola Sturgeon, the SNP's new leader after the resignation of Alex Salmond, for the nationalists usually prospered when the Conservatives were in power across the border. The result also made Scotland look starkly different, a country whose political currents seemed to be running in different directions from the rest of Britain. What added to this perception was the demise of the Liberal Democrats who lost 49 of their 57 seats across the UK. That meant the SNP was the third-largest party in the House of Commons, and at the set-piece occasions like weekly Prime Minister's Questions, they had a great deal more exposure than in the past. And as a much larger party, the SNP received what is known as 'short money', a subsidy from the public purse that was very welcome in a party that depended overwhelmingly on private donations. The SNP's success sometimes made Scotland look like the opposition not to the Conservative Government but to England itself since there were only three other MPs who could speak directly on Scottish matters. The sole Conservative, David Mundell, of course became Secretary of State for Scotland, but he appeared more like a viceroy than a government minister.

On 12 May 2016, the weary Scottish electorate went yet again to the polls for the third major vote in three years, the Scottish Parliament election. The SNP lost their majority, but with 63 MSPs, they remained the largest party and opted to go into coalition with the Greens, who held six seats. The most dramatic outcome was the steep decline of the once-dominant

Labour Party. They lost thirteen seats and were overtaken by the Conservatives. With 31 seats, they became the second-largest party and the main opposition to the SNP. But that was by no means the most important or decisive poll in 2016. Voters knew that they would once again be returning to the church halls, schools and other venues that served as polling stations.

In what some commentators described as the greatest act of recklessness since the British invasion of Egypt and Suez in 1956, Prime Minister David Cameron committed to a referendum on the United Kingdom's membership of the European Union. There was no great groundswell of dissatisfaction in the years leading up to 2016, or many calls for another referendum. There had been a decisive vote 40 years before. With only a slender majority in the House of Commons, Cameron wanted to consolidate control of his party and that meant silencing dissent from a small, right-wing group known as the Eurosceptics or the European Research Group. He also wanted to neutralise Nigel Farage's UK Independence Party (UKIP). Although they had won only one seat in 2015 (and that was a defecting Conservative), they had attracted 4 million votes, enough to split the Conservative vote in future elections, and a referendum that showed Britain wishing to remain in the European Union would undercut their appeal.

And so, principally for reasons of internal party management and personal ambition (Cameron was 49 in 2016 and must have hoped to continue in office for some time), the Conservative Government committed to a referendum to be held on 23 June 2016, six weeks after the Scottish elections. The narrow majority of 52 per cent to 48 per cent for leaving, across the UK, was more than surprising; it was a shocking, earth-shattering result. The Leave campaign had focused on emotive issues like immigration, sovereignty, patriotism and a cloying, and historically misleading, hankering after a past that never really existed. Outrageous lies were told about the effect of coming out of the European Union, the most notorious being a promise on a bus that the NHS would benefit by an additional £350 million a week if Britain could be unshackled from the continental yoke. There was also an unmistakable undertone of xenophobia.

In England, the result was even more emphatic than the overall picture with 53 per cent supporting Leave and 47 per cent with Remain. In Scotland, it was very different. By a very large margin, 62 per cent to 38 per cent, Scots voted to remain in the EU, and there was a majority for Remain in all 32 local regions. On the morning after the poll, the United Kingdom seemed less united than ever before, with a clear victory in England for anger and disconnection, while in Scotland the result was both confusing for some and clarifying for others. The immediate political reaction to these contradictory votes was clear. Nicola Sturgeon, the SNP First Minister, and her party believed that circumstances had changed radically and that a UK decision would be imposed on a nation that had voted against it. And that meant that there should be another referendum on the issue of independence.

Soon after defeat in the Brexit poll, David Cameron resigned, and Conservative prime ministers followed in quick succession. When Boris Johnson entered Downing Street, it was another political gift to the SNP as he proved to be an effective recruiting sergeant. Yet another Old Etonian was in charge. Promising to 'Get Brexit Done', he secured an 80-seat majority in the 2019 general election, many of the Conservative gains coming in the North of England, in what used to be known as the 'Red Wall' of safe Labour seats. It was hailed as a tremendous achievement, the outcome of an excellent Conservative campaign, but in truth it was nothing of the kind. In Jeremy Corbyn, Labour had an unelectable, left-wing leader whose attitudes as much as his ideas drove support away from his party. Like Theresa May before him, Boris Johnson had no intention of co-operating with the SNP Government or facilitating another referendum, and a bad-tempered stalemate seemed to descend. The arguments traded across the border were quickly silenced as disaster burst on the world in the early months of 2020.

*

In a corner of my office, hidden behind piles of books and papers, sits an old, red plastic phone, so old that it has a rotary dialling system. I never use it to make outgoing calls, having preferred a mobile for many years, so only a handful of family and old friends have the landline number. One morning in late January 2020, I jumped out of my skin when it rang.

'Listen,' said a familiar voice, an eminent medical professor at one of Scotland's ancient universities and an old friend. 'You're not as young as you used to be.' I wondered what was coming. 'You'll have read about this virus from China. You mustn't take any risks. It's going to be really nasty. It affects your lungs, and you don't want to end up in an ICU, intubated and stressed, or worse. It'll go for older people. Don't go anywhere, and if you absolutely have to, wear a face mask, don't touch your face and wash your hands thoroughly, *really* wash them, and often.' All of which was said slowly and emphatically. I suspected I'd been on a list of calls that had included parents and family as well as friends, calls prompted by some insight the press didn't have. 'This is going to be something,' my friend said before he hung up. 'This seems to be spreading faster than anything else I've seen.'

We did exactly what we were told. And we were very lucky to be told it. From the second week in February, my wife and I stayed on our farm, had everything delivered by drivers who left the green plastic crates outside the porch. After we had picked them up and stored the food, we washed and scrubbed like surgeons. And we watched the news as events unfolded and the COVID-19 pandemic swept across the world.

Accounts varied, but in a city few had heard of, the virus that became known as COVID-19 appeared to be spreading very quickly indeed, and fatally. Amongst Wuhan's population of 10 million, the first case may have been detected in November 2019, and many more were certainly reported in December. But the Chinese did not inform the World Health Authority until 11 January 2020 that the deadly virus existed. And it seems that they did too little too late to prevent its initial spread. Wuhan is a major transport hub, and many carriers left the city in all directions, including international destinations. In only a few weeks, it became clear that a juggernaut was developing a fatal momentum, and on 11 March 2020, the WHO declared a pandemic. Nightmares seemed to be coming true, and another call on the red phone advised me not to think that because China was on the other side of the world that distance was any protection. COVID would reach Scotland within weeks. And it did.

On 22 February, the new virus was declared a notifiable disease in Britain, one whose cases had to be reported to the authorities. By 1 March, these were multiplying quickly, and as the scale of the nightmare became clearer and clearer, the Scottish Government advised people against non-essential travel and to work remotely if possible. Health was a devolved matter in Scotland, Wales and Northern Ireland, and so four, occasionally different, sets of advice and restrictions were heard across Britain and Ulster. On 23 March, what became known as the first lockdown came into effect. All schools and public spaces were closed, and the entire population was instructed to stay at home. On the same day, fourteen deaths were recorded in Scotland as the virus began to bite.

A series of daily TV press briefings were broadcast where politicians and their scientific advisors reported on developments and passed on statistics on the rate of infection, continually emphasising how important the restrictions were. We had to protect each other and protect the NHS. No government had exercised such direct control over its citizens since the Second World War, and almost everyone complied. Almost everyone. As First Minister, Nicola Sturgeon was often flanked at briefings by Catherine Calderwood, the Chief Medical Officer for Scotland. On 5 April, it emerged that, far from staying at home, she and her husband had driven twice from Edinburgh to Earlsferry in Fife, where they had a second home. A photograph of them walking on the beach with their dog was published by a tabloid newspaper. At a press conference, she said, 'I did not follow the advice I was giving others,' and repeatedly said how sorry she was. But instead of resigning, Calderwood merely promised to 'do better'. Apparently, Nicola Sturgeon had persuaded her to continue. Given the sacrifices, and indeed the hardship millions were enduring as they dutifully stayed at home, many trapped in flats with no ability to go outside, far less stroll with a dog along a beach, her hypocrisy made her position untenable. Catherine Calderwood may have been the first powerful individual to believe that the regulations she helped formulate applied to other people, but not to her. In fact, she turned out to be the first of a long sequence of hypocritical and arrogant public figures who showed their contempt for what ordinary people were going through.

By 1 May there had been 11,500 cases of COVID in Scotland and 1,525 deaths. The daily press briefings talked, sometimes obscurely, of statistics and R values, showed graphs and tried to explain how decisions were arrived at. But there was only one curve the public wanted to see and that was one travelling downwards. Knowing that lockdown was paralysing society and the economy – Scotland's GDP had declined by 19.5 per cent between April and June of 2020 – politicians wanted to ease restrictions. Scotland's view of risk began to diverge from England's, and while Prime Minister Boris Johnson announced that lockdown would end on 11 May, Nicola Sturgeon's government kept it in place for another ten days. That had meant isolation for many vulnerable people for two months. No evidence has since emerged to confirm or deny that Scotland's more cautious approach made any appreciable difference.

Meanwhile, scientists were working flat out to find a vaccine. And, miraculously, they did. It was – and remains – an extraordinary scientific achievement, something that gives one faith and hope for the future. Perhaps human ingenuity, driven by extreme, urgent necessity, could solve the problems of the world, or at least mitigate them. Although 2020 saw more lockdowns across Britain, the picture was much more optimistic and the ordeal more endurable as it became clear that vaccines were trialling successfully. They would be available within months and administered first to people who were not as young as they used to be. Even though Christmas 2020 was severely disrupted, with too many people on their own, the New Year promised the possibility that the nightmare would end, or at least subside. Having followed the regulations (which were much easier for us than for many others), my wife and I had avoided the virus and we were vaccinated with the first dose on 9 February 2021. It was almost exactly a year since the red phone had rung.

A few months later, it emerged that Catherine Calderwood's selfish behaviour was by no means unique. Over Christmas 2020, when it really had been a bleak midwinter for millions, when they were unable to see family and friends, restrictions on social gatherings were being routinely and repeatedly ignored in 10 Downing Street. Partygate was the name given to a culture of drinks parties where bottles of alcohol in suitcases had been smuggled into the workplace for staff consumption. An emblematic photograph of Boris Johnson toasting an illegal gathering was published widely, and a screenshot from a CCTV camera showed the Health Secretary, Matt Hancock, in a passionate clinch in a corridor with a woman who was not his wife. His hand was clamped to her backside as they kissed. It was an image that disgusted many, and with good reason. The public concluded, at best, that these were not serious people who could be relied on to behave decently, far less govern effectively in the midst of an immensely destructive crisis. Or indeed obey the laws they themselves had made. Hancock resigned, and Johnson's lies and his behaviour – and how it was seen by the electorate – eventually led to him being forced out of office by his party.

In July 2021, the WHO revealed that out of ten COVID hot-spots in Europe, six were in Scotland. The situation was worst in Tayside, where, at one point, there were 1,002 cases per 100,000 people. As it became clear that the vaccination programme had been largely effective, the curve shifted downwards and restrictions were finally removed at the end of August.

The social and economic damage had been tremendous, unprecedented since 1945. By May 2022, more than (perhaps many more than) 2,174,265 Scots had contracted COVID, and 17,599 had died, some of them alone at the height of the lock-downs. In church halls, schools and other handy public spaces, around 15 million vaccines had been administered by an NHS at full stretch. These routine, everyday acts of heroism happened despite a chronic lack of essential equipment, especially personal protection equipment (PPE) such as gowns, masks, gloves and other coverings. In order to speed up the faltering process of sup-ply, a panicking government bypassed all sorts of controls and opened up unofficial VIP lanes, a means of direct access to minis-ters and their departments by companies who could manufacture what was so urgently needed. This arrangement was immediately abused, and off the back of the misery of millions and the her-culean achievements of the people of the NHS and other public agencies, obscene profits were made. In late 2023, Michelle Mone, a Scottish businesswomen who had been elevated to the House of Lords by David Cameron, confessed that she had lied about using her contacts in government to lobby for lucrative contracts for her husband, Douglas Barrowman. Through a company called Medpro, he had supplied PPE and other items – much of it useless – and made an eye-watering profit of more than £60 million.

The COVID virus continues to infect people, but its existence has been, to some extent, normalised, like other debilitating diseases. On 5 May 2023, the WHO declared that the pandemic had ended. But its effects continue to make an emphatic mark. In Scotland, 187,000 (3.5 per cent of the population) have been felled by Long COVID, a condition where symptoms persist for months, even years. What has been dubbed Long Social Distancing has also had an impact. At the height of the pandemic, people were advised to maintain a distance of at least two metres between themselves and anyone they encountered (there seemed to be no scientific basis for this), and it was known as social distancing, even though that seemed like an oxymoron. A significant minority are now permanently fearful of getting too close to others, dislike large groups, feel uncomfortable on public transport, especially aeroplanes, and socialise much less. During the pandemic online meetings through platforms such as Zoom and Teams became commonplace, and they have become part of everyday life for many, also enabling them to continue to stay at home to do their jobs rather than commute to an office. Society has become much more fragmented, atomised – and suddenly very different. All sorts of longer-term questions now hang over transport infrastructure, half-empty city-centre office blocks and centralised resources for communities. People who were at first forced to stay at home are now choosing to remain there.

By 2023, it had become clear that COVID had had a devastating impact on the economy. Closed during lockdowns, many pubs, hotels, cafés, restaurants and other businesses related to public gatherings simply ceased trading, and staff lost their jobs.

As tax income fell and costs soared, Scotland's budget deficit doubled. At the end of 2023, it stood at 22.4 per cent of GDP compared to 14.2 per cent in the UK. The Scottish Government is unable to borrow and therefore in the future will have to cut public services or raise taxes – or both. These necessary measures are likely to herald an era of political upheaval and radical change. The pandemic has altered the world, in ways that will not be fully understood for some time to come.

That upheaval and radical change arrived sooner and more dramatically than anyone predicted. On 22 May 2024, I watched an era in British politics come to a soggy and almost farcical end. After the richly deserved defenestration of Boris Johnson, the members of the Conservative Party, approximately 172,000 mostly older people, decided that Liz Truss should follow him into 10 Downing Street. An endless litany of lies, contempt for the electorate and pure farce were followed by 45 chaotic days of utter madness as she launched a 'mini budget' of unfunded tax cuts that would supposedly stimulate economic growth. In fact, it stimulated a widespread and profound crisis of confidence in the bond markets, and the cost of borrowing immediately rocketed. The Bank of England was forced to intervene to stabilise the situation. One newspaper commented that governments were supposed to defuse crises, not create them, and another, the *Daily Star* tabloid, put up a livestream of an iceberg lettuce placed next to a portrait of Liz Truss. The lettuce comfortably outlasted her reckless premiership, what had become an international embarrassment.

Truss was quickly replaced by Rishi Sunak, who announced in a downpour outside 10 Downing Street that there would at last be a general election on 4 July 2024. As his grey suit became saturated, the rain glistening as it ran down his shoulders, the end of a disastrous period in British politics seemed to be in sight. The unnecessary and destructive Brexit referendum called by David

Cameron had led to paralysis in the short-lived premiership of Theresa May, the disgraceful deceit and ludicrous trivialities of Boris Johnson, what I believe was criminal lunacy from Liz Truss and, finally, an election called by Sunak that seemed destined to put the crumbling Conservative Party and the country out of its collective misery.

The exit poll on 4 July confirmed a universally expected outcome. Labour gained a huge majority of 172 seats and the Conservatives had a catastrophic night. They lost 251 seats and were reduced to a rump of only 121 MPs as the electorate punished them and huge constituency majorities tumbled. But as I watched the results come in – especially enjoying Liz Truss' childish petulance when she lost her previously safe seat – I felt a sense of anticlimax. There seemed to be no great enthusiasm for Labour under the capable but uninspiring leadership of Sir Keir Starmer, only a wish to eject the Conservatives after their years of bungling, corruption and contempt for the electorate.

However, that dynamic was not the sole decisive factor in the dramatic outcome. On both sides of the border, nationalism played a decisive role. After seventeen years in government in Edinburgh and a history of major failure across the devolved functions of government in Scotland, ranging from the near-collapse of reliable ferry services on the Atlantic seaboard to a sustained decline in educational standards, the SNP's Westminster representation collapsed. From 48 seats won in 2019, they returned nine MPs, most of their 39 losses turning into Labour gains.

After its unexpected triumph in winning the Brexit referendum, English nationalism, in the shape of the Reform Party led by Nigel Farage, transformed the electoral landscape in England. They bit hard into the Conservative vote and ensured they lost many more seats despite Reform returning only five MPs to Westminster. Just as eye-catching was their total popular vote across Britain (they did better than anticipated in Scotland with

168,000 supporting them) of just over 4 million. It compared with 3.5 million who voted Liberal Democrat. And just as significant was Reform's second place in 98 English constituencies.

The general election of 2024 will be remembered as a massive Labour victory and the reduction of the Conservative Party to a rump, their worst result in their history. But more significant in the longer term was the performance of the Reform Party. With few identifiable policies beyond their fierce views on immigration and a proposed tax policy that would scare the bond markets even more than Liz Truss's idiotic proposals, they nevertheless established themselves as a significant force even if our first-past-the-post system gave them only five MPs. This general election showed how volatile voting has become. Labour's similarly huge majority in 1997 ensured that they had three consecutive terms of office. But all that Sir Keir Starmer can be sure of is one five-year term. If the Conservatives can lose 251 seats in a single election, then any party can.

The impact of the British election of 2024 as an event may or may not be temporary. But its consequences are as nothing compared to another crisis that is already having an immense, life-altering impact all around the world. The climate emergency is turning out not to be an existential problem for the future but one that has already begun to change our planet as a series of natural disasters seem not be episodes but part of a developing pattern with clear preludes.

Wednesday, 27 December 2023 turned out to be an emblematic day. On the BBC website's weather pages, this surprising sentence appeared: 'Storm Gerrit is the seventh named storm of the current UK storm season which started in September and runs until August next year.'

The use of 'season' here seems at best problematic. Most people think of there being four seasons in a year, but the BBC seems to be saying that storms can occur at any time in a twelve-month season, or a year. The Met Office report for the previous year offers this analysis: 'The 2022/23 storm season saw only two named storms across the year, with these two storms coming late in the season, with Storms Antoni and Betty impacting the UK and Ireland in August 2023.'

Despite the uncertainties over definitions, one thing at least became clear on 27 December 2023. The number of named storms is multiplying fast, with seven in only four months compared to two in the previous year, or season. On the same day, weather reports from across Scotland showed extreme conditions. More than 400 cars were trapped on the A9 in a snowstorm that engulfed the Drumochter Summit. Streets in Cupar in Fife were so badly flooded that houses were evacuated, high winds battered the Borders, and in Manchester a tornado ripped the roofs of several houses. On the front page of the *Daily Mirror*, above pictures of the damage, the headline 'Twister Terror' employed language that seemed to be imported from the USA.

The weather has always been important in British culture, living as we do on the eastern shores of the Atlantic Ocean, what defines our climate. It is enshrined in the language of our greetings and as a topic of enduring interest, and the weather can be a good way of initiating conversation. But as the weather has begun to change radically, so has the language used to describe it. Not only do we now have storm seasons, we are also assailed by tornados, hurricanes and monsoon-like deluges. The ubiquitous use of mobile phone cameras now records these extremes as never before, and online and on TV we watch in horror as trees are blown down like matchsticks and roiling rivers burst their banks. There is now an unmistakable sense of the world's weather in turmoil, almost as though the planet is angry, punishing us for how badly we have abused it. Who can forget the images of thousands of terrified Australians fleeing to the beaches of the eastern coasts as bushfires raged inland, as day turned to night when smoke filled the skies and fireballs exploded in the air? To many it looked like Hell on Earth, like Armageddon.

On 27 December 2023, the National Trust released the findings of an exhaustive audit. 'Weather changes are causing chaos for UK flora and fauna' was the headline, and below it was a long list of species that had suffered badly because of 'the disappearance of reliable seasonal weather patterns and [the coming of] more extreme weather events'. Ben McCarthy, the Head of Nature and Restoration Ecology, said, 'The shifting weather patterns we're seeing, particularly the warmer temperatures, is continuing to upset the natural, regular rhythms of the seasons. This loss of predictability causes chaos for the annual behaviours of animals in particular but can also impact trees and plants.' The lack of long periods of frost meant that, for example, insects such as moths and their caterpillars can survive through the winter and attack trees, and that beetles can kill off heathland plants. Hibernators such as dormice are waking up too early and finding that there is little for them to eat, red deer are rutting later, and calves now born in the summer have too little time to store fat for the winter. Floods are driving riverbank animals like voles from their burrows, and storms are destroying the winter roosts of seabirds all around our coasts.

On 1 September 2023, NatureScot published a similarly alarming report, saying: 'Considerable and rapid change across all aspects of society is needed to stop further nature loss in Scotland.' Changing weather and its warmer, wetter winters and hotter, drier summers 'is clearly the cause of widespread chaos'. Six major changes were listed: more extreme weather events, more long spells of hot weather, higher maximum temperatures, fewer periods of frost and snow, longer periods of dry weather in spring and summer and more rain on the wettest days of the year.

All of which mirrors our lived experience on our small farm in the Borders. Thirty years ago, we had 'reliable seasonal weather patterns'. There were of course exceptions, but generally speaking, after cold and sometimes snowy winters, the weather warmed, April showers fell, our grass grew, and the younger animals especially thrived on its fresh sweetness. Our well on the higher ground above the eastern meadows was a constant and reliable source of pure water for us as well as some cottages and the neighbouring farm. The hay harvest could be chancy (one summer we had to bale and then burn the whole crop because persistent rain prevented us from turning it, and it rotted black on the underside) but was generally good, and the spiky marsh grass in the wetland area around our burn could be kept in check.

By 2017, it was becoming clear that our well was drying up. Known as St Mungo's Well, it had been an ancient source of water for the nearby town of Selkirk, filling a tank at the Pant Well in the town market place. We began to find that our 7,000-gallon holding tank was filling slowly, too slowly to keep up with consumption. In 2020, at great cost, we were forced to connect the farm to the mains water supply. In the same year, very unusual weather nearly killed my wife. In summer, when the trees are in full leaf, each one acting like a little sail, a very high wind blew down a major bough from an acer that stands next to the gate into the stable yard – only a second or two after my wife passed it. Marsh grass is now everywhere, even in free-draining fields, and we now buy in all our hay and hayledge.

The look of the land has also altered. Long periods of heavy and persistent rain, especially between the end of June 2023 and the December of the same year, have turned some fields into quagmires, the entries badly poached, and even the higher ground to the south of the east meadow is sodden. Downpours have washed away the gravel on our tracks and made access difficult, to say nothing of the wear and tear on vehicles' suspension. Newspaper reports and footage of extreme weather events as well as charts and statistics describe what is happening around the world and experts make predictions. But our experience is that the climate has already changed – and profoundly. That unwelcome future is here. Now.

Ben McCarthy of the National Trust went on to say: 'We need to see more action from politicians . . . to ensure tackling the nature and climate crisis is a top priority.' These are clearly global problems that require global solutions and international co-operation on unprecedented levels. But the rise of populism/ nationalism will probably prevent that. It is in part a reaction to the globalisation of the economy, the atomisation brought about through the use of algorithms and faceless transactions, and a per-ceived loss of identity. Populist politicians offer simple answers to complex issues, and their actions are governed by short-termism and an unwillingness to take unpopular decisions that might lose them electoral support. The world is also disfigured by war in Europe and the Middle East, conflicts that might subside but that look insoluble. And there is also a renewed threat of nuclear war. Hope can be hard to find.

Once again, on the emblematic day of 27 December 2023, human ingenuity offered the beginnings of a possible solution. The climate crisis is the consequence of global warming, which in turn has largely been accelerated by huge increases in the use of energy, much of it polluting and damaging. At the Lawrence Livermore National Laboratory in California, it was announced that scientists have managed to repeatedly produce nuclear fusion ignition for the first time and produce a small amount of energy. It marked a milestone on the road to achieving near-limitless clean energy at scale. On 8 December 2023, the world's largest nuclear fusion reactor began to operate in Japan. It will conduct experiments to create the same natural reactions found inside the Sun. Nuclear fusion requires no fossil fuels and leaves behind no hazardous waste. The Japanese reactor is a joint project, with funding from the European Union.

These are clearly early glimpses of a better and brighter future, one that might not require the intervention of politicians to succeed. The world's only superpower, one of the very largest single markets and the world's fourth largest economy have all invested in this enormously important project. Economics, not politics, will make it work. Human ingenuity produced remarkable results when vaccines were created during the recent pandemic. Let us hope that urgent creativity of a similar sort can save our planet before time runs out.

14

To See Ourselves

The first of January 2024 dawned damp and grey. The Met Office had promised sunshine for New Year's Day, but when I drove down to Kelso, the rain was lashing down. The Teviot roiled and foamed, flood-brown, as it surged into the Tweed, and when I parked in the Square, I had to rummage for an umbrella. My plan was to walk, to follow old familiar routes, the way to school, my paper round, my milk round, to gather a sense of the last 75 years and how the place where I was born and raised had changed in that long time. But not in the pouring rain, not half-blinded by the brim of a dripping umbrella.

It was 9.15 a.m. Perhaps a warm and welcoming coffee shop would be open on the holiday. Just off the Square I found Naked Sourdough, where I ordered an excellent latte and a comforting croissant with jam and extra butter. Even in my one-minute walk from the car, I could see how much Kelso had gentrified. High-end retailers like Farrow & Ball, Fat Face and shops selling cookware, cashmere and expensive gifts had replaced the Co-op menswear department, two chemists, the newsagent where I queued for the *Pink*, Lombardi's Café, Jock the Box, two grocers and Frank Frost, the tobacconist. In contrast to other towns, and perhaps confirmation that there was money in Kelso, there were branches of the Royal Bank of Scotland and the Bank of Scotland.

Two grand, neo-Georgian buildings sit next to each other, dominating the south side of the Square, their air of respectability and solidity much dented by the antics of Fred Goodwin and others in 2008. As I hurried through the rain, I could see that much had changed, but some things had endured. Opposite Naked Sourdough is James Stewart & Son's hardware shop and the offices of the electrical contracting business my dad worked for all his adult life. And next door is Blair the Jeweller whose owner had been the town's Provost when I was young.

By 10 a.m. the rain had eased, and I decided to drive to Inchmyre, to where the prefab I'd been raised in used to stand. In its place, I found some evergreen bushes and miniature, municipal trees that had been savagely pruned. In the middle of them lay a discarded red bicycle.

Despite the puddled pavements, despite the bleak low-rise blocks of flats whose guttering was leaking badly, the weeds and the cold north wind, and the air of neglect, I could see that behind the gauze of grey clouds a faint sun was beginning to brighten the morning. When I crossed the road to our corner of the New Jerusalem, where Bina had sat smiling a long time ago, cuddling me in the crook of her arm, I felt tears prickle. I turned to look along the road where Sandy Purves had herded his cows with his collies, and I saw the old man waving his crook, heard his boots clacking on the tarmac. And I saw the little boy on the pavement, cold hands shoved in his pockets, scuffing along on the edge of life. My tears were not for him or for some obscure sense of loss, but for a life that had been lived and all its joys, the sensual memory of lost summers that will never come again. Not tears of regret or of self-pity, but tears for what had been forgotten or misunderstood.

I walked back along the road where I had delivered scores of *Sunday Posts*, passing only the occasional dog walker. On the morning of 1 January, most sensible people were probably sleeping

in, sleeping off the effects of the night before – what we used
to know as Old Year's Night, when we celebrated as we waited
for the Bells. Leaving the flats at Inchmyre, I reached the small
council estate we moved to in 1952. The variety of front doors, the
extensions, porches, carports and garages told me that Margaret
Thatcher's bargain offers of the 1980s had been enthusiastically
taken up. All these well-built, two-storey houses with gardens
front and back had been bought by their tenants. The grim, grey
harl had gone, and many were brightly painted. Our house, 42
Inchmead Drive, looked spruce, and a large garage at the back
and a driveway leading to it had taken advantage of its being at
the end of a short terrace. When I walked on, following my route
to primary school, I could see that the wish for privacy had raised
high, screen-like fences and thick cypress hedges around front
gardens. Nana Hawkins' house on the corner looked a bit like the
cavalry fort in *Boots and Saddles*.

I crossed Inch Road into another world. Forestfield is bounded
by hedges and railings, behind which stand a score or so of splendid, well-set houses. Not 25 yards from our estate, this enclave of
the professional middle classes was home to doctors, businessmen,
dentists, bank managers and solicitors. Two of the properties
were, and still are, church manses. There may have been a gulf in
income and assets, but Kelso was too small for social apartheid.
I had good friends in Forestfield, and with the exception of one
or two wealthy families and surrounding farmers who sent their
children to boarding school, almost all the children in Kelso went
to the local high school. And with the coming of the Robbins and
Anderson reports, those with ability (to pass exams) went on to
university. That window of opportunity made for a brief sense
of near-equality, of the possibility of a bright future. James Clow
and John Knox lived in Forestfield and won the dux medal, but
so did Nanny Hall and my big sister, Barbara, and they lived in
Inchmead Drive.

Kelso is tiny. I had forgotten that it took only ten minutes to walk from our house on the northern edge of the town to the southern side where our primary school was. On the way, I met no one I knew. Only ghosts. The ancient human geography of the place has lodged indelibly in my memory. As I walked, I could remember the faces and voices of many who lived on these streets: Matt Ballantyne, Dr Poole, John Middlemas, Tinkle Laidlaw and Mrs Black all lived within 60 yards of each other, three of them in detached houses at the foot of Forestfield and the others in a Victorian terrace 50 yards further on. All changed now, and perhaps those people who passed me thought I was a ghost from the past. I suppose I am.

My final destination was one of life's departure gates. At Kelso High School, I manage to pass enough exams to get into university, and the certificates were passports for a journey to a different sort of future. The gates were barred because of building work, but beyond them the old school looked superb, freshly minted. A more modern high school was built on the edge of town a few years ago, and this, the original building, was converted into apartments for the elderly. As an alumnus, I had been given a tour of what was to be renamed Poynder Apartments, and because this was a development of social housing, accessible to all, I'd done a video interview supporting the project.

But before I could walk around to the far side of the site, where there was an open gate, I had to cross a field of dreams. Poynder Park is the home of Kelso Rugby Football Club, where Ian Hastie and many other heroes had played. The last time I walked out onto the pitch was in 1972 to play for Kelso at the annual Sevens tournament. Starting from the clubhouse, I walked across it, hearing echoes of the roars, the ooohs and aaahs of the crowd, the grunts and shouts of the players. Scoring in the corner, kicking a goal that just scraped over the bar, throwing a dummy, an altercation with the then captain of the Scotland team – all of that was for me part of this place of spirits. On the sign that advertises forthcoming fixtures, I read an attractive motto I hadn't seen before: 'One Club, One Community – History Is Our Strength'.

When at last I walked into the grounds around the Poynder Apartments, the reluctant sun was blinking between clouds, lighting the façade of the building. Perhaps I'd end up here, back where it all began. Perhaps it would be good to complete a wide circle that had taken me around the world. From the top floors of the old school, where there were at least a dozen new apartments, I knew I would be able to see Inchmyre, Inchmead Drive, the spire of St John's Church and the rugby pitch at Poynder Park. My beginning, my past, and a map of how much and how little my Scotland had changed since 1950.

Acknowledgements

Writers who say their editors are wonderful, creative, empathetic, who whine that they could not possibly go on without their support, who go into a decline if their editor moves or retires – I used to think these people needed to get out more. Authors should write what they mean, mean what they write and be prepared to stand up for it!

I'm very grateful to work with two first-rate editors at Birlinn. Andrew Simmons has been my editor there for almost twenty years, and I have appreciated his considered and sensible comments on many manuscripts. My copyeditor, Alison Rae, immediately got what I was trying to do, and made it better. Simple as that. Thank you, Alison. You are wonderful, creative and empathetic, and if you don't do my next book, I'll whine like someone who needs to get out more.

Jan Rutherford of Birlinn always believed in this unlikely project and never wavered in her support and belief. And nor did Hugh Andrew, Birlinn's managing director. My agent, David Godwin, also has a great deal of faith, and stamina. We have done thirty-six books together.

Thanks also to those who kindly read the first draft and offered excellent comments: George Rosie, Gordon Brown and Walter Elliot, all still friends.

Further Reading

Personal recollection is a central part of this book, and not only my own memories but those of many others. I found the vast majority of this material online, on social media platforms, especially those carrying contributions from my contemporaries. These recollections offered not only detail and richness but also fresh and often unexpected perspectives. I am very grateful to all those who took the time to write their versions of a personal history of Scotland since 1950. I also delved deep into newspaper archives, and the staff of the National Library of Scotland were unfailingly helpful and kind. The following books also offer fascinating insights into British and Scottish life during a period of immense change.

Devine, T.M., *The Scottish Nation: A History*, London 1999

Dudgeon, Piers, *Our Glasgow: Memories of Life in Disappearing Britain*, London, 2010

Ewan, Elizabeth, Innes, Sue and Pipes, Rose (ed.), *The Biographical Dictionary of Scottish Women: From the Earliest Times to 2004*, Edinburgh, 2006

Faley, Jean, *Up Oor Close: Memories of Domestic Life in Glasgow Tenements 1910–45*, Glasgow, 1990

Glasser, Ralph, *Growing Up in the Gorbals*, London, 1986

Hennessy, Peter, *Having It So Good: Britain in the Fifties*, London 2007

Hunter, James, *The Land of the Free: A Millennial History of the Highlands and Islands of Scotland*, Edinburgh, 1999

Kynaston, David, *Austerity Britain, 1945–51*, London, 2008

Kynaston, David, *Family Britain, 1951–57*, London, 2009

Kynaston, David, *Modernity Britain 1957–62*, London, 2015

Kynaston, David, *On the Cusp: Days of '62*, London, 2021

Kynaston, David, *A Northern Wind, Britain 1962–65*, London, 2023

MacFarlane, Colin, *The Real Gorbals Story: True Tales from Glasgow's Meanest Streets*, Edinburgh, 2007

Rodger, Richard (ed.), *Scottish Housing in the Twentieth Century*, Leicester, 1989

Roy, Kenneth, *The Broken Journey*, Edinburgh, 2016

Smith, Rebecca, *Rural: The Lives of the Working Class Countryside*, London, 2023

Index